Actions
Speak
Louder

Actions Speak Louder

A Management Guide to Corporate Social Responsibility

DAVID CLUTTERBUCK with
DEZ DEARLOVE and DEBORAH SNOW

published in association with

KING*f*SHER

KOGAN
PAGE

First published in 1990 by George Weidenfeld & Nicholson Limited, entitled *Working with the Community*.
Second edition 1992 entitled *Actions Speak Louder*.

Kogan Page Limited
120 Pentonville Road
London N1 9JN

British Library Cataloguing in Publication Data

A CIP record for this book is available from the British Library.

ISBN: 0-7494-0810-3

Typeset in Great Britain by Saxon Printing Ltd, Derby
Printed and bound in Great Britain by Clays Ltd, St Ives plc

Contents

Foreword

by Howard Davies,
Director General of the Confederation of British Industry

Actions Speak Louder is a comprehensive and realistic guide for business managers. Its strength lies in its emphasis on the practical steps companies can (and, in many cases, already do) take to be excellent suppliers, purchasers, employers, investors, neighbours and partners with the wider community – in other words, to fulfil their social responsibilities.

The guide addresses the challenge faced by all businesses, neatly summarised by one manager who took part in a recent study on community involvement, "It is easy to give money away; it is more difficult to make it truly effective." It is not just community investment decisions, but all aspects of a company's social responsibility policies, which risk losing effect for being *ad hoc* or piecemeal. Just as a company must have a clear idea of where to position itself in the market, so it must develop a guiding concept of social responsibility.

By drawing on examples of good practice, this guide shows how hard-pressed managers can ensure that every decision counts. The answer lies in setting clearly focused goals, and then building up comprehensive strategies to achieve them. There is no shortage of good practice on which to draw: examples include partnerships between purchasers and suppliers; first-class employment and training policies; protecting the environment; urban renewal; forging links with schools. Advice on these and other areas is brought together to form a strategy, rightly recognised to be as much a part of mainstream business, as, say, production or marketing functions.

A well formulated and managed approach to community involvement strikes a chord with employees and potential recruits and investors, purchasers and suppliers, as well as with local residents and the voluntary and charitable sectors. Kingfisher is just one of a growing number of companies who are in no doubt of the resulting commercial as well as social benefits.

The emphasis on *how* rather than *whether* to give priority to social responsibility policies is a good measure of the extent to which the debate among business managers has moved on over the decade. This is a fitting testimony to the leadership by example given by world class companies, large and small. I am delighted to commend *Actions Speak Louder* as a timely and useful handbook, and to congratulate Kingfisher on once again making it available to all.

Preface

When we sponsored the first edition of this book two years ago, we were determined to re-emphasise that social responsibility is an important – indeed, essential – element of our business philosophy. It could hardly be anything else when our bottom line is so dependent on our reputation with our customers, who make up the local communities in which we trade.

It is true that Kingfisher and its operating companies have put a great deal of time, effort and resources into becoming leading players in community involvement. But so have many other companies, including many of our competitors. The more we become involved in social responsibility issues, the more we recognise how much we need to learn, and the greater value we place upon learning from the experience of others. The spirit of this book, like its predecessor, is very much one of sharing of good practice, wherever it occurs.

Our own understanding of social responsibility has evolved over time. It was originally characterised as "charitable donations". Then it progressed to the concept of "community investment". More recently, it has become a much broader concept, encompassing the environment, employment practices, equal opportunities and a wide spectrum of issues affecting our stakeholders.

The broader and more complex our definition of social responsibility, the greater the need to apply the high standards of management we expect to apply to commercial activities. This is, in many ways, a fledgling science. It is not enough simply to have a portfolio of worthy activities. They must form part of a coherent strategy, which assigns responsibilities appropriately to the corporate centre of our highly devolved business units. The policies arising from our strategy must be communicated effectively to both internal and external audiences and the effects of our policies on each audience must be measured and used to stimulate continuous improvement.

Hence the increased emphasis in this edition on management processes. The research has identified good practice in a wide range of organisations, of all sizes, in many sectors. It is our belief that applying good practice in social responsibility will become an increasingly important factor for every company, not least because there are considerable mutual benefits to well-managed community involvement programmes. For example, directing attention towards social problems which themselves affect profitability of businesses, such as crime prevention, helps contain a major problem. Other benefits come in the form of increased corporate reputation or direct employee benefits such as the personal and management development of staff through equal opportunity action and secondment schemes.

Added together, the multiple benefits of an involvement in social responsibility provide the basis for significant competitive advantage. By enhancing the relationship with all our stakeholders, we enhance our capability to perform well, whatever the measurement.

One measure of the effectiveness of this study will be if it provides the ammunition to help some companies improve the organisation of their social responsibility activities. Another will be if it gives hesitant companies the confidence to start along the road.

Finally, I would like to say thank you to all those who have made this book possible by telling the research team of their experiences in this rapidly developing area of management.

Geoffrey Mulcahy
Chairman and Chief Executive
Kingfisher plc

Introduction

The first edition of this management guide appeared under the title *Working with the Community*. Sponsored, as is this edition, by Kingfisher plc, it aimed to illustrate best practice among UK companies in approaching their responsibilities to a broad range of "communities" or stakeholders. From hundreds of interviews and documents, we distilled seven key stakeholders, demanding attention from socially concerned companies:

- customers
- employees
- suppliers
- shareholders
- the political arena
- the broader community
- the environment.

While not all these have a voice of their own, all have someone to speak up for them. Those voices have the power to influence the fortunes of the organisation for better or worse.

In this edition, we have focused more closely on the *management* of social responsibility. The second issue of our detailed survey into social responsibility practice, carried out by The ITEM Research Unit, has provided much useful information on how the most forward-thinking companies manage their activities in all of the stakeholder areas.

The concept that such "soft" areas require management is not always accepted by companies. Yet there are very strong arguments for insisting that social responsibility is managed with all the rigour and commitment that would be applied to core activities within the organisation.

For a start, there is the amount of money involved. Membership of the Per Cent Club (companies that donate 0.5% or more of profits to charity) is growing and there are many companies who are not members, yet who make substantial donations each year. Shareholders have a right to insist that top management uses their funds wisely – and the only assurance of that is if the process of giving is managed effectively. Managing effectively means having clear policies; practical guidelines and procedures to implement them; and working systems to measure performance and instigate improvements.

A more important consideration for many companies is the amount of time and creative energy of employees at all levels being invested in social responsibility issues. Increasingly, the leading companies in community investment, for example, are refocusing their activities away from giving cash and towards lending expertise.

On the negative side, the cost of social responsibility failures – whether from poor environmental management by water utilities or from dishonest behaviour, as in the Guinness and BCCI affairs – can be high. Negative publicity can cause loss in share price and downgrading of borrowing status, as well as loss of customer trust. In many cases, the subsequent exit of senior management (who may not be guilty of anything more than paying insufficient attention to social responsibility issues) adds to the casualty list.

Putting a value on corporate reputation is not easy and is certainly not just a factor of the bottom line. In many cases, it is only something you value once you lose it! After all, whose self-respect will propel them to work for an *ir*responsible company?

We have therefore placed additional emphasis in this edition not just on where companies should get involved in social responsibility but on:

- how they can select and prioritise involvement
- how they can ensure that social responsibility activities contribute to the well-being of the company and all its stakeholders
- how to involve the entire organisation
- the management processes that will support all these activities.

Our aim, and that of our sponsors, is to help more companies formalise best practice so that it becomes part of the normal routine of business. It should therefore be of practical assistance both to companies with strong social responsibility programmes and those in the process of starting their involvement.

At the same time, we are conscious of a significant shift in approach among the most forward-thinking companies. From something companies did *to* (or *for*) the community, social responsibility activities have become something the company does *with* a growing list of partners. "Enlightened self-interest" has given way to "mutual benefit", with both companies and voluntary organisations seeking genuine partnerships.

One of the reasons for writing this book was to encourage the continued exchange of best practice. We would be very pleased to hear about your social responsibility activities and how they are managed, for the next edition.

David Clutterbuck

1. The case for management

Not so many years ago, how a company's management team ran the business was pretty much its own affair. Shareholders rarely asked questions, let alone insisted that the board change its policy or practices. If the company got into financial difficulties, they might be vociferous in their complaints and even demand a change in management – but the day-to-day running of the company was not their affair.

The senior manager of the 1990s could be forgiven for thinking that how he/she does the job has gradually become everyone's affair. *Government* has crept into every functional aspect of how businesses behave:

- corporate governance legislation and City regulations are making a minefield of boardroom discussions
- employment legislation places increasing burdens on the company to ensure fairness of treatment for all
- data privacy legislation affects information technology departments
- monopoly legislation restricts the degree to which they can co-operate with competitors

and so on into every nook and cranny of the business edifice. In many cases, government pressure to behave in socially desirable ways is through moral obligation rather than legislation – for example, to meet minimum standards of employee training, or to settle small suppliers' bills promptly. But moral pressure tends to give way in due course to legislative pressure, especially when voluntary pressure failed to achieve the desired results.

One result of expanding legislation is that directors and individual managers find themselves exposed to significant risks of prosecution or pursuit through the courts by dissatisfied shareholders, especially in the United States.

A notable characteristic of the 1980s was that this was the decade when top management learnt what it was like to end up in the dock. On both sides of the Atlantic and as far away as Australasia, a steady stream of CEOs has been arraigned for actual or alleged corporate misdemeanours. Milken, Trump, Saunders, the BCCI cabal – the list is like the roll call of the famous. Some, such as Robert Maxwell, escaped trial through premature death. Some executives, while taken to task for unacceptable behaviour, also escaped prosecution.

Some of those prosecuted and convicted were out-and-out crooks, who set out to cheat their stakeholders; others received relatively little personal gain. What they did, they did in the belief that it was for the good of the company and therefore justified – Ernest Saunders would be a typical such case: perpetrator and victim at one and the same time.

These much publicised cases are but the tip of an iceberg. Over the coming decade, if experience in the United States is any guide, we can expect to see an increased rate of prosecutions, both at the executive level and further down. In particular, companies and their executives will find themselves in the dock for breaches of:

- environmental regulations
- misdemeanours of corporate governance (the law in the UK and many other countries is increasingly tightening up on the responsibilities of all executives, including non–executive directors)
- employee relations.

The range of actionable behaviour by corporations is expanding all the time, with responsibility being increasingly shared by middle managers. Take the following examples from the United States:

- a company storing chemicals had a serious spillage, which contaminated soil for some distance around its perimeter ditch. When the case came to court, it was not just the company that was sued. The training department was also in the dock on the grounds that, had the operators at the plant been better trained to deal with emergencies, the spillage could have been contained within the depot grounds.
- rejecting a 58-year-old-man for a job because he was "overqualified" landed another company's managers in court. The company argued that the man couldn't possibly be happy in a job so far beneath his capabilities; the court decided it was age discrimination.

- another training department found itself in court for attempting to prevent the release of transcripts from training sessions designed to combat discriminatory behaviour. In the sessions, managers had been encouraged to search their deepest prejudices, on the grounds that bringing them into the open was a critical element of therapy in overcoming them. Then a group of women filed a suit against the company and demanded that the transcripts be revealed as evidence of the degree of discrimination practised by the company. The lower courts agreed with them. The case continues, but meanwhile companies have become much more wary of investing in anti-discrimination training.

Closer to home, the County Natwest/Blue Arrow affair eventually resulted in the departure of a number of senior executives at the bank. Some of the issues, relating to executive liability, are covered in more detail in our chapter on business ethics (page 268).

Employees are demanding a greater say in policy making and more information about the company's plans and performance. At the same time, there is increasing pressure from top management in many companies for greater employee involvement. These companies recognise the value of harnessing the commitment and creativity of everyone in the company.

At the same time there is a growing connection between ethical reputation and employee goodwill. Most people like to be thought of as honest and trustworthy, so they tend to avoid seeking employment with companies that don't have an ethical "feel" to them. Labour turnover is frequently much higher and the calibre of recruits available is lower in companies with a poor social responsibility image.

There is also evidence to suggest that theft or "shrinkage" is less of a problem in companies which have a strong ethical culture. In particular, if a company is not wholly fair in the way it treats its customers and suppliers, it cannot reasonably expect employees to behave ethically towards the company. Other benefits from a strong ethical culture may be higher motivation, lower absenteeism and improved communications.

A recent example illustrates some of the results of a poor ethical stance. A major furniture retailer was disturbed to find sales assistants hiding from customers. On investigation, it found that the problem stemmed from an instruction requiring staff to promise customers their orders would be delivered in six weeks. Staff hid because they knew that whenever a customer approached they would either have to lie to them, or listen to their complaints about late delivery. What seemed like a good idea to entice customers to place orders turned out to erode the goodwill of both customers and employees.

Customers are increasingly using their muscle to insist on changes in the culture of the organisations they do business with. Marks and Spencer's long-standing tradition of imposing its own standards of good practice on suppliers is no longer a quaint oddity; indeed, it has rapidly become the rule, for example, that large companies insist their suppliers institute total quality programmes.

Customers are also being brought into the battle between companies and social pressure groups. The US campaign to boycott Exxon over its Alaskan oil spill is merely the visible tip of a very large iceberg. Millions of customers every day avoid particular companies or brands because they have been influenced by organised negative publicity.

A positive social responsibility image also helps in *customer* recruitment and retention. Put at its most basic, people prefer to do business with someone they can trust. This, on its own, is a strong argument for integrating social responsibility activities – having a good customer service record can be undermined, for example, by a poor reputation as an employer, or on environmental issues. Similarly, much of the goodwill generated through community sponsorships can be wiped out by claims of insensitive treatment of customers, as some of the high street banks recently discovered to their cost.

The *investment community*, too, is showing a much stronger interest in how companies operate. Ethical investment funds demand copious information on companies' policies and activities in a host of areas previously considered none of their business.

The fact is, how a company behaves *is* now everyone's business, whether managers like it or not. Among the critical implications of that change is an obligation for executives to ensure that they apply the same level of management expertise and competence to social issues, as they have traditionally done to operational issues. That is easier said than done. Social issues tend to be "soft" and therefore difficult to measure and categorise; the answers aren't always straightforward, because they frequently involve conflict between the interests of different groups; and appraisal/reward systems in most companies still tend to emphasise short-term results rather than reflection.

Yet the need to manage and to be seen to manage a wide range of social responsibility issues is becoming increasingly urgent, as each audience raises its expectations of the company.

Investment funds, whether ethically based or not, are increasingly taking social responsibility performance into account as an indicator when rating shares, although as yet only a handful openly use this as a criterion for investment. The perception that companies which have an open, socially conscious climate, are less likely to have skeletons in the cupboard, clearly has some validity. It is logical to assume, too, that companies which are sensitive to the external social environment will be better and faster at reacting to change in their markets. However, social responsiveness can be a two-edged sword. After years of rapid growth, based in part on environmental campaigning, Body Shop shares were reportedly marked down by the City for fear the commercial objectives were being lost!

The problem is that the pay-offs will remain largely theoretical and the discussions largely philosophical unless there are practical and adequate management processes for making social responsibility goals happen. The fine words have to be translated into fine deeds, through commitment at the top and innovation and initiative throughout the rest of the organisation. Every company will want to arrange its social responsibility approaches differently, according to its own priorities, but it will need at a minimum:

- a system to generate and review social responsibility policies at the highest level and, in most cases, at individual business level. This system must be capable of helping the companies develop business strategies that lead to competitive advantage through its public reputation.
- a system for gathering information about social responsibility trends and about the organisation's performance.
- a system for stimulating change and, where necessary, for enforcing it.

In companies which have gone furthest along this road, one can usually trace an evolution along the following lines:

- recognise the existence of different communities of interest
- understand these communities' needs and their legitimate demands on the organisation
- develop policies to cover each issue, taking into account conflicts of interest between those communities
- establish priorities for action
- design and implement procedures to put the policies into action
- measure and review.

Let's look at these in turn:

1. Recognise the existence of different communities of interest

Essentially, a community is a grouping of people with common background or interests. The source of their commonality may, for example, be geographical (they all live in the same village), occupational (they all work for the same employer), religious, or to do with a leisure pursuit. From a corporate social responsibility point of view, the key questions are:

- To what extent do the company's activities impact upon these people's lives?
- How does the company benefit from meeting people's needs?
- What do people have a right to expect from the company?

An interesting and different way of looking at the various communities with which a company becomes involved, is as a series of concentric circles. In the centre is the individual employee, a community of one. There isn't much the individual can do to influence community involvement, unless she/he is one of those highly motivated individuals whose enthusiasm captivates and stirs others; or unless she/he is in top management.

The company has a series of responsibilities to this individual, from providing opportunities for personal growth to ensuring that she/he works in a safe environment. She/he may have strong ambitions to advance within the organisation, or may be content with the responsibilities she/he has now. The potential variance in domestic circumstances, education level, personality type, functional discipline and so on is enormous. The challenging task of those responsible for personnel management (including the line manager) is to apply mass approaches while still treating that person as an individual.

The individual employee is part of a larger community, the team. The team will have a common set of objectives set by management, but it will have its own way of doing things and its own culture. The interaction between the motivation levels and behaviour of the team and the individual is substantial and two way. The team is the most important functional unit in both controlling social responsibility processes and motivating employees to undertake community activities. The company's responsibilities towards the team consist in the main of supporting it in supporting the constituent individuals; in practical terms, this usually means providing quality of leadership.

Above the team is the business unit, or company. We can define two distinct layers of responsibility here. One is local, in the sense of the communities that have a frequent, direct link with the organisation. This includes the employees *en masse*, customers, suppliers and the local community. The local environment, while not a community as such, can be considered in the same light, from a responsibility point of view, with the local community as the primary spokesperson. Depending on how close the company wishes to be in its relationships with shareholders, they belong either in this layer or the next.

Beyond this layer is the national community, where relationships with government and national lobbies (often the national chapter of international organisations) become important. Outside this are in turn, the European community (small c to include non-Common Market countries) and finally, the global community. The European dimension is becoming increasingly significant as multinational companies coordinate social responsibility initiatives across borders. The Third World, while generally a low priority for such initiatives, is gaining greater attention under the twin pressures of economic disaster and the need to adopt and spread good environmental practice.

This relatively straightforward model (overleaf), with all its flaws, permits serious discussion of where to focus corporate attention at the macro-level. Which areas can we afford to ignore for the present? Which are vital to our future well-being?

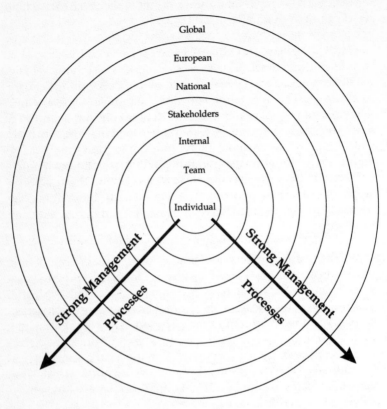

2. *Understand the communities and their legitimate demands on the organisation*

Understanding the nature of each community – its aspirations, limitations, hopes and fears – is an important step in designing initiatives towards it. The process of doing so is essentially the same as would be applied by the marketing function to market segments. In essence, it involves:

- defining precisely who the community is
- assessing to what extent it can be segmented even further
- using market research techniques such as surveys, focus groups, advisory panels and so on to explore their perceptions
- developing relationships with key influencers within each community
- communicating regularly with them
- gaining their input into initiative design.

Relatively few companies have a structured database of this kind of information, but it is not difficult to develop; nor, for most companies, should it be difficult to develop the kind of dialogue that will provide useful data. A word of warning, however. Just as many employers made the mistake in the 1960s and 1970s of listening solely to trade union officials on matters of employee interests, on the assumption that the officials genuinely represented employee needs and perceptions, so it is very easy to assume that a few, vociferous voices in a community fully understand its needs and aspirations. Although relying on a few sources of information may be relatively cheap, it is often better to have other, more direct channels to receive feedback from people within a community, rather than to rely solely on the interpretations of a third party.

3. *Develop policies to cover each issue, taking into account conflicts of interest*

Policies can be generated in detail at the functional level (human resources, information technology, public affairs) and ratified by top management; or they can be outlined in broad principle by top management and passed down to be worked into detailed guidelines by function managers. In practice, most companies seem to combine both approaches in an iterative process that, at its most successful, integrates the authority of the board with the functional department's day-to-day closeness to the issues.

The solutions companies have adopted for policy development vary widely. Compare, for example, the following approaches to community investment policy:

Case study: Marks and Spencer

Marks and Spencer has a general policy set by the main board, to support the communities in which it operates. Beyond this, policy on how to allocate and manage the £5 million annual budget rests with a community involvement committee with five main board directors. Three specialist sub-committees, each chaired by a director, deal with health care, the arts, and community services, which includes education, training and secondment.

Case study: Allied Dunbar

Annual reports from Allied Dunbar Charitable Trust state: "Responsibility and accountability for our community affairs activities have been delegated away from the board. Having made the important decisions in respect of principles, general direction, and resources to be made available, directors rely on trustees, in conjunction with professional staff and advisors, to develop and implement appropriate programmes."

Whether it retains or delegates policy making, the board has a responsibility to ensure that the organisation has a clear statement of principles. It must also ensure that any subsidiaries and all functional departments both adopt those principles and develop their own more detailed guidelines, relevant to the social responsibility issues they face.

The board is also the point at which policies need to be integrated, to make sure that effort is not duplicated and that the efforts in one area are not undermined by problems in another. A graphic illustration of the kind of problems that can occur if functions are allowed to develop policies independently, is an airport. The marketing and human resource departments spent heavily, training staff to be polite and helpful to customers and promoting this to the public. Then the security department, anxious to prevent its staff colluding with other people to avoid immigration and customs controls, forbade them to talk to anyone while on duty. Inevitably, this led to staff turning away in embarrassment when passengers asked for directions, undermining the customer service initiative.

Because concern for different areas of social responsibility action has arisen at different times and within different business functions, it is hardly surprising, for example, to find there is little co-ordination in many companies between purchasing policy and environmental policy. This normally has to be done at functional level rather than at organisational level.

Although chemical and manufacturing companies, for example, often have a board member responsible for co-ordinating all environmental policies, few companies have a board member responsible for all social responsibility activities.

One of the best ways to organise social responsibility issues is to have regular meetings between function heads, who report to a board member responsible for ensuring that the company activities in this field are documented and publicised.

Part of the responsibility of this gathering must be to ensure that no key issues fall through the cracks. It should ask such questions as: who takes responsibility for making sure the company's marketing practices are fair and ethical? It should also ensure that every business function does have clear, written guidelines, job descriptions/mission statements and targets; and that they are mutually supportive.

Who participates in these discussions will vary according to how responsibilities are divided. For example, do the company's links with schools and universities come under human resources, public affairs or community affairs? It is critical that responsibilities are clearly defined and that social responsibility issues are not simply "dumped" on one individual or department.

Checklist

1. Does our business mission deal with a sufficiently broad spectrum of stakeholder interests?
2. What values do we hold/want to hold towards each stakeholder group?
3. Can we encapsulate in no more than one page:
   - the fundamental responsibilities of the company to its main stakeholders?
   - responsibilities by the stakeholders towards the companies?
4. How will we communicate our values?
5. How will we police them?

4. *Set priorities*

No company has the resources – either financially, or in manpower, or in simple energy – to tackle all the social issues that it might legitimately become involved with. Moreover, dissipating its resources by trying to deal with too wide a range of issues brings little benefit to either the company or its communities.

In setting priorities, it is helpful to follow a reasoning process along the following lines:

1. What are our *legal* responsibilities towards each community? Now? Likely in the next five years?
2. How are we doing against each of these?
3. What are our *moral* obligations towards each community?
4. How are we performing against each of these?

5. Where will the greatest impacts on the *business* (both positive and negative) come from, in dealing with each of these communities of interest?
6. How are we doing in terms of meeting each of those business challenges?
7. What resources do we have, that we could apply to these issues?
8. What resources should come from functional budgets (because they are primarily commercial goals) and what from community investment?

There will inevitably be grey areas, demanding discussion and sometimes compromise, but the key is to follow a structured analytical process (like the one in the box below) that allows decisions on priorities to be made on a rational basis. It also helps ensure that major issues are not left out simply because there was no obvious route to bring them up for consideration.

Prioritising social responsibility issues

1. Who are our key stakeholders?

2. What do they demand of the company?

Legitimately	Of debatable legitimacy	Of no legitimacy

3. How strongly are the legitimate and debatably legitimate demands held? (Score 1 low to 10 high.)

4. What would be the severity of impact on the company's reputation if we did nothing? (Score 1 to 10.)

5. What would be the impact on the company's reputation if we were perceived to be a leader in this field? (Score 1 to 10.)

Case study: The Co-op

The Co-op took an unusual step in establishing its priorities for community action – it surveyed its members. Under the title "Your opinion matters", it invited members to "help us by completing our care poll. It will make sure our community action plans focus on the issues that you care about."

Among questions asked were:

- how important people felt it to be kept informed on issues such as solvent abuse or diet and health
- what really concerned people about community life
- whether the Co-op was right to refuse to stock irradiated foods, or ban hunting with hounds from its 30,000 acres of farmland, or whether it should provide bottle banks outside the stores, and so on
- which of a list of charitable causes the Co-op should support.

Although the level of response was not as high as hoped for, one positive result was that two-thirds of the Co-op's customers felt that major retailers should get more involved in local issues. The data from the survey was also helpful in allocating priorities for action.

American Express also asked its card members for their opinions on where to focus its community activities. It invited them to write in to nominate a charity they thought the company should support. From the hundreds of nominations, Amex was able to select five for priority attention: aids charity AVERT, Help the Aged, The Greenpeace Environmental Trust, Shelter and UNICEF.

5. *Procedures for putting the policies into action*

By and large, we will cover these in the chapters that follow. Suffice it here to say that the same basic procedures and controls used to implement any other business programme or project can and should be applied towards social responsibility issues. These include:

- having very clear objectives
- a detailed plan of action, with budgets, clearly assigned responsibilities and specific milestones
- communicating both the objectives and the plan
- providing training and other forms of support as needed
- having strong, practical feedback mechanisms.

6. *Measure and review*

The maxim "What gets measured gets done" applies here as much as to any other form of management activity. The question is: what do we measure?

The clearer the objectives and the more directly implementation is under the company's control, the easier it is to devise realistic measurements that will be useful both to management and to the communities which have a legitimate interest in the issue. For example, Superdrug's avowed intention to increase the proportion of women in middle and senior management posts to 20% by 1997 should pose relatively few problems in tracking.

Measuring the impact of a specific charitable donation or a sponsorship initiative is often much more difficult. Here, it may be more appropriate to measure changes in public perception to a programme of related activities over a period of time.

Whether measurements are "hard" or "soft", they also need to be tied into the organisation's motivational systems. Few if any companies make social responsibility issues a direct and significant aspect of performance appraisal for managers – yet. However, specific targets (for example, minority recruitment) are becoming more common, and so is a general pressure for managers to be seen to set an example in community involvement.

Where possible, in the following chapters, we have tried to suggest ways in which each aspect of social responsibility can be measured, and how to use measurement data for continuous improvement.

Structuring social responsibility activities
The cascade of activities, from policy making to implementation, perhaps by individual employees at scattered sites around the country, requires clear thinking through. The following template has been designed to help the thinking process.

A draft code of conduct

The need for guidelines and how to use them

Your role in maintaining the corporate reputation
- behaviour towards people outside the company
    - customers
    - suppliers
    - the general public
    - etc
- behaviour towards your colleagues at work
- behaviour towards the company and its property
    - time
    - assets
    - intellectual property
- confidentiality
- activities outside working hours
- conflicts of interest

What to do when you are concerned about other people's behaviour or about company policy

What the company owes you.

The campaigning company

A significant development in recent years is the adoption of overt campaigning on social responsibility issues by companies. Traditionally avoided as stepping outside a company's legitimate area of interest, the campaigning approach is rapidly gaining legitimacy where:

- the campaign theme is relevant to the company's area of business
- the campaign addresses a serious issue of legitimate public concern
- the company's stance will be regarded as reasonable by at least a majority of people in the target audience.

Companies which have adopted the campaigning approach include:

- Manchester Airport, which has supported the environmental charity ARK in its Green Travel Bug Campaign. The airport has published a lengthy article in the newspaper it gives to passengers, promoting the aims of the campaign and educating holiday makers in how to be friendly towards the environment of their holiday destination.
- The Co-op, which has mounted campaigns to educate youngsters in the dangers of smoking and parents in how to prevent their children from starting smoking. Another campaign stresses the dangers of solvent abuse.
- Benetton, which has chosen to emphasise in its advertising controversial social issues, in particular the values of racial harmony. Benetton's use of powerful visual images, intended to shock, has earned it both praise and condemnation around the world – but the approach has raised the company's profile both in brand terms and as a caring organisation.
- Body Shop, which has, for example, involved staff in collecting petitions against animal testing and the destruction of tropical rain forests.

    It has raised its public profile to international status in large part by the scope and intensity of campaigning on environmental and other social issues. Environmental campaigns have included a membership drive for Greenpeace in 1986, Stop the Burning in 1987 (raising over 1 million signatures in a matter of weeks to protest against the destruction of the Brazilian rain forest) and two major campaigns against animal testing of cosmetics (one of which raised 2.6 million signatures and was instrumental in changing a proposed EC directive).

The benefits for these organisations lie in public image building. From one point of view, they can be seen as cynical market manipulation. However, the likelihood of implementing a sustained programme of campaigning without a deep and genuine commitment to the cause in question seems low. The problem with this high profile campaigning is that the company must go to extraordinary lengths to avoid any suggestions of being hypocritical. The more strident the campaign, the greater the temptation for journalists to put the company's own performance to the test.

Alliances

Just as companies throughout the world are leveraging their resources by forging strategic alliances, so companies can put more muscle behind social responsibility initiatives by spreading the burden. Of course, where part of the motivation is image building, there is a danger of diluting impact – sharing the glory as well. In practice, however, some large companies are overcoming this difficulty (and in some cases enhancing impact) with innovative segmenting. For example:

- the Co-op's Care Grants scheme offered voluntary groups grants of £500 to £5000 for community projects. Three of the award categories – environment, streets and towns, and helping others – were funded by the Co-op itself. But two were funded by major suppliers: Flora margarine for health and fitness projects and Comfort for projects to do with children. The shared sponsorship was the result of an active approach by the Co-op's buyers to encourage supplier participation. All the suppliers who participated received a mention in the Co-op's customer newspaper (delivered to 2.6 million households) and on point of sale promotional displays.

  The Co-op has also forged an alliance with Tetley Tea to revitalise and relaunch the Cycling Proficiency Test for children.
- some multinational companies are encouraging national units to collaborate on community initiatives, particularly for international events.

Delivering results

Ultimately, the success or failure of companies' efforts to manage social responsibility issues as an integral part of executive responsibilities will depend on three factors:

- the degree of focus they can apply to ensure that efforts are not diluted
- the relevance of the initiatives they undertake, both for the company and for the various communities of interest
- and the commitment, particularly among top management, to developing the kind of climate, where socially responsible attitudes and innovation in community involvement can flourish and become a natural part of "the way we do things here".

No single company has all the answers to managing social responsibility. However, in the following chapters we have tried to capture some of the experience of a sufficiently broad spread of organisations, to at least point in the right direction.

Case study: IBM UK

IBM internationally has devoted a lot of time and effort over the past 30 years to developing practical management systems for social responsibility. The result is a complex yet integrated matrix of policies and responsibilities, as illustrated in the diagram:

At IBM's international headquarters in the United States, an ethical subcommittee advises the global board on broad policy issues. The European board interprets these in equally broad terms and monitors the social responsibility performance of each national subsidiary. It may also promote pan-European initiatives. Within each subsidiary, community involvement is part of corporate affairs, which reports to the national board through the personnel director, effectively tying external and internal social responsibility management together at the business policy level. There is a similar structure across the world, in each major country where IBM does business.

Sarah Portway, the UK public affairs manager, has responsibility for external relations, government relations, issues management and community relations. These functions were only brought together four years ago. She explains:

I recommend the sort of areas we should operate in, the budget we should have and the organisational structure for the department.

We decided to coin the phrase community investment so that the rest of the company could see what we do as a business investment rather than something attached to the chairman's office as a philanthropic activity. We

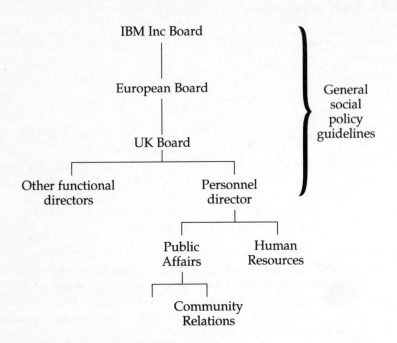

also wanted people externally to see it as something we expected to make a return on. We are working on how to develop measurement processes – it's a very tough problem.

We decided we should invest in areas most important to IBM. It was very important for our public policy agenda to be aligned with areas of our business where critical things were happening:

- industry policy
- education and training
- the environment.

We concluded we could develop meaningful community policies in the last two. To these we added the issue of disability with an emphasis on IT as a means of alleviating many of the problems people with physical or mental disabilities may have. The products we bring to market can have a real benefit for these people. Also add voluntary sector empowerment – helping them become more effective and efficient.

We started by analysing what strengths we had as a company. One of the conclusions we came to was that we knew how to manage, but that many charities lacked skills in that area. "Creative management skills" is a programme based on our own management development course and has been going for six years. Just being replaced with updated version: "Creative management in a changing environment."

Under the same banner we set up a fund for community computing. It came about because we were involved in a study by the Community Development

Committee into how voluntary organisations used computer equipment. The study found that they didn't use it efficiently because they didn't invest in training. So we instituted small grants of £1000 to buy computer training for them.

Another important form of voluntary sector empowerment for us is through secondment – lending people. It makes better use of the skills and resources we have, of our unique values.

It's hard to hold the line, to maintain our focus. There are a lot of pressures from inside and outside the organisation to make exceptions. We usually say no. We make sure people understand the strategy, especially at the most senior levels, so they will feel comfortable arguing the company's case when they are approached.

The management process

There is an annual strategy review by the main management committee for the UK company. I take to them our proposals in terms of strategy and funding. They give me direction on the proposals. It's a very healthy, educated debate.

The plan is also reviewed at European level – mainly for information and confirmation. They check that our spending is appropriate and reasonable and give some international guidance on areas to focus on.

The US headquarters has a public responsibility committee, which looks at ethical considerations and includes people from the external world. The IBM board in the UK doesn't have such a committee. Instead we have a Community Advisory Panel of four people – currently executives of National Council for Voluntary Organisations, Citizens' Advice Bureaux, the J. Rowntree Foundation and Earthwatch. It is a rolling membership (we don't want people to become too close to us) and we use it to advise my functional managers about social responsibility issues. None of the advisors receives a salary for their work, but IBM pays a contribution to their organisations instead.

The first of the four quarterly meetings sets the broad agenda for the year. Information and views from the committee members is supplemented by feedback from employees and elsewhere.

I have a central budget, but our programmes are a mixture of national and local, so budgets are also dispersed through regional directors. They have the discretion as to whether they should pass spending authority down to the individual location managers. We've been enthusiastic to encourage location managers to develop programmes consistent with national strategy. It's more difficult here at the South Bank in London, because most people who work here don't feel a strong identification with the area. But in areas such as Leeds, where people do identify with the city, it is much easier.

We educate the location managers in a variety of ways. For example, every manager can call up on his screen the full community investment strategy. We also run a community investment forum, where we and the regional directors meet quarterly to talk about top-down and bottom-up issues. Then every year we bring all the location managers together to discuss a wide range of activities they could undertake.

Involvement in community investment is not mandatory in performance assessment for managers – but it is part of their job specification and is taken into consideration.

We tell location managers to look out for critical local issues, such as AIDS in Edinburgh, where the local office has helped provide an education programme. We also encourage them to develop their own local strategies and the systems to run them.

Bottom-up input of this kind helps drive the national and international community investment strategies. For example, a major new issue for us is ageing. The Leeds office initiated a project in that area, which has led us to review our priorities. In order to keep a strategic focus, we would normally expect to change priorities, rather than simply add another priority area.

Some locations have community investment committees, where the employees become involved in deciding what activities to get involved in.

We recognise local community investment efforts through a formal chief executive's award. Locations nominate themselves and the award is given on an assessment of good practice in strategy, project management and originality of the programmes themselves. The winning locations receive a cheque to go towards the activity their entry was based on and an additional sum is made available to hold a celebratory event with the community partner.

Local environment action teams – groups of employees who get together under their own initiative to tackle a local environmental issue, such as a derelict piece of land – can also apply for specific awards from the centre.

Another award goes to individual employee volunteers. It consists of a trophy and some money for the organisation, to which they volunteer their time.

Measurement

We have two key measures:

- is it helping the business interests?
- is it helping the community?

We participate in a MORI survey on what people think about community investment. It's a helpful umbrella, but it doesn't tell us much else.

Last year we piloted in Bristol and Greenoch a more detailed survey of three audiences:

- employees
- opinion formers
- the general public.

We asked questions such as:

- what role should companies play in the community?
- what did they think about IBM in this context?
- what did they think about individual programmes?
- what should we be doing?

There were a lot of correlations between local and national opinions.

We also asked what people thought were the most important resources IBM had to offer. Every group put people resources first. This has helped us think through some of the strategic issues around whether to give money or time. We were also able to use some of the data on what people knew about us to refine the emphasis of some of our community activities.

At the individual project level, we aim to set clear objectives at the beginning, and gain the agreement and understanding of the partner organisations. Then we track progress closely against those objectives. For example, we review regularly with the subcontractors the contract stipulating what's needed for our Creative Management Skills programme. We also evaluate each week-long course, both immediately afterwards and six months later. In the six-monthly review we ask the participants from voluntary organisations:

- How do you rate the CMS you attended as an effective use of your time?
- How do you rate the course as an educational or developmental experience?
- How do you rate what you learned on the course in enabling you to do your job better?
- Do you currently use any ideas which you developed during the course?

Another form of measurement is what would be called repeat business in the commercial sector. In 1991, 45% of voluntary organisations using the scheme did so more than once.

We are also participating in a J. Rowntree Foundation research project to assess the impact of our community activities on the recipient organisations. Has our involvement made a real difference to them?

Individual locations provide annual reports on their activities, in which they assess their performance against broad strategic objectives. For example, IBM Edinburgh's report for 1991 contains five sections: strategy, implementation, results, project areas and a brief summary. An abbreviated version is reproduced here:

IBM Edinburgh statement of activity

Strategy

To support the community in areas of clear need through activities where IBM's contribution is recognised for its

- Value
- Effectiveness
- Quality.

Implementation

The strategy is achieved by:

1. Continuing people involvement

Approximately 50% of our 180 employees are involved in community projects as volunteers. They must want to be involved and must be given clear roles.

2. Continuing impact
We have an established process of

- Understanding the requirements of the community
- Defining our contribution to match
- Monitoring delivery and implementation.

This is driven by a Community Investment Committee consisting of staff from all levels and all functions.

Results

Our value to the community in the Edinburgh area in 1990 was £300,000 including cash, equipment and employee time (all given voluntarily without reduction in workload).

This covered 16 major projects and 20 smaller projects involving one or two people. Our efforts were recognised by us winning IBM UK's chief executive's Location Community Investment Award in 1990. Despite the recession and lack of funds, our level of employee volunteering has continued in 1991.

Project areas

Projects cover the areas of:

1. *Voluntary sector empowerment*
   - Citizens' Advice Bureaux – Cash, equipment, training, specially written software (600% productivity gain in handling money advice cases) and management advice. Scottish project managed from Edinburgh with a total value of £185,000.
   - Microbeacon – Personal computers for training people with disabilities. Cash, equipment and skills.

2. *Social concern*
   - Apex Trust – Training for young offenders.
   - Edinburgh Health Initiative – Drugs/AIDS working group.
   - Craigmillar Initiative – Urban regeneration advice and guidance.

3. *Environment*
   - IDEAS (Information Database for Environmental Action in Scotland) – Cash, equipment, training, advice and guidance.
   - National Museum of Scotland environmental exhibition – Cash, equipment and development of special software for their needs.

4. *Education*
   - School visits
   - Teacher placement
   - Work shadowing.

5. *Employee fundraising*
   - The Sick Kids Appeal – this was our single largest project of volunteers. They arranged fundraising events –
     - Sponsored Ten Step Award event at Meadowbank Stadium open to all Lothian Schools
     - 10K Race – Sponsored open to the public
     - Fun Run – Sponsored open to the public.

These events expect to raise over £10,000 and required significant commitment from all employees involved.

Measuring the impact on the business is much more difficult, however. You can't put a specific cash value on our activities for a particular year. You can only measure gradual changes in the way people think about us.

Communication

Historically, we have been ambivalent about publicising our community involvement. Only in recent years as we have brought it closer to the business have we begun to place more emphasis on communicating what we do. We tell the employees by electronic-mail and in the company newspapers and we produce simple informational booklets. But we don't take out big glossy advertisements or produce a social report.

Most of our publicity comes from being talked about by our community partners – and particularly from the members of the Advisory Committee.

Alliances

We have done some work with dealers as partners in projects. For example, when the Rediscovering Pompeii exhibition, in which IBM Italy was closely involved, came to the UK, we offered the opportunity to one of our dealers to supply the PCs.

We have also recently introduced in our local award scheme a category for projects that involve one or more of our business partners.

Case study: Whitbread plc

Although Whitbread has one of the longest established Community Investment programmes in the UK, the management team responsible for the day-to-day operations takes the view that it is only the beginning. The structure and organisation of the community activities have evolved significantly over the past decade, and particularly during 1991–92.

The first few years, explains vice chairman, Martin Findlay, ''were about getting board backing for the general direction of community investment policy and agreement that it should be involved. We developed a corporate activity where the board approved resources and major projects. Our goal was – and is – to set an example others could follow, to take the lead in new initiatives.

Driving the new thinking in social responsibility was a steering committee consisting of people from a variety of Whitbread backgrounds, who developed policy proposals to put before the board.

Since 1991, the focus of activities has begun to swing away from the corporate centre towards the operating divisions.

The corporate community investment team retains responsibility for developing a three-year business plan, which the board approves. Within the plan are defined both the objectives of the community investment plan and some broad overall guidelines for how they should be implemented. The objectives are summarised as follows:

- to help improve local communities economically, socially and environmentally

Organisation

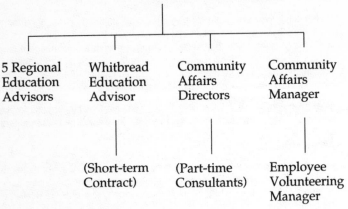

Director – Community Investment Programme

| 5 Regional Education Advisors | Whitbread Education Advisor | Community Affairs Directors | Community Affairs Manager |

(Short-term Contract)   (Part-time Consultants)   Employee Volunteering Manager

- to build Whitbread's corporate reputation and image by being (and being seen to be) actively involved in the community
- to encourage other non-competing organisations to get involved in community development activities by adopting a high profile in chosen areas
- to involve a wide range of Whitbread people to provide a broadening and satisfying experience for them.

The guidelines for implementation say that there should be:

- locally delivered activities with some centralised initiatives
- objectives set by the divisions, to fit their own business objectives
- a close alignment between the Community Investment Programme, corporate reputation and image, and the business needs of the divisions
- a shift in focus of community investment activities away from arts and small business development and towards education, volunteering, inner-city problems and communications
- a shift in emphasis from donations to involving the time, skills and enthusiasm of Whitbread people in their local communities.

Under a new structure, introduced in 1991, activities throughout the UK are supported by a complex regional network of regional education advisors and community affairs directors. The five education advisors are career Whitbread managers seconded to the task, who will usually move back into normal line management roles in due course. Supporting them is an education specialist. Their role is to support the divisions in the implementation of their education partnership plans at regional level.

Alongside them are seven community affairs directors, who are senior Whitbread managers who have retired and now work on a consultancy basis. Their job is to encourage a wide variety of other community initiatives,

Regional Network

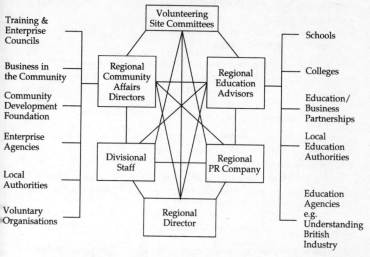

building bridges between the divisions and organisations such as Training and Enterprise Councils or local charities. They are supported by a community affairs manager at corporate headquarters. Among his responsibilities are communications (both internally and externally) and promoting employee involvement. There is also a manager, who works full time on developing the Volunteering Site Committees, of which there are now 12.

The local structure is also strengthened with input from a regional public relations company and the Site Volunteering Committees, which help both by putting forward ideas for involvement and providing the manpower to make things happen.

One of the big problems within a highly decentralised management structure such as Whitbread's, however, was how to provide firm leadership and direction within a region. A single area might have sites belonging to all four of the divisions. To resolve potential conflict and confusion, the company has designated a single senior manager in each area as regional director in addition to his line role. Their task is to raise the profile of Whitbread plc in their region. The Community Investment Programme is a major tool in achieving this task. There is a ceiling of 10% of the managers' time involved in this role. A high proportion of that time tends to go on maintaining communications between the various parts of the network and representing Whitbread at appropriate functions/activities.

Measurement is seen by the Whitbread team as a sign of maturity in social responsibility management. Key measurement criteria relate to both the objectives for community investment. Examples are:

- corporate reputation: measured through surveys of employees, shareholders and other observers
- recruitment figures from schools where the company has an education partnership (both numbers and quality of recruits)

- staff motivation: measured through attitude surveys and staff appraisal
- attitudes of local authorities towards Whitbread: measured by surveys and by the outcome of local authority decisions, in which Whitbread has an interest
- government contacts, in both Westminster and Brussels; how these influencers regard the company.

Although none of these measurements directly affects the bottom line, they do have an impact on the ability of the company to operate effectively. The director of the Community Investment Programme, Bryn Smith, has started to look at the possibility of measuring the impact of community investment on product and service sales, and on profits.

In the future, says Martin Findlay, the emphasis on regional responsibility for community investment will increase under the impact of the divisions assuming ownership of the programme. In line with that, charitable giving, which currently accounts for about 20% of the company's annual Community Investment budget, should gradually move away from the corporate centre until 75% is allocated in the regions.

Case study: Allied Dunbar Assurance plc

Allied Dunbar has an established community affairs department staffed by nine externally recruited community affairs professionals. According to community affairs manager, Des Palmer, the decision to delegate community affairs away from the board was an important one. He explains: "It's very important, too, that the community affairs budget is built in to the way the company operates. Other companies have a system where the board decides what the budget will be each year, which does not allow for long-term planning for community programmes. We, on the other hand, know that we'll get 1.25% of the profit the company makes and the board won't touch it."

Annual reports from the Allied Dunbar Charitable Trust state: "Responsibility and accountability for our community affairs activities have been delegated away from the board. Having made the important decisions in respect of principles, general direction, and resources to be made available, directors rely on trustees, in conjunction with professional staff and advisors, to develop and implement appropriate programmes."

According to Palmer, an invaluable mechanism for any company trying to establish a co-ordinated community policy is some sort of a safety valve to prevent accidental sabotage by senior managers who are constantly approached to contribute to worthy causes and sometimes find it impossible to say no, even when the cause in question does not match the company's policy objectives.

At Allied Dunbar the safety valve is the Special Projects Policy (formerly called the *ad hoc* policy) which:

- enables the company to respond to applications of "exceptional merit" which fall outside the corporate affairs department's current terms of reference
- enables the company to respond to appeals which, by virtue of its position in the financial industry, it is appropriate to support

- gives the opportunity to support charities with which employees are connected
- allows the chairman and other senior directors to respond to appeals from peers which benefit the company and the trust particularly when the time comes to return the favour.

"What we've done", says Palmer, "is allow board members in particular a small budget to support their favourite charity when they feel they can't say no. They don't have time to make themselves aware of current issues and needs, and so in this way we avoid contradicting or weakening our strategic policies."

The administration of the budget, however, remains firmly in the community affairs department, so directors have to make a direct application for it and can't release it without the department advising them on whether the company already supports the charity in question. Since they have a set allocation for the year, directors also tend to be more frugal with their donations. The take-up in 1990 was just £7000.

Allied Dunbar has very definite ideas, too, about selecting which projects to support. Says Palmer: "A fundamental principle of the Allied Dunbar approach is that you go and look or invite someone from the charity in before you fund anything. Going to see what's going on changes your prejudices; you find that what looked a bad bet on paper has potential and vice versa."

Far from raising expectations as one company said it would, the community affairs team at Allied Dunbar have found that charities are very pleased they take an interest by visiting them. Palmer and his colleagues have also found that on many occasions, although they are unable to fund a charity, they can offer advice or point them in the right direction for other available funds.

"We act as a conduit of information and ideas," says Palmer. "And because we see when things change, it can change our views sometimes."

Palmer also emphasises the importance of familiar management concepts for managing community programmes. In particular, he says, most programmes would benefit from greater emphasis on the processes of:

- assessing
- monitoring
- evaluating
- reviewing, sharing and feeding back into systems.

For example, when Allied Dunbar was setting up its schizophrenia programme, the community affairs department invited applications from a number of charitable projects. One application was submitted in an inappropriate format and was therefore returned with some strong recommendations for changes to the application.

The action caused a misunderstanding whereby the project concerned thought that it was being rejected, so panicked and attempted to lobby the company through the House of Lords.

Says Palmer: "We tried to rush the programme and as a result caused a lot of unnecessary heartache to all concerned. But when we evaluated what we'd learned, we introduced a two-phase procedure for all subsequent programmes. We now invite organisations to submit a draft application which it is understood we will make recommendations on. The recommendations are considered and usually incorporated in the final application. It's a very simple system, but it avoids misunderstandings that can lead to panic."

Another aspect of the Allied Dunbar approach is the importance placed on monitoring progress through annual reports compiled by programme charity participants. The requirement to prepare a report is included in written contracts drawn up between Allied Dunbar and the recipients of its support. Charity personnel are also invited to the company's head office to make presentations to the board.

Another method of monitoring programmes is through survey questionnaires sent out to those involved in the programmes asking what could be changed to improve things. In the case of the Open University diploma course the company sponsored for community affairs management, Palmer enrolled himself for the first course to evaluate the curriculum and teaching materials used.

What happens next?

The trend continues for concepts and methods in social responsibility to flow from North America to the UK and thence to the rest of Europe. So it pays for companies, which aspire to be at the leading edge of this area of management, to keep a close eye on developments in the United States.

The rise of new social issues seems inexorable and business can easily be caught in the cross-fire. For example, some US companies which thought they were displaying socially responsible attitudes by discouraging employees from smoking, have recently found themselves accused of discrimination against employees who smoke out of working hours. These companies had over-reacted against the need to protect non-smokers from passive smoking – one had even fired a female employee because a urine test indicated traces of nicotine. (The extra health care costs of smokers might also have been a contributory factor.)

While the UK and Europe will hopefully not follow the US down the sterile path of "political correctness" (which tends to cast social issues into rigid, black and white contrast), taking note of US experience is an important element in developing proactive social responsibility policies.

David Grayson, managing director of Business in the Community's strategy group, recently spent several months in the United States examining community involvement projects.

His conclusion is that the United States is entering a "third wave" of community involvement. He explained in Community Affairs Briefing: "If the first wave was philanthropy (ad hoc, responsive, driven by the CEO's whims); and the second wave involved focus and drills; then a third wave is now discernible [which] integrates this activity with all other aspects of the business. It relates the activity closely to the bottom-line concerns and treats the corporate community involvement function as a source of advice and expertise across the business – especially in developing global programmes."

Grayson points to a number of US attempts to measure the impact of social responsibility on business performance, including a study by UCLA, which suggests links between community involvement and the morale and productivity of employees, as well as financial indicators. In the UK, a recent study attempted to link investment in good people-management (training, fair compensation systems and so on) to financial performance. In our own researches, we identified a strong desire among managers responsible for social responsibility programmes, to have data they could use to demonstrate the benefits to top management and the investment community.

Among other trends identified by Grayson are:

- increasing internationalisation of community involvement programmes, with multinational companies exploring the potential to allocate programmes to different brands in different countries. (In fact, the key example he gives is a UK company, GrandMet, which has a very active US subsidiary.)
- increasing emphasis on partnerships between industry and the not-for-profit sector, with government often joining in as a third party. One result has been that the not-for-profits are becoming increasingly entrepreneurial and results-oriented in the way they approach business. Educational partnerships are particularly common and are expected to be a strong growth area (as is the case in the UK, according to our survey).

The time gap between the development of concepts in the United States and their application on the Eastern side of the Atlantic seems to be reducing rapidly, with some ideas making the crossing almost simultaneously. Could it be that within the decade we will see an equal two-way flow of ideas and methods?

2. Responsibilities towards customers

On the face of it, behaving responsibly towards the customer is the most obvious area of self-interest for commercial organisations. Public sector organisations, too, will normally have their objectives written in terms of fulfilling specific customer needs. Certainly, there is considerable evidence – for example, from PIMS data – to suggest that organisations which are truly customer-focused tend on average to have returns on investment as much as six times that of companies which are not. And, certainly, many more companies are now recognising that the value of a customer lies not in a one-off sale, but in ensuring he or she comes back again and again and again.

The aim, put simply, must be to be seen as "good business to do business with". In practice, such a public perception is only sustainable if the company goes to very considerable lengths to ensure that it is not undermined by contrary behaviour.

Companies serving industrial and commercial customers are increasingly learning the value of establishing long-term partnerships with them. Travel agency Thomas Cook, for example, has made this a fundamental element of its global corporate strategy. As a result, customers such as IBM now have direct access to Thomas Cook's own computer systems, so employees can book their own travel arrangements, when and how it is convenient to them. Agreements such as this require transparency of costs and a great deal of *trust*.

The customer element of a social responsibility agenda will normally consist of:

- customer responsiveness
- provision of information
- product safety
- ethical marketing.

2.1 Customer responsiveness

Thundered the *Financial Times* in February 1990: "Successful shops will be those which give the shoppers what they want in terms of what products they want, at the price they are prepared to pay, in the surroundings they find convenient. Like many things which seem obvious, these ideas are too often missed by those involved." Much the same applies to any business. The key to delivering what the customer wants lies in:

- having systems to listen to customers
- having systems to make sure that necessary improvements happen.

There are three main times when a company comes into contact with a customer:

- at the point of sale
- for servicing
- when it receives complaints.

Astute companies are increasingly dedicating significant resources to training people at the first two points.

Case study: Dell Computer Corporation

Dell Computers has evolved what it calls a "direct working relationship" with its customers. The American-based company pioneered unlimited telephone support for the life-time of a product via a toll-free telephone "hotline" and claims its engineers can solve 90% of customer problems over the phone.

Dell takes 25,000 phone-calls world-wide a day and its engineers can pull up on-screen details of equipment sold to its 750,000 existing customers at the touch of a button. Clearly, there are important spin-offs from such a close day-to-day dialogue with customers. For example, one customer-led innovation was the company's offer to ship systems fully loaded with applications software if required. The move enabled corporate customers buying large numbers of machines to save hours of time loading the software manually.

Companies are also finding, however, that training alone is not enough. The vast majority of failures to meet customers' needs arise because of systems, standards or structures outside the control of the people at the front line – i.e. most problems are management problems. Customer service programmes that work are those which recognise that the management issues need to be tackled first, or at least in parallel with the general smile training.

For example, Mastercare Ltd, which handles customer service warranties for the large electronic retailers Dixons and Curry's, estimates that 30% of all call-outs are because customers don't understand instruction manuals. Mastercare has repeatedly called upon manufacturers of electronic consumer goods, particularly Japanese and Korean suppliers, to improve the quality of instruction manuals provided with their products and to make operating procedures user-friendly.

As for complaints, companies should ensure:

- there is one clear address for all product complaints and queries. People need to know exactly who to call or write to. Ideally, this information should be on the product itself, rather than in operating literature that can be lost or destroyed.

    For service operations, however, the complaint should be dealt with at the point of delivery. Compare the following experiences:

    A large financial institution directed complaints to head office. The department responsible grew to the extent that, at over 100 people, it was no longer possible to accommodate it in the building. Meanwhile, line managers failed to put complaints right, because they understandably felt that this was now a head office function.

    Avis calculated the cost of dealing with complaints centrally and found that the extra paperwork, loss of time and other indirect costs came on average to more than £20. Added to this was the frustration of the customer at the desk, who has to wait days for his or her problem to be sorted out. Now Avis encourages its desk staff to resolve customer problems, up to the £20 level, entirely on their own authority.

- queries are turned around rapidly. Ideally, written complaints should be acknowledged by return – preferably with a telephone call. Every hour's delay allows the customer to grow more and more frustrated and to tell more people.

- there are technical experts within the company who will investigate complaints with the customer.

- there is a director with responsibility for ensuring that complaints are:
    – handled properly
    – analysed for trends
    – brought up for discussion at board meetings.

A handful of companies has also experimented with rotating responsibility among the top team, a month at a time, for answering all complaints that arrive by letter or telephone.

- a check is made into whether the customer is satisfied with the actions taken to put his or her problem right. Some companies have also appointed an ombudsman to represent the interests of the customers who are dissatisfied with how their complaint has been handled.
- that people at all levels in the organisation realise how valuable complaints are in identifying areas for improvement. By constantly taking notice of complaints, companies can achieve competitive advantage, simply by becoming better at the operational activities that affect customers.

So valuable does Corning Glass in the United States regard complaints, that it produced a booklet for customers, guiding them on how to complain.

Companies in the food manufacturing industry, which have experienced sympathetic complaints experts on call, have found that in a recent spate of queries about food hygiene and product safety, these travelling troubleshooters have more than earned their keep. The sight of a company employee on their doorstep to sort out the problem convinces customers that the company really cares. If customers believe that the company, or at least someone in it, is on their side, their goodwill towards it and their confidence in its products will rise.

Although effective complaints handling creates customer goodwill, ideally companies will identify most problem areas – and opportunities to improve products and service – by actively asking for customers' opinions. Normal market research techniques, such as opinion polling and mystery shoppers, can provide some useful information. But many companies are finding greater value from approaching customers direct, either inviting them in to talk about their problems and needs, or sending employees out to find out for themselves. Some, such as BT, are also making very effective use of customer panels.

Case study: Wessex Water plc

Wessex Water operates a Customer Service Charter to ensure customers receive the attention they deserve. The Charter lays down procedures for dealing with queries and complaints and emphasises the importance of rapid response either by telephone or in writing to establish a dialogue with customers.

Case study: British Telecom

In June 1992, in recognition of its responsibilities to all potential customers, including those with special needs, BT funded the launch of a national telephone exchange for deaf and speech-impaired people. Called Typetalk, the new exchange is run by the Royal National Institute for Deaf People (RNID) and based at Speke on Merseyside. Typetalk enables its users to communicate with other people through the operators provided. Through another scheme run in partnership with the RNID, BT gives rebates on text communication telephone bills.

In 1991 – in partnership with the Royal National Institute for the Blind – BT offered Braille and large print bills to customers with poor or no sight. In addition, a new telephone called Converse was produced to meet the needs of people with disabilities.

Case study: Safeway plc

Safeway, part of the Argyll Group, has taken a strategic decision to achieve differentiation from other food retailers by developing a reputation as the most responsive to customer needs, both nationally and at store level.

Every week, the directors visit about seven stores and look at them through the customers' eyes. They note details such as signage, product ranges and the amount of car parking space available.

When a store opened at St Helens, Merseyside, in July 1989, the company set up a customer suggestion scheme inviting customers to comment on its supermarket and to offer suggestions on how to improve it. The scheme was so successful that it has been extended to 14 other stores from Penzance in Cornwall to Irvine in Scotland. The St Helens branch took the scheme a step further by organising a customer conference. A hundred people were selected from more than 1000 who had sent in comments at St Helens. The participants spent the day grilling Safeway executives. Many of their suggestions have already been put into action. For example, the store used customer complaints about a dangerous exit to put pressure on local planning authorities to permit a second exit from its car park and to install a pelican crossing. It has also changed trolley designs because many customers complained the handle was too high, making it difficult to pick things out of the trolley.

Case study: British Gas plc

British Gas has published a guide entitled, "Commitment to our customers", laying down the standards and quality of service customers can expect. Customer relations managers are being appointed, who have the authority to award compensation payments up to £5000 and to deal with any outstanding customer problems.

Case study: Kwik-Fit

For Kwik-Fit, one of Britain's leading car servicing and repair companies, safety comes first from good workmanship and extensive guarantees.

When cars are brought in for repairs, customers expect that to be the end of the problem. Kwik-Fit goes to remarkable lengths to make sure that this is the case. It does so by

- training every member of staff so that they know exactly what to do, before they are allowed to work on customers' vehicles and by insisting on frequent refresher training
- showing the customer what is to be done before the job is started, and what has actually been done when the job is finished
- offering guarantees over and above those from the manufacturers
- publishing its own code of practice, which is monitored both by internal auditors and by independent organisations.

Checklist

1. Does your company have effective systems for listening to its customers?
2. Does it have a customer champion and/or ombudsman?
3. Are complaints regarded as a problem or an opportunity?
4. Does your company measure and analyse all complaints and use them to improve products and service?
5. Are employees empowered to resolve customers' problems on their own initiative?
6. Do you have a service quality policy and is it published for both employees' and customers' benefit?

2.2 Provision of information

Over the past decade there has been a growing expectation among consumers for accurate, relevant information about the products and services they buy. In part, this arises from a desire for reassurance; in part because people who want to make informed choices need information.

Case study: Tesco plc

Tesco has been at the forefront of nutritional labelling on its products. Customers can pick up a selection of free booklets from Tesco's branches covering topics such as fat, salt, fitness and health, vitamins and minerals.

In addition, the company publishes a cheap booklet on nutrition to help the customer understand its products.

Case study: Safeway plc

Safeway publishes a series of booklets on nutrition. The Safeway Nutrition

Advice Service is a department set up to extend the company's customer service. It aims to ensure that Safeway products comply with the highest dietary standards.

The service is responsible for ensuring that products carry nutrition information. Eventually, all Safeway food will carry this information, in addition to the list of ingredients, which is required by law.

Customers can contact the advice service to help with any diet, nutrition and health queries and for further nutritional information on health products.

Safeway, voted the "greenest supermarket" in *The Green Consumer's Supermarket Shopping Guide* by John Elkington and Julia Hailes, also gave out free "green action" calendars in late 1989. The calendars highlighted different environmental problems. Solutions ranged from building a bird table, through converting the car to lead free petrol to using bottle banks.

Eco-labelling

Perhaps the most burning issue of customer information is eco-labelling. The labelling of consumer goods to inform consumers of their environmental impact has been on the green agenda for some time. West Germany introduced its "Blue Angel" scheme as long ago as 1978. In the past few years Canada and Japan have both launched their own versions, while a number of other countries, including Britain, are poised to follow suit.

A decision by the Council of Ministers in December 1991, which gave the go-ahead to a European eco-labelling scheme, was welcomed by many green consumers within the EC. The European scheme will assess products on a cradle-to-grave basis taking into account the manufacturing methods used in their production. An eco-label will be awarded to those which meet specified environmental standards.

While its passage through the Council of Ministers reflects the growing power of the green consumer lobby, the voluntary nature of the scheme has drawn criticism from some green lobbyists. Friends of the Earth, for example, whose Green Con Awards did much to draw attention to the case for eco-labelling, is campaigning for tighter legislation in the UK to stop false and misleading labelling. The pressure group would like to see an amendment to the 1968 Trade Descriptions Act to cover environmental claims made by companies on behalf of their products.

Peni Walker, consumer products campaigner at FoE, stresses that the voluntary scheme proposed does not go far enough. "This scheme is better than nothing", she says, "but in order to have a lasting and significant effect on the environment, it should be mandatory. Protecting the environment should not be a voluntary option for industry but an absolute imperative."

A survey published by Mintel in May 1991 suggests public interest in buying green products is stronger than ever. Of those questioned in the survey, 39% said they always, or nearly always, bought "greener" products, while a further 20% said they tended to buy them. Against this background, the eco-labelling debate looks unlikely to end with the voluntary scheme currently proposed. More likely, it seems, is a series of steps in the next few years leading eventually to compulsory disclosure of the environmental impact of all products on sale to the public.

Clearly, it falls to businessmen to weigh up the strategic advantages of addressing their customers' preferences for environmental disclosure through eco-labelling. The growing influence of the green consumer lobby suggests, however, that companies would be wise to consider voluntary assessment before they are compelled to by new legislation.

Further unanswered questions on the subject of eco-labelling relate to the model that will eventually be adopted for assessment. For one thing, working out the environmental implications of a product is no easy task.

The voluntary schemes currently proposed by the UK and the EC use broadly similar models. They take a simple pass/fail approach based on "cradle-to-grave" or "life-cycle" analysis of the product applying for an eco-label.

The model takes the view that products impact on the environment in a number of ways: consumption of raw materials, consumption of energy, noise, the pollution of water, land and air and the generation of solid wastes. In awarding an eco-label each of the environmental impacts will be taken into account using an "assessment matrix". A final score will be arrived at which by this model is classified as either a pass or a fail.

However, Friends of the Earth favours a graded system so that products would not be simply passed or failed, but awarded green stars to indicate how the product affects the environment. If this system were to be adopted, companies would have to add a product's environmental rating to the list of competitive variables which currently include price, performance, appearance and convenience. More sophisticated consumers would no longer be appeased by the simple assertion a product is environmentally friendly, but would compare its green star rating with that of similar practices.

Checklist

1. Does your company have a programme to identify what information customers require and to ensure they receive it?
2. Could you comply now with the requirements of eco-labelling?
3. How will you ensure your suppliers provide information for product safety and eco-labelling?

2.3 Product safety

The legal requirements upon companies to ensure the safety of their products are becoming tighter and tighter. Debate within the European Commission as to how – and how far – to extend product liability has been heated and is likely eventually to require manufacturers to demonstrate more rigorous preventive systems and to raise the level of penalties for failing to react sufficiently rapidly to real or potential problems.

Customers, too, are becoming more demanding in terms of product safety. Reaction to food safety problems of listeria in eggs and soft cheeses and to BSE in beef demonstrates that the perception of risk is enough to persuade people to exercise the power of negative choice – at least until the publicity dies down.

Companies wishing to keep ahead of the legal requirements and to reduce the risk of customer distrust of their products should ensure they have:

- a monitoring system to give early warning of real or potential problems and to bring them to top management attention
- a network of experts who can be trusted to give truly impartial analysis of any problems (rather than give the answer they think the company wants). Ideally, any potentially serious problems should be put out to several organisations, to ensure a representative spread of expert opinions.

- a system for rapid response – e.g. to remove suspect stock from the shelves. Wherever possible, those systems should be tested from time to time with a "product fire drill" to make sure they work in practice.

Case study: Texaco

Texaco's policy is to ensure that all its customers are supplied with accurate and up-to-date product safety information on any products they buy. To support this policy and in response to the Consumer Protection Act, in 1988 Texaco Ltd established the Product Safety Information (PSI) Database.

This computerised system currently holds the product safety information on all Texaco products sold in the UK. This involves approximately 700–800 Material Safety Data Sheets giving detailed information on the safe handling and storage of individual products.

Whenever a customer's order is placed through the computerised ordering system, PSI automatically picks up the order and allocates the appropriate safety sheet, which is then printed that night and placed in an envelope for next day's first post. In this way the Material Safety Data Sheet reaches the customer at the same time, and in many cases before, the arrival of the Texaco product.

Product safety information is constantly updated by Texaco's product safety specialists. Any significant changes in health, safety or environmental information automatically results in the reissue of the appropriate data sheet to all customers who have made purchases in the last two years.

Case study: ICI Group

ICI states that it is determined to encourage the responsible use of its agrochemicals. The aim is to maximise their effectiveness while minimising the risks inherent in their use. ICI's Product Stewardship programme looks at every step from manufacturing through marketing and distribution, to final use and impact on the environment.

The risks are not always the obvious ones, says ICI in its annual report for 1989. For example, some years ago ICI discovered that its leading herbicide could be mistaken for cola or coffee. The risks were increased because farmers, in the Third World especially, sometimes stored leftovers in old bottles against the advice on the label. The company immediately changed the colour of the product and added an unpleasant-smelling agent.

In Malaysia, ICI uses posters, radio advertising, training sessions and videos to teach good practice to dealers, smallholders and estate managers. It also spends time designing clear, informative labels to ensure that distributors and users understand each product and its related dangers.

Case study: W.H. Smith

W.H. Smith's rapid response procedures mean the company is able to remove a faulty product from the shelves of its 500 high street stores within hours of an alert. On Tuesday 17 January 1989, for example, complaints from six members of the public alerted the company to a faulty switch on an illuminated globe which led to its removal from shelves in all 500 stores in under four hours.

Complaints about singed carpets and blown fuses alerted the company to a potential danger to customers. A decision had to be made on whether to operate a recall on 40,000 globes supplied from the Far East. W.H. Smith acknowledges that there was a temptation to wait and see if further complaints were received, but the need to present the company as a caring and responsible family business took precedence.

The company's PR department was concerned that a member of the public would complain to their local newspaper and the situation could escalate. Fortunately, the company had proactive crisis management procedures in place to ensure a rapid response. On Thursday 19 January, after negotiations with its insurers, an *ad hoc* emergency recall committee made up of the managing director, the marketing director, the buyer concerned, and representatives from the company's PR and distribution function was convened and the decision was taken to issue a recall on the product.

The company's PR department was instructed to place advertisements in national newspapers to inform the public of the potential danger. PR decided to pre-empt the inevitable press interest the advertisements would cause and turn the situation into a positive one. It arranged an interview on Breakfast Television which was broadcasted at 8 am the next morning and immediately followed it with a press statement sent out on the WIRE news service to all national and provincial media. The release stated that customers could return their globes for a cash refund.

W.H. Smith's branches reported that several customers returned their globes that morning. A number of press enquiries followed and resulted in coverage in both national and local newspapers. As a result of its swift action, however, the message was controlled with no negative comments whatsoever.

On Monday 23 January, posters were displayed in the company's stores and on Wednesday 25 January advertisements appeared in the national newspapers.

In a review of its own performance during the crisis, W.H. Smith's PR department observed:

- Working closely with the product team we were able to contain and control
- No damage was done to the company's reputation
- We acted as a responsible company with the customers' safety maintaining paramount importance.

Checklist

1. Does your company seek to more than meet the legal requirements for product safety?
2. Does it have systems to provide early warning of possible safety hazards?
3. Does it have a disaster plan, to withdraw a suspect product rapidly?

2.4 Ethical marketing

The Advertising Standards Authority regularly has to deal with companies that have misinformed the public. Its case report for June 1990, for example, adjudicates on a double glazing advertiser, which illustrated leaded glass windows, but quoted prices which did not apply to leaded glass.

Says the report: "This is a technique which understandably irritates most of us. More important, it fails to meet basic standards of straightforward information, which readers have a right to expect from such advertising. It is unrealistic to list all prices, and every detail for every type of product, but if any prices are quoted they must not mislead."

Every month the authority has to deal with hundreds of complaints referred by the public about advertising by companies ranging from large multinationals to small local concerns. The range of complaints extends from dubious taste to deliberate deception. Common problems currently include false environmental claims and sales promotions which do not mention important conditions attached.

Most of the companies involved could have saved themselves embarrassment by contacting the ASA in advance.

In March 1992, the *Financial Times* reported that proposed legislation to ban tobacco advertising throughout the EC looked less likely to come into force. Yet, regardless of the final outcome, the debate in Europe about whether tobacco advertising should be outlawed as unethical or allowed to continue as a legitimate expression of freedom of choice serves to illustrate one of the many grey areas of ethical marketing.

In the US, where the controversy about tobacco ads has been equally heated, there have been particularly fierce exchanges over promotions which allegedly target "vulnerable" consumers deliberately. In one case, a campaign to promote Camel cigarettes featuring a cartoon dromedary named "Old Joe" led to calls from the US Surgeon General for a voluntary withdrawal of all Old Joe ads. Old Joe's problem, according to the medical lobby, is that children like him too much.

In the UK, car suppliers have been criticised for advertising which could encourage dangerous driving and for making safety claims which could be misleading. Reporting in January 1992, the

ASA upheld complaints over an advertisement by VAG UK, the Volkswagen-Audi distributor which claimed that "the Audi 100 is the safest luxury car ever tested". The authority ruled that the car had been tested only for frontal collisions. Its report also stated that an article supplied by VAG to support its claims "did not conclude that the Audi had beaten the other models tested".

The authority also upheld complaints against Renault UK for focusing on the rapid acceleration and top speed of the Clio model, singling out the use of "blistering" and "exhilarating" for criticism. A campaign by Vauxhall which included a claim that the new Astra model has a "pedestrian-friendly front" and referred to the vehicle as "thiefproof", was also criticised.

The issue of green advertising illustrates how marketing enthusiasm can undermine ethical marketing practices. To quote the *Financial Times* in June 1990: "Green advertising is challenging. The arguments are often more abstract or bogged down by complex scientific issues. It is arguably easier to seduce someone into buying something with an image of ostentatious opulence, than with an intricate explanation of how a disposable nappy manufacturer has eradicated dioxins from the pulp production process."

Some large companies came under severe attack for their cynicism. People aren't green about green issues and the *Financial Times* goes on to record:

"Saatchi's research shows that people now expect companies to be environmentally aware in every area of their activities. Companies cannot expect people to be impressed by their new advertisements if they do not take a responsible attitude to the environment in areas such as corporate strategy and production planning."

Case study: Friends of the Earth and the "Green Con"

The international pressure group, Friends of the Earth (FoE), has been at the forefront of the campaign to change companies' environmental behaviour.

According to a senior information officer at FoE the green revolution started in earnest after the widespread deaths of North Sea seals from an unknown disease. "It was at this point," she says, "that the wider media such as *The Sun*, *The Daily Mirror* and *Today* started covering environmental issues on a regular basis."

But as companies struggled to compete for this affluent and growing slice of the market, FoE identified a disturbing trend towards inaccurate labelling. Otherwise reputable organisations started to make banal claims about their products. For example, a 1989 advert for a popular car claimed:

"(This car) is capable of running on unleaded petrol. This means it's as ozone friendly as it is economical."

As Neil Verlander, information officer at FoE explains: "The statement was ridiculous since lead is too heavy to reach the stratosphere and doesn't interfere with the composition of the Earth's ozone layer. There is no connection therefore between the use of unleaded petrol and damage to the ozone layer."

In response to the growing number of spurious environmental claims, FoE began collecting examples of blatant eco-hypocrisy, launching the Green Con Awards in December 1989.

Since then the awards have become an annual event used to spotlight companies abusing public concern about the environment by providing false or misleading information.

For 1991, a number of new categories were included in the awards. The aerosol industry, for example, received special attention for making its third consecutive Green Con appearance. The Still Blowing it Award was given because a number of aerosols still contain ozone-destroying chemicals despite being labelled in a way that implies they don't.

Other new category awards included: The Sir Robert Armstrong Award for advertisements that were economical with the truth. A Scaremongering Award for using a picture of Britain submerged under water as a consequence of a rise in sea level caused by global warming. And the So What? Award for nonsensical claims – which went to a company for labelling a shampoo bottle ozone friendly!

A disturbing new trend, says FoE, is an increase in the number of companies supplying self-promoting propaganda to youngsters in the guise of objective environmental education. For their activities in this area several organisations were given FoE Pied Piper Awards for telling tales to children.

Checklist

1. Does your company have someone responsible for monitoring marketing practice on ethical and fair practice grounds?

Managing customer responsibilities

In designing a management process to ensure that the company meets all its responsibilities to customers, you should start with the following questions:

1. Who is responsible at board level?
2. Is there a structure to ensure that all relevant issues (including product safety and environmental issues) are raised with this director?
3. Is there:
   - a system to monitor and analyse complaints and produce regular reports?
   - frequent market research to test customers' opinions (of the company as well as its brands)?
   - procedures to bring managers into direct and frequent contact with customers?
   - procedures to resolve disputes with customers?
4. Do customers/employees perceive these to work?

If you can answer yes to all of them, you have the basis for building a relationship of trust with your customers. However, it is still not enough. The systems and structures within an organisation are frequently designed to filter out proper consideration of issues important to the customer. (It rarely happens from malice; merely from an excessive focus on operational needs.) British Rail conducts numerous customer surveys, for example, yet it apparently failed to take sufficiently seriously the problem of deaths when passengers fell out of trains. The organisation developed a tunnel vision where, because received wisdom said there was no problem, managers were incapable of seeing one, in spite of mounting evidence. In most companies, a major change in attitude, particularly among middle managers, but also in frontline employees, is an essential part of becoming customer oriented.

Making that change happen demands strong leadership from the top, both setting an example and communicating a clear vision of the customer relationships, to which the company aspires. It demands an investment in making change happen, via communications, in training and in adapting the infrastructure so that it supports rather than undermines customer responsiveness. The main lesson from companies that have travelled this road is that it is very demanding of executive energy and that success – in terms of competitive advantage – takes a long, sustained effort, over years.

3. Responsibilities towards employees

One of the emergent issues of the late 1980s and early 1990s is the importance of public perception as a factor in people's choice of employer. It has become increasingly clear that would-be employees, especially those with scarce skills, place a significant value on the reputation of an employer, on two counts: how it behaves towards the world at large (i.e. is it a quality organisation which cares for the community?); and how it treats its employees.

These issues affect not only recruitment but how people perform at work, how long they stay and how they speak and behave as ambassadors for the company (an important marketing issue). The cost implications of being seen as a poor or indifferent employer can therefore be very considerable. IBM, for example, calculates that it costs £150,000 to replace a qualified engineer; Pilkington calculates the cost of losing a graduate trainee after two years at around £50,000. Both of these companies have good retention rates; yet both are concerned to increase retention by paying more attention to meeting people's needs for development and job satisfaction.

To a considerable extent, this area of social responsibility has been covered by legislation – for example, on equal opportunities, employee rights regarding dismissal, or on health and safety. European legislation will gradually add to what is already a substantial legislative burden. But legislation generally represents only the minimum of action required in any area; moreover, some legislation, such as requirements for companies with more than 20 people to employ a minimum of 3% disabled, has been largely ignored, even by government departments and agencies. Similarly, equal opportunities legislation has had little impact on the promotion of more women into middle and senior management.

It makes sense, therefore, for the socially responsible company to ask itself:

Checklist

1. Are we sure we are aware of, and have policies concerning, all the issues likely to affect our reputation as a responsible, caring employer?
2. Are we meeting the legal requirements in full, in spirit as well as to the letter?
3. Do we significantly exceed those requirements?
4. Do our employees perceive the company as a caring employer?

To cover all the relevant issues here would require a book (or two) of its own. We have therefore focused on some of the most critical issues:

- equal opportunities
- developing talent
- health and safety
- employee welfare.

The common factor among these issues is that in each case good management practices can benefit both the company and the individual. Although there will always be some tension between the interests of the individual (who wouldn't like more pay?) and those of the organisation, the potential to establish win-win situations is very high. If employees are seen as a long-term investment, rather than a bought-in consumable, then the concept of partnership has strong validity here, too. One of the most encouraging signs of organisational maturity in the 1990s has been the growth of a range of agreements between individuals and the organisation (for example, personal development plans), which trade the commitment of the individual to the company's objectives for a commitment from the company to assist the personal development and general welfare of the employee.

3.1. Equal opportunities

Discrimination at work affects a wide variety of minorities. If experience in the United States is anything to go by, companies will eventually be obliged to take note of the special circumstances of the over-45s, the obese, homosexuals and even the plain ugly. UK legislation, however, has tended to focus on four main areas of discrimination – racial, sexual, religious and disability. For the most part, legislation is national in scope, but some regulations are regional in their application – for example, recent employment regulations in Northern Ireland are designed to ensure that programmes of positive discrimination in hiring are not decimated by last-in, first-out redundancy policies.

There is no general body for enforcing equal opportunities in the UK. The Equal Opportunities Commission, set up in 1975, handles women's issues, the Commission for Racial Equality deals with race and the disabled have to make do with a set of voluntary bodies, whose task is to make sure they get a fair hearing in the workplace.

"Lip-service to an equal opportunities policy is not enough", said Employment Minister Robert Jackson speaking at the launch of the government's Ten-Point Plan on equal opportunities in March 1992. "For any policy to be effective, employers must take action to make it work."

Advocated by the Department of Employment and supported by both the Equal Opportunities Commission and the Commission for Racial Equality, the ten steps are:

1. Develop an equal opportunities policy, embracing recruitment, promotion and training.
2. Set an action plan including targets, so that staff have a clear idea of what can be achieved and by when.
3. Provide training for all staff to help people including management, throughout the organisation, to understand the importance of equal opportunities, with additional training for staff who recruit, select and train employees.
4. Monitor the present position to establish the starting point and monitor progress towards objectives to identify successes and shortfalls.
5. Review recruitment, selection, promotion and training procedures regularly, to ensure good intentions are put into practice.
6. Draw up clear and justifiable job criteria and ensure they are objective and job-related.
7. Offer pre-employment training, where appropriate, to prepare potential job applicants for selection tests and interviews and positive action training to help under-represented groups.
8. Consider the company's image within the community to see whether it encourages applications from under-represented groups, and feature women, ethnic minority staff and people

with disabilities in recruitment literature to ensure the company is not seen as an employer that marginalises these groups.

9. Consider flexible working, career breaks, provision of childcare facilities and so on to help women in particular meet domestic responsibilities and pursue their occupations; and the provision of special equipment and assistance to help people with disabilities.

10. Develop links with local community groups, organisations and schools to reach a wider pool of potential recruits.

Despite a spate of equal opportunities legislation, employers are continuing to discriminate against women, disabled people and ethnic minorities, according to the TUC, the Equal Opportunities Commission and organisations, such as the Spastics Society, which represent the disabled. All of these organisations are advocating affirmative action programmes to combat discrimination. These should be based around a detailed and comprehensive equal opportunities policy and programme.

In theory, predicted shortages of entrants should have stimulated companies to greater efforts, to ensure that they recruit from minority groups, pay them at the same rates, and promote representative proportions of those minorities into supervisory and management positions. Certainly, there are a number of well-publicised examples of companies that have done so. For example, several retailers have announced programmes of positive discrimination in favour of over-50s; others have deliberately located new factories in inner-city areas with high black unemployment. But evidence that companies in general have increased activity in this area is rather more difficult to find.

What evidence there is, from both sides of the Atlantic, suggests that equal opportunities will only be achieved if companies take the following steps:

1. Have a policy outlining the company's standpoint on this issue and clear goals to achieve.

2. Have an active programme to identify and encourage candidates for recruitment or promotion to come forward, and to help them overcome any disadvantages that reduce their eligibility. For example, when personnel staff from some companies visit inner-city schools, they take with them black and Asian managers and apprentices to create rapport with minority students, who feel less threatened and more

encouraged to ask questions about opportunities within the company.

3. Measure current performance in a manner that allows progress to be monitored year on year. In practice, this requires the company to gather sensitive data about the people who work for it and to analyse carefully the proportions of key minorities in relation to the population as a whole and in relation to the spread of people at different levels in the organisation. The very sensitivity of the data can make this a difficult task. Ingrained suspicion may make people question what the data is used for. Hence it is essential for the company to explain carefully how the information will be processed and that only anonymous statistics will be released. When the data is collated, it should be released as quickly as possible into the company newspaper to reassure people that the company's intentions are genuine. Where possible, it is also advisable to get people to fill in questionnaires about racial origins themselves. It increases their confidence in the programme and also causes far fewer errors.

Other, rough and ready, methods of establishing a company's equal opportunities performance include simply asking people whether they feel they are being discriminated against. In spite of the growing popularity of the attitude survey as a means of determining how employees view their work, their immediate boss and the company as a whole, it is scarcely ever used to ask employees how they view the treatment they receive as compared with the treatment of other workers around them. Yet what better way to detect discrimination than through the eyes and ears of the people who suffer it?

4. Be alert to unintentional discrimination. The classic case here – certainly the most frequently quoted – is the New York Police force, which insisted on a minimum height for applicants of 5 feet 10 inches. This discriminated not only against women but against Hispanics and Orientals, who are often smaller than the average Northern European male. Analysis of the job content showed that the only time height was required was to fire over the top of a car. Even then the person only had to be 5 feet 8 inches. The force reduced the height stipulation after a woman brought an action against it. The resultant publicity made organisations on both sides of the Atlantic look closely at their recruiting policy for unintentional discrimination.

In the following pages we have attempted to focus on some of the more innovative and socially responsible companies where positive discrimination has become a requirement. The principal groups these companies are tackling are racial minorities, the physically handicapped, women and the mature employee.

Checklist

1. Do you have a written code of practice on equal opportunities?
2. Is your equal opportunities policy led at board room level?
3. Do you have a senior manager responsible for monitoring and implementing equal opportunities?

3.1.1 Ethnic minorities

The industrial history of the British Isles is one of gradual assimilation of ethnic minorities. The beginnings of industrial-isation were fuelled by Huguenot immigrants, bringing new technologies of cloth making, and their absorption into society was not without heated discussion and antagonism. At the turn of the twentieth century, London and Liverpool were the focus for immigration of large numbers of Jews from Russia (many of them under the impression, initially, that they had landed in the United States). In the near-century since, Britain has also absorbed waves of Chinese, Cypriot, Caribbean, African and Asian immigration. The degree of discrimination – or difficulty in becoming absorbed into working society – these immigrants experience depends on a variety of factors, of which the most important may be:

- the level of technical skill/education they hold
- the degree to which they are noticeably "different" and determined to preserve their difference
- the scale of immigration
- the prevailing economic climate
- the homogeneity of the society, which they are trying to enter.

Depending on these factors, a group may be fully assimilated immediately, at one extreme, or only after several generations, at the other.

The socially responsible employer will want to establish the demographics of the local labour pool; to understand the cultural background from which major ethnic minority groups come; and to recognise that the organisation may need to adapt its requirements as much as it requires minority employees to change their behaviour to fit the established working culture.

Only then can it construct viable programmes, which will lead to fair representation at all levels in the organisation.

Checklist:

1. Do you have a clear statement of policy on racial discrimination, and on objectives in equal opportunity hiring and promotion?
2. Have you communicated this fully to the local community?
3. Do you know the ethnic composition of your workforce and the local community?
4. Do you have proactive measures to:
   - attract higher percentages of ethnic minority job applicant?
   - help them qualify for recruitment?
   - promote ethnic minorities into junior and middle management positions?
5. Do you provide training for managers and other influencers in the organisation, to reinforce non-discriminatory behaviour?
6. Have you reviewed all your recruitment and promotion practices to avoid unintentional racial bias?

Case study: Ford Motor Company

Ford has one of the most comprehensive and thoroughly researched equal opportunities policies and initiatives in the country.

Ford also has a joint statement on equal opportunity signed by the company and both sets of trade unions. The joint statement declares opposition to discrimination at work on the grounds of race, religious beliefs, creed, colour, nationality, ethnic or national origins, marital or parental status, sex, non-job related handicaps or age. It commits the company to the elimination of discrimination on these grounds, to the active promotion of equal opportunity and to the provision of training in equal opportunity practices for both trade union representatives and ordinary employees.

To implement these policies, Ford has an equal opportunities department which is based at Warley in Essex and headed by a senior manager, Shanti Selvarajah. Selvarajah has a general personnel background, having joined the company as a graduate trainee in 1986.

The department's role is to develop and update the company's equal opportunity policy and strategy, to monitor and advise management on progress and trends, and to develop and assist in new initiatives. It is also responsible for reviewing opportunities within the community. The company has focused its activities on positive action for ethnic minorities and women with special emphasis on educational assistance.

The company had a firm basis from which to work since it has been monitoring the ethnic background of its workforce since 1967 at its Dagenham plant. Figures at that time showed that 34.7% of all job applicants for hourly paid jobs were from ethnic minorities and 32.5% of these were hired.

A question on ethnic origins was included on a pilot basis in application forms for graduate vacancies in 1978 and 1979. This system of self-classification was extended to all application forms soon after. Any applicant who does not answer the ethnic origin question is classified by his or her interviewer.

Ford also gathers information about local demographics, identifying for example, that 20% of the population of nearby Newham comes from ethnic minority backgrounds. The equal opportunities department believes that the ratio between the ethnic minorities and white employees should be the same at each hourly and salary grade. In reality, ethnic minorities are concentrated far more in the lower grades, with the numbers tapering off as the skill level rises. At present, less than 3% are in the skilled grades. The proportion of ethnic minority technical trainees has risen from 1% in 1977 to 7.7% in 1991 and this should eventually be reflected among the trained workforce.

Selvarajah is determined to bring even more young ethnic minority people onto the apprenticeship scheme, via positive action programmes. The Technical Training Centre at Dagenham organise a careers conference for teachers, parents and careers advisors to discuss the problems of recruiting ethnic minority individuals onto Ford training programmes.

As a result of the discussions, Ford took women and ethnic minority apprentices to local schools, so that prospective candidates could talk to somebody of their age and background about the training. In addition, the recruitment brochure was redesigned to include more pictures of young blacks, women and Asians. Staff awareness of the problem was raised by discussion and company courses. The equal opportunities department sent information sheets to schools describing the entrance test and giving practical examples so that pupils could prepare for it.

The proportion of ethnic minority job applicants rose from 5 to 18% by 1991 thanks to these measures. However, a significant number still did not get through the selection procedures says Selvarajah, due largely to high teacher turnover for mathematical and technological subjects in inner city areas.

The answer was a bridging scheme. Ford now pays £75,000 per annum for a year's course at Newham College, East London, for about 15 youngsters between the ages of 16 and 18. The first course started in September 1988 and was attended by 12 boys from ethnic minority groups and two white girls, but was open to all students regardless of race or gender. More than 50% of the students went on to join the Ford apprenticeship scheme. The company pays them a bursary for attendance, at a rate only slightly less than what the company pays undergraduates and the students are not committed to join Ford afterwards. The scheme proved so successful that it has run annually since 1988.

The equal opportunities department is also taking part in the Newham Compact, a government-sponsored scheme to build up a partnership between youngsters, educational establishments and employers. Selvarajah is on the steering committee and the manager of technical training is a member of the employers' group.

As part of the Compact, Ford gives teenagers work experience at its technical training centre in Dagenham. Managers from the company also go into the schools to work with the children and teachers return the visit with a stint at the technical training centre.

The company also sets goals for the pupils at local schools. These are not based on academic achievement, but discipline. (Among other targets youngsters must reach 80% punctuality and 80% attendance.) If they achieve these goals they can become Compact students on a Ford training programme.

Ford has trained more than 1000 supervisors to deal with any problems that arise such as discrimination and sexual harassment. Ford issued a booklet in the summer of 1990 advising its supervisors how to deal with discrimination. The company also runs equal opportunities courses. Managers, shop stewards and supervisors attend a two-day event called the Equal Opportunities Workshop. Participants are encouraged to plan positive steps to counter discrimination. They study the importance of equal opportunities to the company, how prejudice and discrimination can arise and the legal aspects of these issues.

Ford has also been concentrating on increasing the number of women and ethnic minorities in graduate jobs. Working in conjunction with sixth form colleges in Tower Hamlets, Redbridge, Newham and the North East London Polytechnic, Ford developed a pre-degree foundation course at the polytechnic for 15 youngsters between 18 and 19 years of age. These students have been assessed by their sixth form teachers as having potential but needing help to get through their A levels. Ford provides a bursary plus tuition fees for these students during the extra study year.

Ford's schools liaison department actively encourages female and ethnic minority employees to give presentations to local schools to provide role models and dispel stereotypes.

Case study: TSB plc

TSB operates a structured equal opportunities strategy covering race, gender and disability. Initiatives have included revising recruitment procedures; establishing closer links with ethnic community groups throughout the country; providing pre-recruitment training and rewriting recruitment advertising to include ethnic minority languages.

The TSB has forged links with various community groups but particularly in the West Midlands where the bank's head office is now located. Within the West Midlands, TSB has built up links with groups such as the Handsworth Breakthrough, Out Reach and Acafess.

Pre-recruitment training courses have been run at local colleges with significant ethnic minority intakes. The TSB offered work experience to students, and those candidates who successfully completed the course were guaranteed job interviews. The results were successful with six candidates being recruited. One of the lessons learned by the equal opportunities department was that black candidates often do not apply to financial institutions because they fear discrimination. By offering work experience the TSB hopes to break down those barriers.

TSB is currently developing new recruitment procedures which it is envisaged will encourage more ethnic minority applicants. Recruitment literature is now printed in several minority languages including Urdu and Hindi. The interview process has also been revised so that candidates are now asked to complete a series of exercises that closely resemble the type of work they will be doing in the bank. Such exercises are less open to subjectivity than other methods and mean candidates are selected on their ability to do the job for which they are applying.

TSB's equal opportunities policy is supported at the very highest levels. The equal opportunities policy is coordinated within each operating company by an equal opportunities coordinator. Equal opportunities statistics are monitored on a half-yearly basis and include information on the number of ethnic minority staff by grade and the number of ethnic minority recruits to the bank. The long-term strategy is that the composition of the workforce will reflect that of the external labour force. Final year figures together with action plans for the next financial year are presented as a report to the bank's executive committee.

Case study: The Department of Employment

The Employment Department Group is responsible for employment policy at the Department of Employment. It regards equal opportunities as the responsibility of all its staff.

The Employment Department Group equal opportunity statement sets out policy, the rights of staff and the responsibilities of managers and staff for promoting equal opportunities, within the terms and conditions of employment laid down for the Civil Service generally.

It states: "The Employment Department Group is determined to be an equal opportunity employer. We wish to treat all applicants and employees reasonably and fairly irrespective of ethnic origin, sex, marital status, sexual orientation, age, religion or disability. We want to ensure that:

- opportunities for employment within the Group are made known to a wide range of possible recruits
- no applicants or employees are put at a disadvantage by rules or conditions that are not justified by the needs of the job
- every employee's opportunities for training, promotion, and development are based solely on their ability and needs and the openings available
- our equal opportunity record matches that of the best outside employers.

"To support its policy the group has a network of equal opportunities officers (EOOs) and disabled persons officers (DPOs) from each part of the group. These include head office or regional personnel managers with overall responsibility for equal opportunities in their area. They in turn are supported by equal opportunity advisors who are usually higher executive officers in Personnel Management Branch.

"Since April 1991, parts of the group have had five-year Equal Opportunity Action Programmes in place which aim to increase the representation of women, ethnic minorities, and people with disabilities particularly at more senior levels."

3.1.2 People with disabilities

According to the Royal Association for Disability and Rehabilitation (RADAR) in April 1992 there were 370,835 people with disabilities registered with the Department of Employment. But as Mr Tim Eggar,MP for Enfield North, stated in April 1990, only 23.3% of private sector employers who are required to have 3% or more workers with disabilities, actually do so. Only 4.7% of public sector organisations fulfilled their obligation.

Figures from the Office of Population and Census Studies show that there are 6,202,000 disabled adults in the UK which is over 14% of the total adult population. Of these, 93.2% live in the community and 41.8% are aged between 16 and 65. Yet only 36% of disabled men and 31% of disabled women of working age are in employment.

The *Financial Times* noted recently: "Disabled people of working age are four times more likely to be unemployed than their able-bodied counterparts and earn, on average, about half the salary."

A recent survey by the Spastics Society found that two-thirds of employers discriminated against job applicants who admitted they had a disability, even though the disability would not affect their ability to do the job. The society is pressing for anti-discrimination legislation along the same lines as for race or sex.

Among the reasons companies most frequently put forward for not hiring people with disabilities are:

- trade unions are often more concerned about finding jobs for the able-bodied, who they insist must be given priority
- disabled people will have greater absenteeism and add to insurance costs because they are a safety risk
- people with disabilities can't work as efficiently as the able-bodied.

In practice, most of these assumptions turn out to be at best only partially true. Some years ago, the US chemical company Du Pont conducted a survey of the safety, attendance and job performance records of 1425 employees with disabilities. The employees had a variety of handicaps, including partial paralysis, lost limbs, deafness, blindness and chronic heart ailments. The people with disabilities were found to be better on all three counts than the able-bodied people. In job attendance, for example, 79% had a better than average record. In job performance, only 9% were below average while 37% were above average. In terms of safety they also outscored the able-bodied. More than 50% had a better than average record. The study also recorded how long they had been with the firm. It found that 90% had been there an average or longer than average period. There was comparatively low labour turnover among the disabled.

In January 1992, the Employers' Forum on Disability launched its Agenda on Disability aimed at extending equal opportunities to people with disabilities. The core of the initiative is a pledge by 21 UK companies to a ten-point agenda of action to promote job prospects for people with disabilities and remove discriminatory practices which hinder their careers.

Explains the director of the Employers' Forum, Susan Scott-Parker: "Our aim is to help companies put disability firmly on the equal opportunities agenda. Historically, equal opportunities has been influenced by the legislation focused on women and ethnic minorities while people with disabilities have been overlooked. Employers do not discriminate from ill-will as much as from simply not knowing what needs to be done. This agenda spells out the first priorities."

Key elements of the Agenda for Action include:

- making a positive effort to attract people with disabilities and, once employed, developing their careers to the benefit of the company and themselves
- changing attitudes within the workforce through training and awareness programmes
- monitoring progress through an annual audit of performance towards implementing the agenda, reviewed at board level
- communicating achievements and objectives to employees and a wider audience via annual report.

Case study: Midland Bank

Midland Bank is a core member of the Employers' Forum on Disability and supports the ten-point agenda. In conjunction with Skill (the National Bureau for Disabled Students) and the Birmingham Employers' Network on Disability, Midland is running what is hoped will be the first of many job-search skills seminars aimed at enabling disabled students in their final year at university to acquire the skills necessary to get the jobs they want.

In addition, Midland helped to develop and is the principal sponsor of the Employers' Forum "Guidelines on the Monitoring of People with Disabilities in the Workforce". Launched in 1991 by Midland's chief executive Brian

Pearse, the guidelines provide practical steps for companies to be able to monitor more accurately the profile of disabled people in the workforce through a process of confidential self-declaration by employees.

Midland has introduced its own pilot monitoring programme following these guidelines.

Midland also runs a programme of work experience placements linked with training organisations such as Outset, Action for Blind People and Lambeth Accord. The company is currently in the process of establishing a database of information about these placements.

Case study: Barclays Bank

At Barclays, each regional office has a designated person within its personnel team with specific responsibility for disabled people. A disability equality course is run for a wide group of those likely to be involved in recruitment and selection, as well as internal conferences for personnel managers and recruitment officers.

Case study: London Electricity

London Electricity publishes a wide-ranging statement on equal opportunities for the employment of people with disabilities. Areas covered include recruitment, career development, health and safety, training and publicity, redeployment and re-training, government liaison, consultation and management responsibilities.

As part of its policy on employing people with disabilities, the company regularly reviews its recruitment policy. Included is a review of the language used in application forms; monitoring progress of applications from disabled people, offering assistance in the form of interpreters at interview stage and adapting premises where necessary and practical. Qualified disabled candidates receive automatic shortlisting for interviews.

Regular meetings are held between disabled employees and personnel staff with the aim of involving both in the development of company policy and procedures.

London Electricity has also developed a distinctive policy on its role and responsibility in the London community. Staff are seconded to disability organisations including Opportunities for People with Disabilities; equipment is donated to Oak Lodge School for the Deaf; and financial assistance is provided to organisations such as Riding for the Disabled.

One of the keys to getting the most out of disabled workers is to treat them as much as possible like everyone else. Disabilities can often be overcome through training or minor adjustment to equipment. Most companies experienced in this area avoid creating enclaves of disabled employees or sheltered workshops. In such an environment, it is inevitable that the employees will adapt to a rule where they are not expected to perform as well as others. Most disabled workers neither ask nor desire to be mollycoddled.

French company, Banque Nationale de Paris, has an innovative approach to the disabled. It runs its own training school for the disabled where it teaches them basic banking skills. It started the school in 1965 because so many of its employees had disabled children who could not find work. As soon as the students reach the proficiency level of regular employees in skills such as bookkeeping or dealing with bonds, they are transferred to a full-time job in one of the bank's branches.

Companies like General Electric in the US or Cadbury Schweppes in Bournville, Birmingham, have made it a policy to incorporate ease of access for disabled people in all new offices and factories. Aids that can make access much easier for disabled workers include non-stop flooring, handrails on stairways and lower than normal drinking fountains and public telephones. The most practical way to establish where access improvements are needed is to ask handicapped people. It is very hard for the able-bodied to appreciate the difficulties of being confined to a wheelchair or of lack of sight.

People with learning disabilities also have a role to play in today's workforce. All that it requires is that the personnel department thinks a little harder about job content.

Supermarkets and large stores are increasingly using such people to stack their shelves. These workers gain immense job satisfaction from doing dull, repetitive tasks and by doing so they free other workers to do more demanding work elsewhere. Fast food outlets are using them to clean the tables and floors throughout the day, leaving others to man the tills.

While there are problems with using these workers – they need more supervision, they cannot be hurried because it destroys their concentration and they may have to be transported to and from work – the benefits tend to outweigh the disadvantages.

Case study: The Post Office

The Post Office's long-standing commitment to equal opportunities is contained in a joint policy statement agreed with the unions.

This declares opposition to discrimination at work on the grounds of race, colour, nationality, ethnic or national origins, religion or creed, sex, sexuality, marital status or disability.

The Post Office was one of 20 employers invited to support the launch in 1991 of a new disability symbol, indicating commitment to providing real opportunities for people with disabilities. It is now being used in job advertising and recruitment literature. Twenty corporate personnel attended external courses held by Disability Matters Ltd, and links are being forged with appropriate agencies to match people with disabilities with jobs.

Case study: The Littlewoods Organisation

The Littlewoods Organisation is one of the UK's largest private companies. Its business activities include retail chain stores, agency home shopping, Index, the catalogue shop outlets and an interest in the Littlewoods football pools and competitions partnerships. It has a turnover in excess of £2 billion.

As part of a long-standing commitment to equal opportunities, Littlewoods is actively involved in providing opportunities for people with disabilities, both in terms of employment and career progression.

The company employs over 400 full-time staff who are registered as disabled and 500 staff who are not registered, but have disabilities such as epilepsy and multiple sclerosis.

Attention has been given to the provision of ramp access, special toilets and other adaptations to meet the needs of employees with disabilities, such as visual fire alarms in buildings where deaf people are employed. In some cases job content has been amended to enable those with disabilities to contribute fully to their work.

A number of pupils with disabilities from the School of the Good Shepherd, Litherland, Merseyside have undertaken work experience at the Littlewood site in Crosby. The visit was so successful that one of the children was offered a place on the YT scheme.

Littlewoods is happy to play host to other companies which wish to see the facilities and discuss the initiatives taken by the company to assist people with disabilities.

Checklist

1. Have you set yourself targets to employ a certain proportion of disabled people by a set date?
2. Have you checked access to factory and office buildings? Can disabled people get into your premises to work?
3. Look at the work stations and the duties of the job. Think of ways of making the tasks disabled-friendly. Install a screen reader so blind people can work on your computers and word processors.
4. Can some work be put out to disabled home workers?
5. Are there any tasks that can be profitably done by people with learning disabilities?

3.1.3 Working for women

According to the Henley Centre for Forecasting, women are expected to make up more than half of Britain's workforce by the turn of the century. At present they occupy one in three jobs. Henley expects three-quarters of all new jobs to be filled by women and the proportion of women in full-time professional occupations or senior management will increase from its present 5%.

Leading corporations, such as the high street banks, are trying to make it easier for women to return to work after having children, and to encourage older women to work. For example, Lloyds offers career breaks to both men and women who have been with the company more than five years. Its ultimate aim is to encourage all eligible staff to take a career break. The bank will give consideration to requests for several breaks with a total absence of not more than five years and guarantees that the employee comes in at the level he or she left. This is mainly because of a predicted skills shortage.

"Women on the Board", a report published by the Policy Studies Institute in October 1991, examined the under-representation of women in the boardroom. Research for the report included two surveys: one of chairmen of companies known to have appointed women non-executive directors and the second of the women appointed. It concluded that:

- companies continue to neglect women for boardroom appointments. Fewer than 5% of directors are women, even though the pool of talented and experienced women available for such appointments continues to expand
- company chairmen continue to hold stereotyped views of who makes the best boardroom director, too often seeking the chief executives of other companies to be their non-executive directors
- companies that have appointed women non-executive directors have reaped the benefits of independent thinking and new perspectives
- companies need to change their strategies for appointing non-executive directors, by re-examining their selection criteria and recognizing the value of more varied, less conventional and often richer female careers
- companies need to expand the sources they use to locate potential non-executive directors to include the voluntary sector, the civil service and local government.

Opportunity 2000

Prime Minister John Major's backing ensured widespread publicity for the launch of Business in the Community's Opportunity 2000 initiative in October 1991. The initiative, which aims to improve the prospects of women in the workforce by the year 2000, is supported by 61 founder member companies. All 61 have publicly pledged to set and meet measurable goals to improve employment opportunities for women at all management levels.

Opportunity 2000 is a purely voluntary scheme, but Business in the Community hopes its high public profile will raise expectations and encourage companies to meet their stated targets. By May 1992, a further 49 companies had joined the Opportunity 2000 initiative making a total of 110 participants in all, covering 20% of the British workforce. Participating organisations include 20 government departments, the five main high street banks and a number of local authorities. It is also anticipated that peer pressure will continue to boost the number of companies supporting the initiative in the next few years. Some of those participating, for example, also plan to encourage good equal opportunities practice among their suppliers.

Speaking at a reception to announce the new signatories, Lady Howe, who chairs the Business in the Community's women's economic development target team leading the initiative, said: "None of us would claim that Opportunity 2000 will solve everything on the equal opportunities front. But we hope we can persuade more businesses that it is in their commercial interests to participate."

It is also anticipated that peer pressure will boost the number of participating companies in the coming months. The companies supporting the initiative have introduced a variety of measures aimed at achieving equal opportunity goals. These include:

- training schemes for senior and line managers
- board-level awareness programmes
- progress updates in annual reports
- building equal opportunity objectives into appraisal schemes
- targeting maternity retention rates.

Case study: Cadogan Management Ltd

Cadogan is a seven-year old management services company with ten full-time staff and 30 part-time associates. The company has always nurtured what it describes as a learning culture by offering staff continuous training programmes and encouraging membership of professional organisations, particularly those for women. Cadogan also offers mentoring, job shadowing and work experience for students and women returning to work after a career break to start a family – in 1991 it provided four such opportunities.

However, with 90% of the company's staff already female – including two directors and three managers – Cadogan's decision to become the smallest participating company in the g company in the Opportunity 2000 initiative presented it with different sorts of problems.

The company's mission, according to its managing director, Janet Brady, is: "To be recognised as a best practice employer; as an organisation that does not waste individual potential; to be seen as a pioneer/role model that encourages other companies to follow, in spite of our size."

In keeping with the principles of Opportunity 2000, Cadogan has set itself the following goals:

- to maintain female staffing levels of at least 50%
- to maintain an open policy for the recruitment of all staff
- to support women looking to start or return to careers in its industry by offering opportunities to a minimum of at least two work shadows and two women returners each year.

In addition, the company is pledged to maintain its flexible working arrangements for all staff. This includes the flexibility to work from home when the need arises; the chance to take career or study breaks; paternity or maternity leave with a staged return to work; encouraging women proprietors among its suppliers.

Janet Brady, Cadogan's managing director, has responsibility for the company's equal opportunities policy and its continuing support of Opportunity 2000. That policy is expressed in its vision statement – towards a balanced workforce – as follows:

"It is the company's intention to create and maintain a working environment where:

- individuals continue to learn and develop
- the best person is recruited for a job, regardless of gender, age, race or disability
- there is flexibility in hours worked to accommodate maternity/paternity leave, child rearing, career breaks, illness and/or care for the elderly.

As part of the company's business planning process, results are measured: at quarterly board meetings; at monthly staff meetings; through individual job appraisals; by comparison with other best practice employers regardless of size.

Case study: Kingfisher

Kingfisher employs over 61,000 people in the UK. Currently 69% of the total workforce and 31% of the managers within the group are women.

A founder member of the Business in the Community's Opportunity 2000 initiative, Kingfisher states that it is "committed to ensuring that the group's policies and programmes operate to provide equality of opportunity based on performance, individual aspiration and potential".

Its principal goal is to "increase the number of women at middle to senior management level".

To achieve this aim, the group's operating companies have set a number of goals as follows:

- Woolworths is pledged to recruit 80% of all management vacancies internally by 1995.
- Superdrug is pledged to increase the proportion of women in middle management from 16 to 20%.

A main board director is responsible for equal opportunities across all companies within the group. And operating companies report progress towards their target annually as part of their medium-term business and management development plan.

Case study: The National Health Service

Under guidelines issued by the government in January 1992, regional health authorities in the NHS are obliged to include a woman in the shortlist for every senior management appointment. By appointing up to 100 women general managers in the next three years, the health authorities are expected to double the number of women in senior management in the NHS.

The scheme, which is part of the government's commitment to the Opportunity 2000 initiative, was launched by Health Secretary Virginia Bottomley, who also set targets for the number of women accountants and consultants. Where there are no suitable women applicants for the management positions, names are to be included from a regional list of possible applicants.

A guide for health authorities and trusts sets eight goals aimed at breaking down barriers to women's careers. The guide includes targets for a 20% increase in the number of women representatives on health authorities and trusts and calls for initiatives on recruitment and retention.

Managers are asked to ensure that women returning to work after maternity leave or a career break are offered work on a similar grade to the one they left.

Authorities and trusts will be expected to give reports on progress made towards the targets set, which will be monitored by the NHS women's unit. Regional registers of suitable women candidates will be drawn up during 1992.

Case study: Audi

German car manufacturer Audi has been hiring women as apprentice tool makers and mechanics since 1978. Since 80% of its jobs are technical in nature, the company saw the initiative as vital to increase the number of women employees.

The original goal was to increase the proportion of female apprentices to 25%. But although over 700 women aged 15 to 20 have taken places on these training schemes, the target has not yet been reached.

One of the biggest problems, Audi has found, lies in persuading the women themselves to train for technical jobs. The company has found that the majority of women applicants would prefer to go into sales.

To change attitudes, Audi runs advertisements in German newspapers pitched specifically at female recruits. It also sends members of staff to give talks in schools to parents and students to explain the potential for women coming into their factory, to overcome the traditional image of the automotive industry as masculine.

The company has learned from experience that the best way to integrate women into the company is not to put them in all female teams but to mix them with the male apprentices. But women apprentices are encouraged to attend seminars where they can swap experiences.

Audi staff are offered over 50 different types of part-time work. Mothers can take a career break of up to seven years with a guaranteed job at the end of it and can retrain with Audi during their maternity leave.

To ensure the initiative receives the attention it deserves, a board director has overall responsibility for women's development.

The range of measures leading equal-opportunities oriented companies have taken to encourage more women back into the workplace, and into management positions, is considerable. Among them:

Company sponsored childcare

Midland Bank was one of the first organisations to tackle the issue of childcare when it opened a 45-place, wholly owned nursery in Sheffield in October 1989. The nursery, which charges £42 for each child, is subsidised by the bank and was the first of 115 introduced by 1992 providing 800 nursery places. All the nurseries cater for children from six months to five years and are supervised by qualified nursery nurses.

In 1990, Midland piloted a holiday play scheme for school-aged children during the summer and now has 50 self-financing play scheme projects in operation.

Midland calculates that its childcare policy has resulted in substantial savings in recruitment and training costs by retaining skilled employees who might otherwise have left.

Midland's equal opportunities director, Anne Watts, says: "Parents leaving to care full time for children represent a serious loss of skills. The costs of paying for childcare facilities is far outweighed by the savings made in other areas."

First Leisure employs women of all ages in its bowling centres and has solved the child-care problem in a slightly different way. Each centre has a children's playroom which operates during the day for customers who bring in their under-six-year-olds. Staff also take advantage of the supervision by qualified child minders.

Case study: The Body Shop

When the Body Shop day-care centre opened in January 1990 at a cost of just under £1 million, it was the culmination of two years work. The 6500 square foot building is the first purpose-built company nursery in the UK and is designed to be energy efficient with sophisticated heating control systems, low energy lighting and double glazing throughout.

The decision to build the day centre came from a workplace survey, conducted in April 1988, which concluded that many of the company's employees would welcome the provision of a workplace nursery. Body Shop recognised that expertise was needed and brought in Kids Unlimited Triangle design team. The relationship proved highly successful and Kids Unlimited now runs the day-care centre on behalf of the company.

Set in 1.5 acres of landscaped playground, bramble and hazel hedges create a natural habitat for wildlife with further landscaping and development planned with parents' involvement.

The day centre provides places for 48 children between the ages of three months and five years. The Child Development Centre also runs an after-school scheme where children are collected from local schools (within a radius of seven miles) by nursery staff and are involved in a range of activities at the centre until the parent finishes work. Holidays are covered by day camps for children aged between five and eleven.

The cost to an employee to keep a child in the Child Development Centre is dependent on his or her income level. Employees earning £10,800 pay £31 per week and thereafter contributions rise by £4 per £1000 earned. So employees earning more than £21,800 pay £80 per week. The Body Shop offers places to other local employers and provides emergency places for Social Services.

Most companies expect a 40% return after maternity leave; so far the Body Shop has achieved 100%.

Says Gordon Roddick, Body Shop's chairman: "Childcare is a family responsibility. The Body Shop is a family company, it is entirely appropriate that we should help share that responsibility."

Positive recruitment and career development

The discrimination chain starts at the point of career choice. In "male ghetto" occupations, for example, women will only apply if they are specifically encouraged to do so. A passive approach to equal opportunities in recruitment is essentially management abdication. Positive management action is needed to:

- identify the reasons so few women apply for jobs in the sector
- examine ways of changing the working environment (including people's attitudes) to make it more attractive
- target potential female employees
- encourage them to consider this occupation, through promotional literature, careers seminars, site visits, holiday work experience and so on.

Case study: B&Q

B&Q, the DIY chain, is making special concessions to bring women into its workforce by offering part-time junior managerial posts and through an advertising campaign aimed at women.

B&Q explains: "Female managers don't apply to work with us because DIY is perceived as a male oriented business. In the light of demographic change, we need to attract more women. This can only be a positive move for us, since our surveys have shown that women stay longer with the company. Their appraisal ratings are very good, too. They are more consultative and see the person as a whole when it comes to people management."

Part of B&Q's campaign includes promoting women into positions which have previously only been held by men. The aim is to give a strong signal to the business that the company is serious about having women in senior management positions. B&Q appointed its first female area manager in 1991 and has since appointed two women senior executives.

At store level, the company introduced in late 1989 a flexible scheme designed to bring more mothers back to work. About a dozen women in the South East have been employed during school term times, leaving them free to look after their children in the holidays. The posts are filled by students during vacation periods. B&Q says: "We introduced the scheme in the South East, where we currently have major recruitment problems, and so far it has been very successful."

Case study: The Littlewoods Organisation

Littlewoods employs 36,000 people, of whom 24,000 are women. The company has been working towards equal opportunities for over 20 years and has developed a comprehensive approach embodied in an equal opportunities policy. The stated objectives of the policy are:

"To ensure that the talents and resources of employees are utilised to the full and that no job applicant or employee receives less favourable treatment on the grounds of gender, marital status, social class, race, ethnic origin, religious beliefs or disability, or is disadvantaged by conditions or requirements which cannot be shown to be relevant to performance."

The following table shows how successful Littlewoods has been.

Women in management at Littlewoods (%)

	1985	1988	1991
Director/senior executive	2.60	4.30	8.20
Senior manager	1.85	5.90	7.50
Middle manager	10.00	15.20	24.40
Junior middle manager	21.70	27.60	37.30
Junior manager	49.65	54.00	57.90

An important factor in the successful implementation of Littlewoods' equal opportunities policy has been the continued personal commitment of John Moores, a main board director and son of the founder of the company.

"We attach a great deal of importance to our equal opportunities programme," says Moores. "It helps us in several ways: to meet our legal and moral obligations; to utilise people's abilities to the full by removing artificial and irrelevant barriers to their recruitment and promotion; to draw from the widest possible pool of talent; to implement good management practice. It is also good for business."

The company's equal opportunities objectives are part of its corporate plan and are monitored at board level.

To manage its responsibilities in this area, Littlewoods has adopted the following procedures:

- a code of practice
- a five year action plan with targets
- the establishment of an equal opportunities committee
- the establishment of an equal opportunities unit
- a comprehensive training programme for all line managers.

The code of practice exists in the form of a 20-page booklet on all aspects of recruitment, career development, terms and conditions of employment and equal opportunity appeals procedure.

A five-year rolling Equal Opportunities for Women action plan is part of the company's corporate business plan. Percentage targets were originally set in 1986 and continue to be adjusted where necessary. Managers are assessed on their ability to meet these targets. As a matter of priority, the initial targets have been set for management levels, with the second phase aimed at the workforce in general. The plan also includes provision for internal management development opportunities such as training programmes, assertiveness training and skills training. Career grooming, offering personal and career development to those at non-managerial levels is also included.

The equal opportunities committee was set up in 1982. It comprises personnel managers and senior line managers of director status from each of the company's major divisions as well as members of the equal opportunities unit. The committee is chaired by John Moores and meets quarterly. Its brief is to ensure targets for equal opportunities are met, problems tackled and initiatives taken.

Littlewoods' equal opportunities unit reports directly to the chief executive's office through the group personnel director. Its brief is to monitor the policies and practices on equal opportunities; recommend changes where necessary; provide training in equal opportunity matters and deal with queries and complaints by individuals.

The company realised from the outset that its equal opportunities code of practice could only be implemented effectively if proper training was given to all concerned. Accordingly, a structured programme was developed to provide staff with the level of skills and knowledge to enable them to implement the necessary changes.

Littlewoods also continues to offer flexible working as a main plank of its equal opportunities approach. In addition, maternity provision has been improved to encourage women in senior positions to come back on a part-time basis. The maternity scheme qualifying period has also been reduced from two years to one year for employees working more than 16 hours a week. Home-working is also encouraged for some types of project work and computing.

To assess progress towards its equal opportunities objectives, Littlewoods has established a computerised statistical monitoring system which produces quarterly analyses of employment by gender and race, broken down to show the picture for different management levels. These form the basis of the report-back process.

Monitoring equal opportunities is aided by specifically designed application forms with a tear-off slip for voluntary self-identification on the part of new recruits to the company. Progress is reported regularly at divisional and group level meetings.

Littlewoods is recognised as a leader in the field of equal opportunities. From its experience it offers the following learning points for companies setting up equal opportunities policies and procedures:

- implementing equal opportunities is not an easy process. It takes time, investment and commitment
- even with large numbers of women in the organisation, it takes a great deal of effort and planning to ensure that women progress through the management structure
- goals are important as an expression of input and output
- goals set by line managers, who are also accountable for them, create involvement and commitment
- commitment from the top is vital to ensure continued equal opportunity success.

Case study: Superdrug

Superdrug introduced a Chief Cashiers Training Programme to improve the promotion prospects of women employees.

Superdrug supports the Opportunity 2000 initiative. It is committed to increasing the number of women managers in the company, and to having more women managers at senior level.

As part of its commitment to Opportunity 2000, Superdrug intends to:

- target a 20% representation of women managers

- target 50% more women at senior management level
- form a pool of potential managers for the future from its chief cashier population (which is predominantly female)
- develop more objective selection techniques
- continue to use attitude surveys to monitor discrimination.

Career break management

Case study: Norwich Union

Norwich Union was concerned at the loss of the training investment it had made in women who did not return after maternity. It also recognised that some mothers prefer a career break instead of returning to work after the statutory 29 weeks' maternity leave after confinement. For this reason, the insurance company has introduced a career break scheme, under which staff with at least two years' service can take a break of up to five years following maternity leave.

Norwich Union offers the career break scheme at management's discretion, rather than as a right for all employees and there will be no guarantee of re-employment. However, for those who are chosen there will be up to two weeks' paid work each year to update on procedures and undertake further training. Other steps will be taken to maintain regular contact. The women will return to the same grades they left. After a trial period, each will be reappointed as a permanent staff member and will be credited with full back service in respect of her pension arrangements.

Norwich Union also revamped its maternity leave in mid 1989. Under the new arrangements, when an employee returns from maternity leave, her period of absence will now count as pensionable service as soon as she continues to work for the Norwich Union for a minimum of a further six months. If an employee should die during her maternity leave, a lump sum payment of three times her salary will be made to her estate in the same way as if she had still been working. Maternity leavers still benefit from insurance premium discounts and can still continue as staff agents during their time away from work.

Once the woman has returned to her former post the company will pay for any additional mortgage costs incurred through the loss of mortgage allowance during maternity leave.

Many women are capable of coming back into full-time employment after their children have grown up, but are worried about being able to cope with the pressures after spending several years at home. Schemes like Norwich Union's help to restore self-confidence by reinforcing their continued value to the company.

Flexible working times

Flexible working hours are now common in many service industries and in a few manufacturing companies. For example, women at the head office of a large building society can work evenings, leaving them free to look after the children during the day. Retail stores already offer a form of flexible hours where women can choose the hours to fit around the children's school times. Many other companies are breaking the old nine-to-five monopoly and taking a closer look at leaving the office open until 9 pm and at weekends. Annual hours, or flexible working years, are also slowly growing in popularity.

Job sharing
The champion of job sharing in the UK is New Ways to Work, a London-based organisation funded by the London boroughs' grants scheme. One aspect of its work is to help companies design and implement job sharing as a flexible working option.

Job sharing involves two or more people sharing one or more full-time jobs between them. They share the work and the pay, the holidays and benefits. It is now an accepted way of easily introducing part-time hours into areas of traditional full-time work. Job sharers may work mornings or afternoons, two to five days a week or three shorter days. The type of work determines how it is shared out. The sharers divide between them the status and promotion prospects of traditional full-time staff. Job sharing does not require changes in establishment arrangements or employment structure.

Secretary Deborah Wilks is in her mid-twenties and before having a baby was a medical secretary with a company in High Wycombe, Buckinghamshire. A major computer shopping company was able to offer her a job share with another woman who was looking for part-time work. Deborah is able to earn more as a secretary than as a shop assistant, which was the only other post open to her because of the hours she could work. And during the school holidays, her job share stays at home to look after her child while Deborah can pick up the extra hours.

She explains: "I was fully trained as a word processor operator and medical secretary, so I do most of the typing. My colleague does filing, phone queries and basic typing. But the job share means that she now has the chance to learn more secretarial skills and I can keep up to date with modern office procedure. When my little boy goes to school, I will be able to apply for higher calibre jobs with confidence or go further with this company."

She adds: "The job share has been a great success and I feel very lucky to get the chance to do it."

Case study: The Boots Company

The Boots Company has 38 job sharers within its retail division, 38 on their register and a husband and wife among others are in the pipeline. The jobs include pharmacists, sales managers and senior sales assistants. The scheme, launched in 1988, allows job sharing at senior assistant and supervisor levels and above in the non-pharmacy grades and at manager level and above in pharmacy.

The scheme was discussed with area managers before it was fully developed. Fears initially expressed by line managers were found to be groundless. Now area managers are behind the scheme and there have been no negative comments from line managers.

Boots feels that the additional costs of employing job sharers are minimal, particularly when compared with total payroll and the cost of replacing lost staff. As the company already has many part-time staff as well as people working term time and variable hour contracts, administration is not a problem. However, it concludes that the training costs may well be higher since job sharers require individual training. In some stores, sharers work three days each to cover a six-day opening; in others they work mornings or afternoons or combinations of days and half days. The suitability of each particular job for sharing is considered individually and so far there have been no unsuitable cases. Boots believes that because job sharers work at times which suit their own commitments, they give 100% effort. By reducing turnover, the company can make savings on recruitment costs and on the training of new pharmacy managers. Boots feels there will be a slow build-up in numbers of job sharers and is now looking forward to job sharing in store management.

Homeworking

Another increasingly popular option taken by forward-thinking companies to help women retain their skills during child-rearing is allowing them to work at home. Dorothy Davies, systems development manager at British Telecom, uses home working as a way of keeping a highly trained workforce. Davies now has some of her most valued programmers and analysts working Telecom computers in spare rooms from Wimbledon to mid-Wales. The programmers' computers are fed their work through modems during the night at cheap rate.

ICL has taken to home working so enthusiastically that it even has home-based managers, because it found that on-site managers did not know how to manage a home-based workforce.

Assertiveness training

Assertiveness training is an increasingly popular way of helping women realise their own potential and overcome hesitancy to promote themselves. Among companies that run such courses is Ford. Its courses, run in worktime since December 1988, are targeted at middle graded women, such as accounts assistants, who might not reach their potential without help. They aim to identify the skills, qualities and abilities that the participants already have and examine how these can be developed further; and to help participants improve their abilities at listening, assertiveness, negotiating, coaching and decision-making.

Rank Xerox, ICI and Southern Electricity are tackling the same problem. They have installed an open learning course, Moving into Management, designed to help women build their own career plan, behave more confidently and develop an individual management style. The course has been put together with financial assistance from the Local Government National Training Board and the Co-operative Bank.

Case study: British Telecom

As part of its Opportunity 2000 initiative, BT has embarked on a substantial programme of research, to provide the information it needs to develop effective interventions. The research programme has a number of clear objectives:

- learn more of women's views and expectations
- compare male and female perspectives
- identify positive and negative aspects (of current organisation and management style)
- pinpoint issues (to assign priorities)
- guide the strategy.

Supporting the research is a major communications programme, to encourage participation and help people put it into context.

The research will enable BT to put increased effort where it will have the greatest impact. The company already has an equal opportunities code of practice, a variety of training initiatives (including a professional development programme at Cranfield School of Management for women managers), and flexible work practices, such as job sharing, teleworking.

Checklist

1. Do you have a coherent, written policy and plan for the recruitment and promotion of women?
2. Do you employ a wide spectrum of mechanisms to overcome the problems of women's employments? e.g.
   - childcare provision
   - positive recruitment and promotion activities aimed at women
   - career break management
   - flexible working times
   - homeworking
   - assertiveness training

3. Do you monitor the proportions of women at each level of management?
4. What proportions of senior and middle management are female now?

3.1.4 Religious discrimination

For most of the UK, religious discrimination is not regarded as a significant problem. For Northern Ireland, however, it is the most critical employment issue after unemployment itself. Our case study examines how Shorts has tackled this highly sensitive issue.

Companies in the rest of Britain should be sensitive, however, to the special circumstances of Muslim employees from Asia and Africa. Special dietary and religious observance requirements need not be troublesome to implement if the reasons are understood and they are planned well in advance. Some companies – for example, some airlines – have also recognised that there are benefits in putting this experience to use in improving service to customers.

Case study: Shorts

Shorts, Northern Ireland's biggest private employer, has conducted an affirmative action programme to try and boost the number of Catholics in its work-force and is held up as an example of good employment practice by the Northern Ireland Office.

The affirmative action programme started in 1983 after a survey in the engineering industry found that Catholics were discriminated against for skilled jobs. Between 3 and 8% of Shorts' skilled workers were Catholic against 26% of the population as a whole in Greater Belfast. Only 6% of apprentice recruits were coming from Catholic schools.

The company recognised it had to employ more Catholics. The programme included advertising in Catholic newspapers, increasing contacts with Catholic schools and greater flexibility in the requirements for entry into the company's technician apprentice scheme.

The number of Catholics employed is now about 12% of the 7700 work force. The mid-term target is 25% of recruits being Catholics (i.e. virtual equality of representation).

John Freeman, a former Shorts shop steward and regional secretary for the Transport and General Workers Union, says: "The shop floor used to come under a tremendous amount of pressure from hardliners. While I don't doubt that there is still a certain amount of that feeling about the place, it bears no relationship to the atmosphere that existed before."

3.1.5 Age discrimination

When unemployment reached its peak in the early 1980s, people over 45 were among those who felt the effects most strongly.

Many newspaper articles focused on the waste of talent as well-qualified unemployed people found themselves "too old" for many employers. The UK does not have age discrimination legislation, as do many parts of the United States. But the socially responsible company will want to ensure that this group, too, receives fair treatment in employment.

Companies that do operate age discrimination are losing a valuable resource. A study by US assurance company Bankers Life and Casualty compared the absenteeism rates of 128 randomly selected employees under 65 and 128 over 65. Bankers Life has a long-standing policy of encouraging older workers and has little hesitation about hiring people over the normal retiring age of 65. The study showed that only 13 of the under 65s had a perfect attendance record compared with 34 of the over 65s. The under 65s had, on average, twice as many half-day absences as the over 65s. When employees over 65 became incapable of doing their job, the company found that they usually retire themselves without the need for hints from above.

Case study: B&Q

In May 1989, B&Q opened a store in Macclesfield. Within six months it was staffed entirely by people over 50. B&Q explains: "Over 7000 people responded to our national campaign. We opened the store for two reasons. Firstly, because the demographic changes forced us to look at our recruitment policies, and secondly, we wanted to make a statement that we were interested in taking the older person seriously."

Another store operating on the same basis was opened in August 1990 in Exmouth. Says B&Q: "We have found that older staff not only bring increased stability, expertise and social skills, but also compare favourably in performance terms with younger staff at our other stores." The company now aims to increase the number of staff aged over 50 from 10 to 15% of its workforce.

Case study: Tesco plc

Supermarket chain Tesco has also reaped enormous rewards from its pioneering campaign to recruit older people to work in its stores. The number of over 55s employed by the retail group had risen from about 2000 to around 7000 by the end of 1991.

Its campaign, Life Begins at 55, not only attracted people in the target age group, but also brought a large response from people in their 30s and 40s and, unexpectedly, from people who were past retirement age.

Following the campaign the company now permits employment up to the age of 70 and has equalised its normal retirement age at 65, although an existing employee can be re-engaged at that age and provided with continuous employment into the future subject to an annual health check.

A study of Tesco employees by the World Health Organisation (WHO) in 1991 showed that older workers are better with customers, more reliable, more responsible and less likely to take time off sick than their younger colleagues.

The Tesco study was part of a larger WHO research programme into the prevention of what it calls "retirement disease", accelerated ageing associated with lack of stimulation, motivation and purpose.

A survey of 80 workers aged between 50 and 71 and 10 under 25 at five Tesco stores revealed that the older employees on the whole were more satisfied with their work and conditions than younger staff. One in four of the older age group said their health had improved since starting their jobs – most had been with the company for two years or less. Eighty per cent of the managers asked at the same five stores said the older employees were better with customers and more reliable. The majority of the managers questioned also said that while the older workers tended to be slower, their greater responsibility, reliability and efficiency made them just as productive.

Checklist

1. Make it clear on publicity material that job vacancies are open to people of all ages.
2. Check hiring practices. Do you ask applicants for a photograph of themselves?
3. Base selection criteria on the real physical needs of the work rather than on simple age criteria.
4. Monitor the age distribution in the company and if possible compare that to the composition of the local working community.
5. Improve and expand appraisal systems so that older workers know how they are performing.
6. Examine closely corporate policies on retirement. Can workers be allowed to work beyond 65?
7. Do you have difficulty getting staff? Have you thought of positive discrimination towards the older worker?

3.1.6 Broader issues of discrimination

Some forms of discrimination appear to make business sense when viewed narrowly. For example, most companies will reject job applicants with criminal records. Indeed, some companies go to considerable lengths to weed out anyone with "criminal tendencies". Similarly, people who have been unemployed for a long period because they have obsolete or inadequate skills are difficult to hire because they frequently take a long time to become productive.

However, opportunities to help both these disadvantaged groups do exist. Employers can now arrange fidelity bonds, underwritten at Lloyds. Apex fidelity bonds indemnify the company against any losses attributable to dishonest behaviour by the ex-offender, as long as the offence is not related to the job opening in question (e.g. it would not cover putting someone previously convicted of embezzlement in charge of the company accounts).

A number of companies are also participating in a Business in the Community initiative to help long-term unemployed. Through what it calls "customised training", companies put unemployed people through a tailor-made training programme, which leads to a guaranteed job interview, or a guaranteed job. Pilot schemes for this approach since 1987 have been highly successful. For example, William Hill/Mecca Bookmakers have employed 11 trainee managers using the scheme and Debenhams in Northern Ireland employed 67 sales assistants. Other companies which have been involved in pilots include Barclays, British Telecom, Express Dairies, John Laing, Lloyds Bank, McDonald's Restaurants, J. Sainsbury, Kingfisher, TSB and the International Stock Exchange.

Glass ceilings

For all the progress towards equal opportunities at work, subtle discriminatory practices in many organisations continue to form invisible obstacles to promotion. These so-called "glass ceilings" restrict a large proportion of the workforce to managerial positions beneath their abilities.

In Britain, the glass ceilings debate has tended to focus on discrimination against women. Yet invisible barriers to advancement also exist for individuals from a wide range of other groups including racial and religious minorities and people with disabilities.

The cultures of many organisations and professions remain hostile to social, religious and physical differences so that the abilities of those from minority groups are all too often overlooked early on in their careers. As a result, talented individuals from these groups are not given assignments and training which would develop their skills and pave the way for future promotions.

Bosses may make assumptions, too, about the lifestyle and aspirations of minority employees, mistakenly believing they are acting in their best interests by shielding them from additional responsibilities. For people with disabilities, the problem is particularly severe with discrimination thresholds in many UK organisations so low that they prevent meaningful career entry altogether.

In America, where glass ceilings have long been seen as an obstacle to ethnic minorities, recent re-evaluation of the problem has led some to believe that the answer lies not in the traditional response of positive discrimination, but in making the promotion system itself more transparent.

Case study: Southern Bell

Southern Bell of Georgia, part of Bell South Telecommunications, used a recent shake-up in its management structure to attack glass ceilings in the traditionally white male stronghold of America's Deep South. The company now uses a combination of supervisor reviews and recommendations by an independent panel of psychiatrists and psychologists to select between 12 and 15 potential executives each year, without racial or sexual bias.

Candidates are selected on their ability in key areas of knowledge, drive, organisational and leadership skills, verbal and written communication skills and the ability to make decisions under pressure. Potential executives then enter a one-year training programme which grooms them for senior positions. Critical to the process, all are given a wide perspective – rather than a departmentalised view – of Southern Bell's operations. The new system has allowed the company to produce 500 black, Hispanic, Asian or American Indian managers and 1182 women managers out of a total of 2990 positions.

3.2 Developing talent

Companies which do not provide opportunities for employees to develop their talents almost invariably experience high labour turnover and problems of motivation. The commercial arguments for continuous improvement of everyone in an organisation are well-rehearsed. Yet the UK is near the bottom of the European league in expenditure on training and development.

It is no coincidence that companies which take their social responsibilities towards the external community seriously, also put significant resources into growing their employees' skills and abilities. Many of these companies now include training as a major plank of their business strategy.

One convenient way of classifying employee development is as follows:

- basic employment skills
- skills training
- management development.

3.2.1 Basic employment skills

In spite of free and compulsory education, the UK still has a substantial section of the population who cannot read and write. A similar number suffer problems of innumeracy. Many companies have hidden literacy and innumeracy problems.

Often the needs of these people are invisible. They have developed complex survival skills such as buying newspapers they cannot read. They rely on their families to fill in forms. When they are unable to carry out instructions, they go sick or find ways of avoiding the issue. They and their companies often regard their illiteracy as a personal inadequacy.

Ford is one company that has set about rectifying the problem and for a number of years has used the Industrial Language Training Association to run English language courses for those of its employees, mainly hourly paid, who want it.

Case study: Our Price

Music retailer Our Price is one of several organisations helping the homeless into work. As part of its recruitment, it selected a number of homeless people for what it calls "pre-recruitment training" – preparing them for work in retail. Confidence-building and work-shadowing are important elements of the training. A pilot scheme was so successful that all of the five participants were offered jobs as sales assistants, although there had been only three vacancies. The scheme is part of a larger programme, called Leap, operated by the Industrial Society, which hopes to persuade employers nationwide to provide similar training for the homeless.

Checklist

1. Are you aware how many employees in your company have a literacy/numeracy problem?
2. Do you have a specific remedial programme?

3.2.2 Skills training

The past three years has seen a plethora of initiatives aimed at strengthening companies' commitment to training. In particular, the CBI, the government and the Trades Union Congress have all united behind the Investors in People programme, which aims to ensure that companies of all sizes develop and maintain effective schemes of continuous education and training for all their employees. Introducing the initiative in July 1991, Sir Bryan Nicholson, chairman of the CBI's Education and Training Policy Committee, explained the intention to "ensure that all young people up to the age of 18 are either in education or in jobs with training. For adults, we are setting lifetime learning targets, which seek to make training a priority for everybody and every firm."

The need for such action is great. Says the CBI: "South Korea aims to have 80% of its young people reach higher education standard by the end of the decade and France has a similar target. Sadly, the UK, despite being on an upward trend, has the lowest proportion of 17-year-olds in education and fewer qualified managers, engineers and other key workers than its major competitors. Forty-five per cent of the total workforce have no qualifications of GCSE equivalent."

To become an Investor in People, a company must fulfil four standard requirements:

- make a public commitment from the top to develop all employees to achieve its business objectives
- regularly review the training and development needs of all employees
- take action to train and develop individuals on recruitment and throughout their employment
- evaluate the investment in training and development to assess achievement and improve future effectiveness.

Case study: International Computers plc

International Computers (ICL), now part of Fujitsu, the Japanese electronics company, employs 22,000 people in 70 countries. It has started an Investing in People programme, which is designed to increase training and development for all of them. A handbook, used by all ICL managers and their staff to define each individual's development needs, covers objective setting, appraisal, performance improvement, career development and training. Each employee regularly discusses his progress with his manager to ensure that he is maximising his potential. At the discussion, they define the objectives the employee should achieve in order to contribute fully to the company's business and appraise the employee's contribution, while looking at ways to improve it. They also determine the most suitable career direction for each employee and the specific action plans needed to achieve this. Finally, they plan the necessary training budget of £25 million a year. Through such programmes, ICL aims to achieve the fastest possible growth for both individuals within it and for the company itself.

Case study: Rover Group

Vehicle manufacturer, the Rover Group, launched Rover Learning Business in mid-1990 to help its 40,000 people develop their talents. The scheme has a training budget of about £30 million a year and will operate in partnership with academic institutions including Warwick University, City University and Leeds Polytechnic, which will help provide some of the courses.

Its main product is the design and development of training courses and materials in response to the demands of Rover employees. The training departments of each Rover plant will act as franchisees to Rover Learning Business.

Some companies have recognised the value of having employees develop skills not directly related to their current work. For example, Ford and the trade unions representing the company's 44,000 hourly paid and salaried employees are running an Employee Development Assistance programme, which offers employees a wide range of educational courses as well as schemes to encourage a healthier life style.

Case study: Ford Motor Company

Ford's Employee Development Assistance programme, which is funded by £1.8 million a year from Ford and £150,000 from the government, is believed to be the first of its kind in British industry.

Everyone from factory line workers to management is eligible to apply for up to £200 a year for approved training and assistance. Under the scheme secretaries will be funded to do accountancy training, but accounts assistants will not be funded for accountancy courses since that is covered by other company schemes. The fund does not give money for hobbies or recreational activities.

Set up after the 1987 contract negotiations, the programme is administered jointly by the unions and the management at national and plant level. The local joint programme committees will approve applications for grants, provide necessary services and identify suitable courses to meet local needs.

Ford is offering financial support for employees who want to do basic academic courses, higher educational and Open University qualifications or vocational and careers skills. Employees have enrolled for courses from bricklaying to weight watchers, with languages the most popular choice. Says a company spokesman: "We thought only 5% would apply in 1989, which was the first year, but 13% came forward and the number has been rising all the time."

He adds: "It is a very positive programme because it demonstrates unions working together with management for the good of the workforce. Employees are getting the chance to exercise their minds which makes them brighter and more alert."

Local education assistants, paid for by the DAP fund, assist employees to find the right course for them and administer the plant's budget.

Jack Adams, a national officer of the Transport and General Workers Union and acting chairman of the trade union side of the Ford National Negotiating

Committee, welcomed the scheme saying: "The joint running of the programme, with trade union representatives having a majority on the committees at national and local level, will ensure that course provision and funding is tailored to meet our membership's needs and that the barriers to access to education and training are removed as far as possible."

Case study: Coca-Cola Schweppes Beverages

Coca-Cola and Schweppes Beverages has a different scheme. Everyone in its main locations has access to Lifetime Learning Links Centres. These are unmanned, but contain learning materials including books, audio tapes, video cassettes covering subjects as diverse as French and financial accounting through to DIY and distribution management. Some centres also have interactive videos and computers available. The centres are open during the day and employees can either drop in and use the resource on site or borrow specific items for study at home.

On sites without a Link Centre people can order learning materials from a catalogue which is updated regularly. CCSB set up the centres because it believes that learning is a lifetime experience and is often more effective when the employee manages it him or herself.

Checklist

1. Does every employee have at least some skills training every year?
2. Do you have a scheme to fund employee self-development?
3. Is continuous learning an element of the corporate mission?
4. Is helping others learn and grow a written part of every manager's responsibilities?

3.2.3 Management development

A plethora of reports and studies in the late 1980s identified that the UK lay well behind its international competitors in the attention it gave to management training. One study, by Bath University, revealed that 20% of large companies (those with 1000 or more employees) provided no formal training courses for their managers at all.

This, it may be argued, is a business rather than a social responsibility issue. But it can equally be argued that companies have an obligation to help managerial employees increase their value to the community. Moreover, the implementation of many of the social responsibility objectives elsewhere in this book is only possible when managers are competent, confident and motivated.

In July 1987, a group of companies, educators and organisations representing business and managers came together with government to form the Council for Management Education. The Management Charter Initiative now has several hundred corporate members and aims to persuade thousands more both to understand their responsibilities for developing managers and to introduce effective programmes to promote management development. An early element of the MCI's activities was a draft code of practice, the nub of which we reproduce here in lieu of a checklist:

- to improve leadership and skills
- to encourage continuous development
- to provide a coherent framework for self-development
- to ensure management development integrates with work
- to provide access to training
- to encourage relevant qualifications
- to participate in MCI networks
- to strengthen links with management development providers
- to link with educational establishments (to promote management as a desirable career)
- to monitor progress.

3.3 Health, safety and welfare

Companies that take a proactive approach to employee health, safety and welfare benefit in a number of ways.

First and most obviously, they are much less likely to fall foul of the law if employees are injured – costly not only in cash terms, but in management time, bad publicity and, in a growing number of countries, the possibility of imprisonment for executives, who hold the responsibility for ensuring that health and safety legislation is complied with.

Other, less obvious benefits include:

- reduced absenteeism: a high proportion of absenteeism results from occupationally induced ailments. Teaching employees how to avoid these ailments often has a knock-on effect in their behaviour outside work. The net result: fewer days off sick and the potential savings could be huge.
- reduced claims for occupationally induced illness. A number of employers who refused to take any notice of the potential danger from repetitive strain injury (a condition affecting people who use work processor keyboards for

long, unbroken periods) now face heavy claims for compensation. At one stage in the early 1980s, well over a quarter of Harland and Wolff's employees were reported to be suing the company for loss of hearing as a result of their work.

- health care premiums: the more employees who need treatment, the greater the expense of company-sponsored health insurance schemes.

- more productive employees: people who are under excessive stress – whether work or domestically induced – cannot give their best to their job. The more rapidly the company can help ease that stress, the faster the employee can return to normal productivity. In practice, some companies claim that people who have been helped through a difficult patch by their employer are more loyal and more motivated to work hard to acknowledge the debt of gratitude.

An EC directive on working time which would put a 48-hour ceiling on the working week has caused much controversy in the UK. The British government has repeatedly expressed concern over this and other legislation which removes employers' flexibility. An alternative to "opt-out" from the next stage of EC employment legislation was negotiated by the government at the Maastricht summit. But the future of the working time directive remains uncertain. If it is introduced under health and safety legislation, as has been proposed, it would require only a qualified majority vote to ensure its adoption. However, the Employment Secretary Gillian Shephard has stated that the British Government would challenge the legal validity of such a development.

But even if the 48-hour ceiling becomes law, which currently looks far from certain, a high degree of flexibility in implementation could still be allowed at national level. The UK government's preferred option is to allow work over 48 hours for people who have passed a health risk assessment.

In the form discussed at Maastricht, the directive included:

- a 48-hour upper limit on the working week including overtime, averaged over a given period likely to be set at four months
- a minimum daily rest period of 11 hours, with Sunday "in principle" treated as a rest day

- minimum annual paid holiday of four weeks, with three weeks for the first three years of the directive.

However, in spite of government opposition to the directive, there is a growing feeling among British companies that the best approach is simply to accept the legislation from Europe and get on with it. Some companies see benefits from cutting chronic overtime, while others, such as ICI, are not enthusiastic but say they live with such restrictions in the rest of Europe and with a bit of reorganisation could do so in the UK.

Case study: Repetitive strain injury

According to the *Financial Times* (27 March 1990) British companies lose 70 million man-days a year to absenteeism caused by musculoskeletal ailments, such as repetitive strain injury (RSI). In 1989, a Midland Bank secretary, Mrs Pauline Burnard accepted £45,000 as an out-of-court settlement for RSI. In March 1990, three Inland Revenue computer data clerks received £107,500 between them.

In approaching these issues, companies should have the following objectives in mind:

- making it difficult for accidents and occupationally induced injuries to happen. That means having effective systems to make sure that only qualified and suitable people undertake hazardous jobs; providing training against any hazard, both office and shopfloor or external site; ensuring that tools and equipment are safe; and recording and analysing all accidents or ailments that may be relevant, whether or not there is a legal requirement to do so. In each case, there should be clearly defined management responsibilities and systems for measuring compliance.

  The training issue is probably the most neglected here. Companies in very dangerous operations, such as oil drilling or civil engineering, usually have strong training programmes for everyone who works on site. But relatively few companies provide training for, say, office staff in the safe use of guillotines, or require their field sales staff to take advanced driving courses.
- monitoring where the hazards lie. Some US companies insist that suppliers of everything, from cooling lubricants to stationery solvents, provide details of composition and likely hazards from their use. At the very least, this provides a good defence if employees do develop illnesses related to the use of these products.
- providing a resource, where employees can unburden themselves of stress-inducing problems.

Checklist

1. Does your company have clearly defined responsibilities for health and safety? Who monitors performance?
2. Does your company know where it might be causing or exacerbating occupational ailments and regularly check to ensure that it does not do so?
3. Does it encourage employees to express their concerns about health and safety at work, and take those concerns seriously?
4. Does it have a confidential counselling scheme that employees trust?
5. Does it encourage good safety practice through education, training and incentive schemes?

Case study: The Post Office

In recent years, the Post Office's Occupational Health Service has earned a formidable reputation through a string of imaginative and comprehensive health projects.

Started in 1854 in the midst of London's last great cholera epidemic, it was scrapped with the formation of the National Health Service in 1948, only to be reconstituted in 1969 when the Post Office became a corporation. Today the service employs a full-time professional staff of 14 doctors and 42 nurses, plus seven part-time medical staff. This team is responsible for more than 200,000 employees.

Its single biggest project in preventive medicine is the Well-Woman Programme offering free cancer screening for all 35,000 women staff at or near their work place. A unit built on the back of a 40-foot trailer tours sites providing cervical and breast screening. Of the 4260 women screened since the programme began in 1988, 225 have been referred to their doctors for treatment. In addition, some 5000 men attended nearly 200 seminars on testicular self-examination.

The Occupational Health Service's responsibilities can be broadly split into two areas:

- the more traditional role of occupational health including identifying and advising on potential hazards in the workplace; finding suitable employment for staff with disabilities; advising staff with health problems either caused by or affecting their work; the medical aspects of recruitment and early retirement; and providing professional guidance on first aid.
- the instigation and promotion of health education programmes for all staff. These include encouraging staff to adopt a healthier lifestyle, with exercise and sensible diet; advice on alcohol; advice on the prevention of non-occupational injury and disease; provision of voluntary health checks and screening; and specialist counselling on stress and stress-related illnesses and stress prevention activities.

Recent initiatives include: a year-long coronary risk analysis programme piloted in Birmingham which, from the 650 screened, identified 100 employees for follow-up by Post Office medical staff. And a rolling stress management programme supported by video and booklets which made over 300 presentations during 1990 and 1991.

In addition, as all Post Offices have introduced or are moving towards a completely smoke-free work environment, stop-smoking clinics have been established to help smokers cope with the restrictions by encouraging them to give up or cut down.

In the area of safety, the main businesses and their field districts have policy statements setting out their approach to safety, and there are national safety managers who advise on all safety aspects. There is also a local infrastructure of trained safety co-ordinators and representatives.

According to occupational safety officer, Graham Collins, the Post Office has a twofold approach to identifying new health, safety and welfare issues. Professional staff within the service monitor new developments in the field and make recommendations as the need emerges, and also respond to new concerns voiced by the businesses themselves by providing advice and guidance.

For example, the Post Office welfare team staged a series of Money Matters road shows during 1991 to help staff who were struggling with unexpectedly high mortgage and interest rates. Stress as a result of "assault on delivery" also had a high priority after a spate of such incidents. As well as training for welfare staff, the service also issued a guide to managers on their role in helping staff to cope following an attack.

Pre-retirement planning is also a priority with a recent review making a number of recommendations for improvements. A video "Still Life", commissioned for use at pre-retirement seminars won an award at the New York Film Festival.

Case study: Employee Advisory Resource

Counselling services in the form of employee assistance programmes were virtually unknown in Britain in 1981. It was then that Control Data introduced its own confidential counselling and information service for employees and their families, called the Employee Advisory Resource or EAR.

It was so successful and attracted so much interest that in 1986 the Uxbridge-based EAR began to provide an independent service to other organisations. Companies which subscribe provide their employees with:

- instant 24 hour access and response
- expert crisis intervention
- short-term counselling and assessment
- consultation and support to managers
- referral to specialist services assessed by EAR
- follow-up contact to ensure that individuals have received the help they need.

Case study: Elida Gibbs

Elida Gibbs, the Unilever subsidiary that produces bathroom brands including Timotei, Pears and Signal, operates an employee advisory programme (EAP). Staff at the company are issued with a card listing the freephone number for a confidential helpline which they can ring and, if necessary, arrange to receive independent counselling on drink, debt, legal or marital problems.

Jon Riches, Elida Gibbs' personnel director, hopes the helpline will help to reduce high absenteeism among the company's 700 blue-collar workers. Riches says a cut in the current 8% rate to nearer the national average of 5%, would pay the £25 a head cost of the counselling service several times over.

The helpline is provided by independent counsellors from the Hertfordshire-based group, Focus, which charges the company a management fee, plus a charge for every consultation. According to Riches, the independence of the counsellors is an essential feature of the scheme. Line managers have a coaching and counselling role, he says, but cannot be expected to have the specialist skills needed to deal with an alcohol or drug addiction problem. In addition, the helpline removes employees' concern that private worries revealed to their manager or the personnel department will affect their job prospects.

The counsellors, Focus, estimate that only 50 to 70 companies in the UK currently have employee advisory programmes and EAPs are barely more developed elsewhere in Europe. But in America, where 75% of the US Fortune top 500 companies use them, return on investment is estimated to be between $2 and $16 for every $1 spent.

Case study: BP

BP's alcohol and drug abuse programme in America includes confidential counselling and employee education in tandem with drug testing and disciplinary procedures. The aim is to identify employees with alcohol or drug problems and offer them an opportunity for treatment.

BP's Health and Safety Policy states: "We will strive to create a working environment in which employees, customers, contractors and the public will not be exposed to health hazards. Our employees and site contractors will be trained in workplace health, and encouraged to adopt a healthy lifestyle."

Another, less commonly considered issue in stress reduction is employment security. Lifetime employment practices, for example, have been common among Japanese companies for many years. Clearly, this policy has important advantages for employee morale and recruitment.

In the UK, IBM was well known for operating a policy of full employment for its employees through a commitment not to use lay-offs or redundancies to manage its business, but has recently had to retreat from that position in the face of intensifying commercial pressures.

In this context, Rover Group's decision to introduce a policy of "jobs for life" in March 1992 against the background of intensifying domestic competition and a recession that has severely affected car sales is an interesting development.

In the long run, it remains to be seen whether gains resulting from job security will allow Rover to maintain its policy.

3.3.1 Employees with dependent relatives who need care

One in nine of all full-time employees and one in six of all part-time workers have an elderly or disabled relative to care for, according to the Family Policies Study Centre. Yet, says the centre, British companies have very inadequate terms and conditions of employment when it comes to assisting such employees.

The charity Opportunities for Women paints an even bleaker picture in its report "Care to Work" (June 1990). From surveys of 1000 people who stay at home to look after dependent relatives and 2000 people in employment it found that:

- 50% of carers would go out to work, if they could find a job with adequate support facilities
- 50% of people in employment cared for children, the elderly, or the disabled
- 69% of all respondents said that carers' difficulties were not sufficiently recognised in the workplace
- discrimination against carers leads to stress, blocks promotion and bars carers from jobs.

Employers in America, however, are introducing programmes to help carers, recognising that the ageing of the population means that more and more employees will be affected.

American help programmes for carers include an extensive assistance programme by the Hartford-based Travellers Corporation. This provides lunch-time seminars, care giver support groups, flexible hours and unpaid leave of up to four weeks for personal emergencies. Champion International has established a policy that includes the right of six months' leave of absence for a family crisis. IBM has set up a nationwide telephone assistance line aimed at helping employees to assist their elderly relatives, no matter how far away they live from each other. Pepsico has drawn up a resource guide and outline for employees with specific problems.

Dependent health care in the USA is essentially private-sector driven and organisations develop practices tailored to their own needs. People who have to care for elderly or sick charges often have symptoms similar to those related to drug or alcohol abuse, such as fatigue, poor concentration, excessive absences and lateness. As well as losing productivity from such employees, companies incur costs from increased use of the telephone, increased demands on company health services and benefits and unanticipated extended lunch hours or days off. A company policy towards the issue makes it possible to control the costs while helping employees to cope with the stress of caring.

Checklist

1. Have you surveyed your workforce to identify the scale of dependent-relative care problems?
2. Do you know how much it costs your company?
3. Do you have a programme to help employees cope with this situation?

3.3.2 Caring for pensioners

The day that they retire is a watershed for most employees. Although many companies have generous pensions schemes, and some have schemes of phased retirement, even some of these organisations take the view that the retired employee is no longer the responsibility of his or her former employer.

Yet both the company and the retiree can benefit from a continued relationship. For example:

- some companies make use of retired employees to fill in at peak or holiday periods
- some manufacturing companies bring back retirees on a part-time basis as tour guides; others as part-time tutors for basic skills training of new recruits.

Even if these opportunities are impractical, the caring company can at least keep in touch, by sending the company newspaper, by recognising anniversaries and by inviting retirees to celebrations. This effort can partly be repaid through the ambassadorial role of former employees, who still feel good about the company and its products and services; partly through a recognition among current employees that they will not be forgotten immediately they accept their gold watches.

A number of companies provide pensioners with regular publications of their own, to keep them in contact. Cadbury Schweppes, for example, has a newsletter called *Update* and

Kingfisher has one called *Penfriend*, which supplements pensions information with articles on travel, home security, accident prevention and news of old colleagues.

Case study: Pilkington Group

Pilkington intends that its former employees will live a full and active life in their retirement. Through its Welfare Programme, it helps retirees to keep physically and mentally fit and independent of institutionalised care, but supports those who need such care.

The Pilkington Welfare Programme consists of a range of cash and goodwill benefits given to ex-employees and their spouses with at least five years' service with the company. Benefits include food parcels, Christmas gifts, and optical and dental grants.

An essential element of the programme is a Visiting Scheme involving a team of welfare officers and visitors as well as a committed group of voluntary visitors. Contact is also maintained by means of articles in the company newspaper, a quarterly magazine and a talk-link cassette for the partially sighted. Additional care and support is provided by a meals-on-wheels service, gardening and carewatch schemes and the respite care unit which was opened recently to relieve the burden on carers.

The Welfare Programme is funded by the Pilkington Charitable and Trust Funds which cover approximately 20,000 beneficiaries throughout the UK.

Checklist

1. Do you keep in contact with retired employees?
2. Do you have a scheme/policy to help them in case of genuine need?
3. Do you regard them as a resource?

4. Responsibilities towards suppliers

The importance of social responsibility towards suppliers – and concern for their welfare – is still only an emerging issue for many companies. Yet there are a number of good commercial reasons for top management to take the issue seriously, particularly regarding the organisation's relationships with smaller companies. Among those reasons:

- many multinational corporations are insisting that their suppliers meet strict quality criteria. They are reducing the number of suppliers, in favour of closer relationships with fewer companies, who can guarantee the consistent high level of product and service quality they require. Those companies, in turn, have little option but to insist upon similar relationships with their own suppliers, because they, too, cannot afford for their products and services to suffer from poor input.
- even relatively minor components incorporated into a product, if they are unreliable, unsafe or environmentally unsound, can ruin brands which have taken years to develop
- small businesses are often both suppliers and customers
- suppliers tend to give the best service to customers who treat them best. The notion that the biggest customer usually receives most attention is a myth. To obtain excellent service from suppliers, companies demonstrate that they are valued. The only difference between customers and suppliers is that they are at different points on the same chain.

To a large extent, suppliers can be seen as an extension of a company's own business. Hence they may demand much the same attention to efficiency and solvency as a fully owned operation.

Companies, which have already taken these factors into account are already offering some or all of the following:

- practical help and advice to smaller suppliers
- purchasing policies that ensure that small and local companies have a fair share of the business
- monitoring suppliers' social responsibility performance
- payment policies that help small businesses
- closer arrangements with suppliers through partnership agreements.

Of these, the most important, in our view, is the last on the list. Becoming a good customer is a sensible and practical way of ensuring that, at least at the input end of the logistics chain, you receive good quality and value. The rise of partnership sourcing as a major issue, supported by a CBI campaign, has been one of the most positive developments in business relationships during the early 1990s. It is, of course, the mirror image of the supplier partnerships, we discussed in Chapter 2.

4.1 Practical help and advice

Most of the companies that have substantial supplier aid schemes find that the expertise they lend results in cost savings for the manufacture of their supplies and that some of these savings are passed back to them.

The areas where the big company can use its resources to aid the small supplier are legion. For example, few small companies have the staff and expertise to evaluate diversification plans adequately. To the big company, however, there is much to be said for encouraging its suppliers to diversify. If the big company needs to slow down production temporarily, any supplier with an excessive dependence on it may either experience financial difficulties (perhaps leading to closure) or have to pass on its increased unit costs. Some large companies deliberately help small suppliers find additional, preferably non-competitive customers.

The purchasing manager of the small supplier company may have neither the time nor the staff back-up to search widely for the cheapest and best supplies for his own company. However, big companies such as Sweden's Alfa Laval, which have a variety of purchasing specialists, can make their expertise available for mutual benefit.

Some companies, including Marks and Spencer, give suppliers advice and guidance on a wide variety of issues from the design of washrooms to personnel policies. The theory behind this intervention, according to former chief executive Lord Sieff, is that attention to employee welfare creates a happier workforce, which in turn means that the quality of the goods produced will be closer to M&S' high standards. Every time a disgruntled worker leaves a supplier, the quality of the output will suffer until the new recruit is fully trained into the job.

Another Swedish business offers suppliers the use of its empty road vehicles to cut their delivery costs. In addition, some responsible customers now help potential suppliers by telling them where they lost out on unsuccessful bids. By providing good feedback, the customer encourages suppliers to keep improving. For example, BP Gas not only provides a breakdown of the criteria on which its decision to accept a bid was made, but also gives the scores achieved by the unsuccessful company against those of the successful bidder. Typical feedback of this kind might include scores for meeting the objectives of the brief, the overall package offered, the overall cost and the customer's sense of chemistry with the would-be supplier.

Case study: British Rail

British Rail actively encourages small suppliers to compete for the substantial number of orders placed every week, where formal tendering is neither justified nor sensible.

To help small companies obtain a share of its business, it publishes a booklet "Selling to British Rail", which details British Rail procedures and offers advice.

BR has simplified its purchasing procedures for low value orders to dispense with bureaucracy that might deter the smaller supplier. The booklet lists areas where BR needs supplies, for example, in catering, maintenance and materials. The aim of the booklet, it claims, is to provide sufficient information for potential suppliers to introduce their products and services to the procurement section responsible for awarding contracts for the goods being offered.

Checklist

1. Do you make some of your company's professional expertise available to suppliers?
2. Are representatives from your suppliers invited on your management/customer care/quality courses?
3. Have you carried out research to identify how your suppliers regard your organisation as a customer?

4.2 Purchasing policy

Companies rely on the prosperity and health of their surrounding community. One way of ensuring this is to help small firms in the area make the most of business opportunities.

Large firms can examine their purchasing policies to make sure that they are giving a fair share of their business to small, local concerns. They can appoint a member of the purchasing department staff to take responsibility for this area. Sources of advice include: local enterprise agencies, chambers of commerce and Better Made in Britain.

Better Made in Britain was formed in 1983 to focus attention on the increasing penetration of goods from overseas into certain sectors such as the retail and car industries. Sir Basil Feldman, chairman of the firm, Clothing Little Neddy, started the ball rolling when he organised an exhibition, where retailers put on display the goods they were importing. Potential UK suppliers visited the exhibition to discuss product specifications, price and delivery with senior buyers.

Following the success of the first exhibition, similar events were organised for the furniture, clothing, footwear, home furnishings, lighting, carpets, textiles and building products and hardware sectors.

These exhibitions have encouraged people to think positively about buying British goods and £500 million of lost business has been recovered by British industry. Better Made in Britain organises Challenge Days for firms with high import bills. Participating companies open their doors for the day and allow potential suppliers to suggest where their products or services might replace imports. Senior buyers also have the chance to see and evaluate product lines under development.

Better Made in Britain also runs the Regain programme. Many UK manufacturers assemble products in the UK but obtain materials and component parts from overseas. Statistics and details of imported components, raw materials and finished products are often not available, so Better Made in Britain audits industry on a localised basis. From the audit, opportunities in the region can be identified and local businesses encouraged to manufacture in the market gaps.

This approach has been used in West Yorkshire, the North East and the West Midlands. In all three regions, Better Made in

Britain was able to point to large numbers of imported components that could be made in the domestic market.

Regain auditors then hold seminars, meetings and exhibitions to inform local businesses, which have relevant capability, about the opportunities for import substitution.

Regain also hopes to establish a national database to match up buyers and suppliers.

Case study: Shell

Shell UK has wooed small local suppliers as part of a general good neighbour programme. For example, some years ago the company was planning to build a large natural gas plant in Scotland. It was only going to employ 150 people and the proposal was not very popular in the area. Shell's solution was to explain to locals through open evenings the spin-off effect for butchers, launderers and other trades. The building contractor was told to take on as many local subcontractors as possible. The company had to send a team of advisors to deal with the number of enquiries from local businesses. Under normal circumstances, most of the subcontracting would have gone to larger, better established firms elsewhere in the country.

Shell has produced two booklets to help its suppliers. The first, "Selling to Shell", outlines the company's buying policies and was produced in response to the need to make it easier for suppliers to make approaches.

However, discussions with suppliers subsequently revealed another difficulty that the company had not previously been aware of, namely that because of its size, some suppliers found they were not paid promptly. Further investigation showed that in most cases the problem with slow payment was caused by suppliers not understanding Shell's invoicing systems. The company responded by producing a booklet called "Getting Money Out Of Shell" which explains how suppliers can speed up payment.

Case study: The Littlewoods Organisation

Littlewoods has issued a code of practice to all its suppliers on the procurement of merchandise for resale by Littlewoods. It reflects Littlewoods' own equal opportunities policies.

The code clearly sets out the group's mandatory requirement that any merchandise purchased must have been produced in conformity with the United Nations Charter, Chapter IX, Article 55. This article governs international economic and social co-operation with specific reference to workers' rights and working conditions. The code also calls for adherence to all regional and local laws covering workers' rights, minimum wages and working conditions in the country of manufacture.

In addition, and to protect its customers, the code imposes on suppliers the requirement that goods provided comply with UK consumer protection law and any more comprehensive specifications which may be stipulated by the Littlewoods Organisation.

Case study: Halfords

Halfords, the UK's largest retailer of cycles and car accessories, held a Challenge Day in summer 1989; 180 potential suppliers attended and Halfords was shown so many innovative products that it started discussions with over 25 of them.

Case study: Marks and Spencer

Marks and Spencer prides itself on its Buy British policy, claiming that 87% of stock in its stores is British made.

Some critics argue that many suppliers have an unhealthy dependence on Marks and Spencer contracts, giving the company undue power over them – particularly in the setting of profit margins. However, textile industry commentators have argued that it was the company's loyalty to British clothing manufacturers, when other retailers sourced abroad, which kept many in business during the recession of the early 1980s.

According to the magazine *New Consumer*, the textile division of the Transport and General Workers Union criticised M&S, claiming that a number of British sourced finished garments were made from foreign sourced cloth. In response, the company met union representatives to discuss alternative UK-based sources. The union commended this move, saying it was in stark contrast to the positions of other major UK clothing retailers.

Checklist

1. Does your company have a formal programme to help small business tender to it?
2. Does your company have a policy and/or programme to encourage local buying; or a Buy British policy?

4.3 Monitoring supplier practices

Companies are increasingly having to take into account the social responsibility behaviour of their suppliers. In particular, following increased media and public concern about environmental issues, it now pays to examine whether a supplier operates its manufacturing and sourcing in an environmentally friendly fashion. For example, furniture companies, which operate a "green" purchasing policy, need to know where their hardwood comes from. They need to ensure that timber suppliers in Brazil, Malaysia, Indonesia and the Philippines are operating sustainable yield harvesting and not indiscriminately chopping down vast tracts of forest.

There is no widespread agreement on how to respond to this particular crisis. Some companies now refuse to stock tropical hardwood. However, others are desperately trying to educate people about the complications of an issue often not properly explored in short newspaper articles or television news pieces. At the same time, these companies are sending senior managers to visit suppliers, to ensure that they are practising reforestation and are operating sustainable logging.

James Latham Group publishes up-to-date information about tropical hardwood deforestation in its company newspaper. It also distributes to customers press releases from the Timber Trade Federation, which discuss the issue from a more general viewpoint.

James Latham buys its timbers from reputable mills, in Malaysia and Ghana, which have especially good records in forest management. But it also buys from Brazil after approval from representatives who have visited the suppliers and checked their approach to logging. All the Brazilian mills it uses practise reforestation. The largest of these mills began planting over 19 years ago and has seeded over 1.6 million trees to date. It is currently reforesting 800-1000 hectares annually.

Other companies have taken slightly different approaches. Major DIY chain B&Q has specified to its timber suppliers that it only wants wood from a sustainable source by the end of 1995, the deadline set by the Worldwide Fund for Nature. And contract furniture makers, Hands of Wycombe, have developed methods of polishing alternative hardwoods such as ash, beech and oak to produce finishes similar to those achieved with the exotic rainforest timbers. In this way, the company also contributes to the national balance of payments by saving expensive imports of rosewoods and other tropical timbers selected for their richness of colour.

These issues are only part of a green purchasing agenda and some companies are sending auditors to all their suppliers to examine their manufacturing processes in detail. In many cases, these companies pass the information about the environmental impact of these products onto their own customers.

At the same time, these environmentally conscious buyers can start putting pressure on wayward suppliers to adopt a more responsible attitude to the environment. Shoemakers and retailers Clarks, for example, made a significant contribution in the 1970s to the world reduction in demand for sperm whale oil to treat shoe leather. It instructed its suppliers that it would reject any leather treated in this way and installed monitoring equipment. Most suppliers agreed, removing an important commercial plank of sperm whale hunting.

Another issue causing similar monitoring is animal welfare. Retail companies are increasingly putting pressure on their suppliers to ensure that product research practice meets broad guidelines in this area, producing detailed specifications on how suppliers are expected to handle the issue. For example, several retailers now insist that their suppliers do not test make-up and toiletries on animals. Similarly, some retailers' specifications now stipulate the way animals and fish should be killed and caught.

Case Study: J. Sainsbury

Sainsbury has strict guidelines for suppliers who kill, catch or use animals. It buys all its meats direct from suppliers who use known and approved abattoir sources. It inspects all meat against strict specifications, which cover all aspects of animal welfare and production and follows all relevant legislation and the Farm Animal Welfare Council (FAWC) recommendations.

The company also works very closely with its suppliers to ensure these welfare specifications are followed. Its technologists make unannounced visits to suppliers to check procedures.

Sainsbury's tuna is caught with pole and line rather than by trawling, because it does not involve killing unwanted fish.

In addition, Sainsbury's cosmetics and toiletries are not tested on animals. The company produces a detailed specification and checks the supply of ingredients used. It insists that its suppliers establish that no animal tests are conducted on Sainsbury's behalf in this area. Human volunteers test the finished product. Sainsbury's is continuing to look for alternatives to testing on animals.

Case study: Co-operative Retail Service

The Co-op has brought in David Bellamy Associates to examine the environmental impact of its branded products from raw material purchase through to manufacture, use and disposal.

It asks suppliers a long list of in-depth questions. In the case of paper supplies, the company wants to know what measures are being taken to control emissions and effluent discharge. Other considerations include what waste and by-products are generated during the manufacturing process and, if these are harmful, how they are disposed of; whether the finished product has been tested on animals in the last five years; what percentage of the finished product biodegrades; and to what timescale; is it recyclable; and does it use recycled materials?

The information will be used to formulate a greener buying agenda.

The practicalities of monitoring suppliers are that it will not happen on its own. The mechanisms available to companies range from the relatively low-cost, low-labour to high-cost, labour intensive approaches. Among them:

- straightforward self-audit questionnaires. Regular postal surveys of suppliers ask them to fill in and return responses to basic questions on, for example, production methods, environmental impact, employment practices, or quality procedures. The problems here lie in gauging the honesty of answers (some suppliers simply may not have the necessary information) and in applying sufficient pressure to compel suppliers to respond.

- independent auditing visits by external consultants – of particular benefit when the consultant has experience and can make comparisons with practices in other industry sectors.

- auditing visits by the company's own specialist staff or line managers. This has the benefit that it can help cement relationships between the two organisations and that the customer company gains a better understanding of the supplier's business (and vice versa).

For the smaller company dealing with a much larger supplier organisation, it is not always possible to withdraw custom. Whether you do or not, however, a useful tactic is to take the issue to the highest levels of the supplier company – very often, the decision not to supply the information is taken well down the responsibility chain and may be reversed by senior management with a broader perspective.

Checklist

1. Does your company have formal policies to vet purchases on environmental or ethical grounds?
2. Are you aware of the environmental impact of your suppliers' processes?

If so, have you done anything to change them?

4.4 Prompt payment

According to a survey conducted by the CBI and Cork Gully in 1991, one in five small and medium-sized businesses asked said its survival is threatened by late payment. The surge in bankruptcies since then suggests that in a period of protracted recession the proportion of smaller enterprises at risk may be even greater.

In response to the survey findings, the CBI launched a "best practice code" for prompt payment. It states that a responsible company should:

- have a clear, consistent policy that it pays bills in accordance with contract
- ensure that the finance and purchasing departments are both aware of this policy and adhere to it
- agree payment terms at the outset of a deal and stick to them
- not extend or alter payment terms without prior agreement
- provide suppliers with clear guidelines on payment procedures
- ensure that there is a system for dealing quickly with complaints and disputes, and advise suppliers without delay when invoices, or parts of invoices, are contested.

Small firms have less flexibility in their borrowing arrangements and therefore are more susceptible to cash flow problems. Large firms can help ensure prompt payment by appointing an employee with the authority to chase late payments and by making suppliers aware of his existence.

Some companies admit confidentially that they will pay a small firm quickly, if they have an informal agreement, but our research did not uncover any large concern which was prepared to put that in writing.

Some states in the United States are considering legislation to penalise persistent late payers. They argue that faster payments all round would speed money flow and increase prosperity for large and small companies alike.

Checklist

1. Do you have a policy of prompt payment to help the cash flow of small suppliers?

4.5 Partnership sourcing

An increasing number of UK organisations are moving towards partnership sourcing. It represents an important trend away from confrontational relationships with suppliers towards mutually supportive relationships. The power of collaboration between customer and supplier is something that has long been understood by successful Japanese companies, and is rapidly becoming an important competitive tool in Britain.

The CBI describes partnership sourcing as "an essential set of techniques for improving responsiveness, cutting costs, and seeking world market share". In essence, it involves extending teamwork from inside the company to relationships outside. To be truly effective, it relies on creating an environment where both parties – customer and supplier – see the benefits of working together on a win-win basis.

The essential ingredients of partnership sourcing include top management commitment to making it work and well-trained people to support the relationship. It also requires a great deal of patience to overcome the inevitable teething problems that come with the move to a more demanding relationship. At the same time, partnership sourcing works best in an atmosphere of open communication and mutual trust – both of which take time to build.

Customers committed to partnership sourcing often go to considerable lengths to help their suppliers understand what they need. They are also prepared to invest time, effort and resources to helping their supplier partners to upgrade systems. When things go wrong, they collaborate in joint problem-solving teams. They also make sure that suppliers have all the information they need about future developments so they can plan product and service improvements.

The supplier partner also has to be very open with information. When things go wrong, it should not try to hide or minimise them, but use the situation as an opportunity to discuss improvements. One of the results of partnership sourcing is that individual contracts become less and less important as increasingly it is the relationship itself which counts. However, measurement becomes more important because to make the relationship work effectively, both sides need to understand what is going on.

According to George Neil and his colleagues from the Supply Chain Management Group at Glasgow University, companies should assess suppliers on a broader range of performance criteria than has previously been the case. They recommend measuring supplier performance in the following areas:

- quality performance
- delivery performance
- cost management
- contribution to development
- commitment to total business quality
- management team
- workforce development
- customer base
- financial health
- flexibility of response
- supplier management (the supplier's management of its own suppliers)
- process capability and capacity
- business systems
- administrative support.

The key to partnership sourcing, according to Neil, is trust between supplier and customer. Suppliers, he says, must learn not to make promises they cannot keep, while customers need to be trusted not to use the closer relationship against suppliers' interests. However, research at Glasgow University has revealed that some companies, while claiming to favour partnerships with suppliers, are not above using the privileged information obtained to try to squeeze suppliers' margins by demanding price cuts on top of the benefits from the partnership.

As a safeguard against such unscrupulous behaviour in the future, companies might consider writing specific policies for managing supplier partnerships into their ethical codes. Moves towards open-book costing – which is currently a one-way street which leaves the supplier vulnerable – may in time require attention, too.

Properly managed, however, a more trusting relationship allows the two partners to engage in an open dialogue which can begin to pin-point not only problems, but also the causes that lie behind the problems. Once identified, problems can then be tackled at their root using the expertise of both partners.

Clearly, the other side of the partnership sourcing coin is an increased responsibility on the part of suppliers. George Neil suggests that the most effective means of defence for suppliers who fear they may become victims of the trend for large companies to use fewer suppliers is to become more proactive. By relieving customers of some of their responsibilities, suppliers may be able to protect and even expand their markets.

For example, a number of suppliers are now moving their operations closer to their big customers to ensure they can respond to the requirements of very demanding just-in-time systems. (A process for delivering to a factory only what it requires for immediate production.) The Nissan plant in Washington, for instance, operates systems which give suppliers 45 minutes notice of manufacturing requirements. Clearly, those companies which take responsibility for meeting tight delivery targets of their own free will are more likely to be retained.

Berkshire Gravure, a producer of food product packaging, recognised that new health and hygiene regulations affected its customers. The company therefore approached customers with an offer to implement measures in its own production processes to help them meet their new responsibilities, even though it was not required by law to do so.

Case study: Fullarton Fabrication Ltd

Fullarton Fabrication Ltd began life doing sheet-metal work in the late 1970s with six employees. By carefully targeting a small number of large customers and by aggressively adopting new manufacturing technologies, the company now employs more than 1400 people.

In one case, Fullarton demonstrated to IBM – for which it was a supplier of moulded plastic – that it had the capability to take on additional types of work. So impressed was IBM by the technological competence of its supplier and the production processes Fullarton had in place, including an efficient just-in-time system with its own suppliers, that it invited Fullarton to supply it with finished keyboards and monitors on a just-in-time basis.

Case study: Black and Decker

Through its expertise in set-up management, Black and Decker – the electrical tool manufacturer – has been able to help suppliers identify potential savings of 90% in set-up time. Of that, the suppliers concerned estimate that 50% could be achieved through training provided by Black and Decker with no additional investment on their part.

Black and Decker has also developed a scheme to recognise its best suppliers. Suppliers are monitored and assessed on a number of criteria, with scores allocated by those functions in the company best placed to do so. Scores are then weighted to reflect the importance attached to them by Black and Decker for a given supplier.

Suppliers which achieve an overall rating of more than 86% receive the Black and Decker Supplier of Excellence award, which they can then use in their own marketing. The company has gone some way to strengthen trust with suppliers, too, by identifying "strategic suppliers" which may be given three-year contracts and encouraged to play a bigger role in product design.

In addition, Black and Decker has found it useful to look further back down the supply chain. Through the creation of a new post of supply chain auditor, the company has recognized the role of all members in its supply chain. The supply chain auditor's role is to assess product performance from raw material supplier through to retailer. And it's an approach that is already paying dividends. A 66% improvement in the time taken to get a quotation was achieved through the simultaneous involvement of four consecutive links in the supply chain.

Case study: IBM–Thomas Cook

IBM UK has been a Thomas Cook customer for over 40 years, but in 1991 it took the decision to make the travel company the sole supplier of its business travel needs.

According to IBM's manager of procurement: "Partnership sourcing is about maintaining long-term relationships with 'best-of-breed' suppliers." Thomas Cook, in turn, was flattered to be chosen, says its director of travel management, Clive Adkin.

The partnership arrangement involves a strong commitment on both sides. As Adkin explained in a best practice brochure produced by the CBI: "IBM is very exacting in the way it specifies standards of service and conducts extensive research to ensure those are met."

It's a far cry from the traditional, adversarial relationships so common between purchasing departments and suppliers – the kind of relationship where, says Adkin: "The customer sees everything that goes wrong as more evidence to damn you with. By contrast, if you have a partnership arrangement, you go into it with an attitude that you are going to make it work.

"When a problem arises, you automatically go into problem-solving mode; there's no assigning of blame, simply an understanding that it's in both our interests to resolve it. It's a very different mindset that really pays off on both sides."

One of the results of the partnership sourcing relationship is that every IBM employee can now go directly through the Thomas Cook computer systems to book hotel rooms. And it's an arrangement with benefits on both sides. It allows IBM staff to make bookings with a minimum of fuss and means Thomas Cook only has to handle the administration.

"Part of the arrangement", says Adkin, "is that we have an open book on costs. Instead of a traditional commission arrangement, IBM covers our costs, with an agreed profit margin. Again, we both benefit from the arrangement."

According to Adkin, the trend towards partnership sourcing is fuelled by a realisation on the part of purchasing departments that maximising value is more important than simply concentrating on lowest price.

Case study: Rover Group

The Rover Group has been using partnership sourcing since the late eighties. Mike Farnworth, supply agent, explains that the company calls it the "preferred supplier philosophy". Previously, Rover designed a product then asked for suppliers to tender to make it. Now under the new regime, the suppliers design their own products or components. Says Farnworth, "We believe they are the experts in the market place, so they can come up with the design."

This close co-operation has led to many advantages for the company:

- shorter lead times to develop components
- improvement in quality
- mutual collaboration to reduce the production costs
- best practice teams go out to suppliers and offer help and advice to supply firms. Rover advisers have advised suppliers why certain machines are producing scrap or why there are bottlenecks at certain stages of the production process. It has also advised suppliers on more general topics, such as energy conservation, and told them to switch lights off at lunchtime and recycle waste to bring down costs.

Rover's suppliers also gain from the new closer relationship. They receive continuity of business, which will in turn benefit their own suppliers. They have also become more competitive and have often won additional contracts elsewhere, on the strength of their close association with Rover.

In principle, Rover will invest in new machinery for its suppliers if it will be more cost-effective. But it also expects its suppliers to do the same. For example, a catering company has been asked to share the cost of new canteen equipment.

The company runs a Sterling Award scheme for 40 suppliers yearly. To achieve this award, suppliers must meet a set of criteria that includes environmental excellence and quality.

Throughout the 12 months prior to the awards, Rover assesses the performance of its suppliers in terms of quality, supply, efficiency, innovation and support to Rover's design, product and manufacturing activities.

Rover's purchasing department issues a statement outlining its mission values and guidelines, giving clear indicators of expected standards.

It is unambiguous in its attitude to suppliers. It states: "Suppliers have a choice; our ability to purchase the best goods and services depends on their ability to supply. They need to have confidence in our commitment to them in order to invest in the sort of future products that we will need, to the benefit of both parties. We each depend on the co-operation of the other."

Checklist

1. Does your company operate partnership sourcing?
2. Do you have long-term supply agreements to ensure continuity and allow trust and collaboration to develop?
3. Have you set up joint development teams to look at cost cutting, innovation, design and quality?

The management process

The essentials of a coherent approach to supplier social responsibility can be summed up in the following questions:

1. Who are our suppliers?
Although the accounts department may have a long list of suppliers, the only useful information this will normally contain is where to find them, what they supply and their credit worthiness. None of this helps greatly in establishing long-term relationships of mutual benefit.

Similarly, the data held by the purchasing department will not normally be of much assistance beyond day-to-day management. All too often, the primary role of purchasing is to obtain the best financial terms, rather than to establish lasting relationships of trust.

Part of the problem may be that there are too many suppliers. From the point of view of quality control alone, there is a strong argument for reducing the number to a mere handful (perhaps as few as two) for each bought-in commodity or service. With smaller numbers, it is possible to begin to create partnership relationships that will provide genuine mutual benefit.

By listing all suppliers and gaining a much wider range of data about them (reliability, cultural compatibility, willingness to operate in partnership mode, creativity of approach and so on), you can start the process of numbers reduction. Immediate benefits are likely to flow if you make sure suppliers understand why you want the information – those keen to develop a partnership relationship will react by intensifying their efforts to improve service.

2. What criteria should we set for our suppliers?
The criteria you evaluate suppliers on will vary according to circumstances. For example, technical excellence and R&D capability will be of great importance in selecting a supplier of aerospace components, but not usually for a supplier of stationery.

A useful method of evaluation is to use the technical requirements as a first filter. For example, does the stationery company have the range of stock and the delivery system to fulfil your needs, both now and in the foreseeable future?

A second stage filter will normally be value (as opposed to price, which is simply one of the components of value).

Next, the supplier should be evaluated on fit. Do the two companies share common perceptions about what is important? Is the supplier willing to adapt its processes and routines to meet your needs? Is it willing to learn in association with you? Would you feel confident sharing your medium- and long-term plans with that company?

A final evaluation should match the selections against other criteria, such as policy towards small and/or minority businesses, to ensure that the process is fair and to make any judicious exceptions for companies which could meet the other criteria, with help.

3. *Have we put in place all the requirements to develop trust in us by our suppliers?*
Partnership sourcing is a two-way street. Policies on prompt payment, technical help and so on need to be in place and working before you can expect suppliers to take your overtures seriously.

4. *How will we make sure we make the most of our partnerships?*
Regular reviews and audits both of individual relationships and of the programme as a whole will enable continuous improvement. For example, BP Chemicals, as part of its quality programme, conducts detailed reviews with suppliers at the end of major projects, to explore together everything that went well and badly, and to extract lessons from the future. The key is that, because both suppliers and BP Chemicals view these as an improvement process, rather than as an opportunity to assign blame or take credit, there is an exceptional amount of honesty and openness in the discussions.

5. Responsibilities towards investors

Traditionally, the manner in which companies behave towards their investors has depended on three influences – the law, which prescribes the responsibilities of directors and companies; the Stock Exchange, whose rules are aimed at protecting shareholders from various kinds of undesirable exploitation; and accepted practice. All have evolved in the past decade providing, for the most part, greater protection, particularly for small shareholders.

One strong reason for these changes is that well-publicised cases of malpractice have raised public demand for protection. Another is that both the Stock Exchange and the government have been keen to expand the number of people who own shares. The major privatisations such as British Airports Authority or British Gas have almost all sought to encourage small savers to become small shareholders.

Having a high proportion of small shareholders is expensive – in the sense that they all need to be sent the annual report – but very valuable to top management from the point of view of defence against unwelcome takeover bids. Small shareholders tend, in most cases, to be much more loyal than institutional investors. None the less, the reality for most quoted companies is that the majority of shares will be held by institutions. The way in which the company treats these investors can have a significant effect both on any immediate share prices and on how likely they are to give the management team support when it needs it.

Recent research into the attitudes of managers of failed companies indicates that a poor attitude towards investors – failure to keep them informed, to recognise their needs, particularly for information – is often a strong contributory cause of collapse.

Moreover, institutional shareholders, in particular, are beginning to flex their muscles, with the Institutional Investors' Committee demanding much greater accountability from companies' executives. Observes Garry Wilson, a consultant in investor relations for Georgeson International: "The growing concentration of funds in a relatively small number of institutional investors' hands and the willingness of these investors to voice concern over a company's activities has been a strong stimulation to the development of the investor relations industry in the UK."

Communicating with shareholders is part of a chief executive's job. Yet opinions differ in UK boardrooms as to how the responsibility should be handled. Speaking about his time at ICI, Sir John Harvey-Jones says: "I used to read every letter from a shareholder and make sure I answered it personally, if needs be." At the other end of the scale, another controversial CEO says he regards his personal involvement in investor relations as a waste of time as people buy and hold shares simply on the trading and financial performance of a company.

However, a recent study conducted for head hunters, Stephenson Cobbold Ltd, shows that there is broad agreement among chief executives about the benefits of good communication with shareholders.

The main benefits are seen as stronger and more stable equity values which make it easier and cheaper to finance further investment; and enhanced shareholder goodwill, which can play an invaluable role in protecting a company in hard times and in defence against a hostile bid. "The chief executive who spends his time communicating with shareholders... finds they have the confidence to support him if times get tough," says David Cassidy, managing director of Widney plc.

For all these reasons, it pays for companies to ensure that they maintain a close and responsible relationship with their shareholders, both large and small.

So, what do shareholders need from the board?

Performance

For the majority of institutional shareholders and many private shareholders, the primary requirement they will have of the company is that it delivers good dividends and that the shares maintain a high market value. These objectives are backed up by a legal requirement that the company should act in the best interests of its shareholders.

The difficulty arises in defining what is, or is not, in the best interests of shareholders. A couple of decades ago, many companies justified not giving to charities because they considered that this was an unauthorised use of shareholders' funds. It has now become accepted that this is a legitimate means of protecting shareholders' interests, for a whole variety of reasons covered elsewhere in this guide. More recently, debate has centred around the various "poison pill" options, which companies in the United States have developed to protect themselves against unwelcome takeover bids. Many observers consider that these arrangements are not in the shareholders' interest, because they prevent investors from realising their investment at the higher share price that would normally prevail in a serious bid.

This whole area represents a minefield for directors, particularly in the United States, where increasing numbers of shareholders are suing board members perceived to be acting against their interests.

One protection for executives is for the board to issue a clear statement of how it perceives its responsibility to shareholders and to have that approval at an annual general meeting (AGM). Some companies include references of this kind within their published mission statements.

Most boards appear to have given little if any consideration to these issues. However, rising expectations from shareholders and the general public are likely to force them onto the agenda over the coming decade.

Ease of purchase

Says Wilson: "Although the treatment of private shareholders often remains limited to providing tea and biscuits at the AGM, many companies have recognised the contribution of the small shareholder. They have achieved this through lower dealing charges, dividend reinvestment plans and setting up PEP schemes."

Information

Shareholders need to know accurately and honestly how the company is performing and what its business prospects are. To put across that information they can use a variety of media, including:

1. The annual report

A cynical broker remarks that he only reads annual reports for what they don't say. The great majority of annual reports do little more than fulfil the basic legal requirements of presenting the audited figures. These companies miss an excellent opportunity to market themselves to shareholders and to analysts and institutional investors, who can influence share values. Those companies, for whom a significant proportion of individual shareholders are also customers, can also enhance sales turnover, by encouraging people to support their investments when buying.

Almost all annual reports are made up of a statement by the chairman (often followed by one from the chief executive, if different) and a statement of trading figures for the year, signed by an independent auditor and conforming in presentation to rules set by the accounting bodies.

By custom, companies tend either to include a notice of the AGM in the annual report itself, or send it as an accompanying document. By law, notification must be at least 21 days in advance of the date of the meeting. The company has an option of what other information it should include and how it presents it.

The shareholder needs to be able to understand from the annual report:

- what business the company is in
- how it has performed during the past year and how that compares both with previous years and with its competitors
- what its prospects are for the coming year and what the prospects are for the sector as a whole.

Increasingly, too, many shareholders want to know how the company does its business, not only in ethical or social responsibility terms, but from the point of innovation, management style and operating philosophy – all issues which can have an impact on performance.

Unfortunately, relatively few annual reports cover all these needs. (We have encountered several where it was not possible to identify, except by inference, what the main business areas were.)

Moreover, they can be extremely difficult to understand. As Barbara Conway pointed out, in *Investor Power*, 1980:

"Try one basic test. Read through the annual report of the company into which you are thinking of putting your hard-earned cash, including the chairman's and director's comments. Then ask yourself the following question: 'Do I understand what this business does and how it does it?'"

The basic requirement for most shareholders is that the information should be readily understandable. That means well-written text and well-designed illustrations. Another requirement is that the executives' statements are open and honest. A great many chairmen's statements can best be described as "not dishonest" – they certainly do not give the impression of great openness. How many chairmen, for example, have admitted to making mistakes (rather than ascribing problems to "unforeseen circumstances" or "poor trading environment")?

It has been argued that the City requires information to be presented in a formal, jargonised fashion. But stockbrokers and analysts do not necessarily support this view. When Thorn-EMI sent analysts its simplified employee annual report, it found that many analysts prefer to have information in normal language. Moreover, the employee reports contained more information on business strategies and how they were being implemented.

The more information the company can give – for example about directors' shareholdings, responsibilities and external involvements; or about social responsibility issues, such as community involvement or equal opportunities – the more the company will be perceived as open and honest. While disclosure of most of this information is entirely voluntary, the company that does not provide this kind of background is effectively missing an opportunity to enhance the relationship of trust it needs with its shareholders.

2. The AGM

AGMs vary from discreet events in isolated hotels, attended by the few, to massive events catering for several thousand.

Key responsibilities for companies here should be:

 – to ensure that shareholders have an opportunity to attend.

Few companies, if any, deliberately try to limit the number of shareholders attending the AGM. But relatively few go out of their way to make it easier. A few, such as BAA or British Gas, have chosen to hold their AGMs as centrally as possible, for example, at the National Exhibition Centre in Birmingham, rather than in London. Even fewer have adjusted the hours of their AGMs to meet the needs of those whose work or domestic responsibilities prevent them attending events during working hours.

US company Emhart has experimented with video conferencing to allow shareholders in multiple locations to attend its AGMs. A chairperson at each location ensures that shareholders can ask questions even though they are thousands of miles away. For those who cannot attend in person, Emhart produces a video of the highlights of the AGM, mailing a copy to any shareholder who requests it.

– to ensure that shareholders have the opportunity to ask questions and that they receive fair answers.

Rather than hope that there will be mercifully few questions, so that the meeting can keep to its timetable, responsive companies can encourage shareholders to submit questions in advance, for the chairman or chief executive to deal with in amalgamated form. An honest, considered answer will usually – though not always – be of more value to the shareholders than one off-the-cuff.

– to ensure shareholders understand the issues on which they are to vote.

Proxy voters, in particular, need a clear, factual explanation of the arguments, the implications for the company and for the value of their shares. It would also be helpful if companies were to provide more information about directors proposed for re-election.

3. Stock Exchange and press announcements

Stock Exchange rules require quoted companies to be accurate in the financial information, including forecasts, that they publish. The rules can be very confining. But companies which restrict their efforts to publicising financial and production information, lose the opportunity to enhance share value by promoting their community activities.

4. Ad hoc communications

Some companies have kept in touch with their shareholders through occasional publications on issues of interest. Others have organised meetings, at which analysts and investors – usually institutional shareholders – are invited to meet the chief executive. These occasions often provide an opportunity for the investors to explain what they expect from the company. However, quoted companies have to be careful not to give preferential access to information at sensitive periods – for example, shortly before the announcement of annual results.

But the small shareholder does not usually receive the same attention. Explains Wilson: "Communication with shareholders is being taken seriously with more companies providing newsletters with the private investor in mind. However, personal contact with senior management remains limited."

A handful of companies is also looking at the potential to involve shareholders in measuring and monitoring the quality of the service they provide.

Case study: Shell International

Shell shares, because they have been handed down from one generation to the next, tend to stay within families and have a wider than average spread among individuals. In its shareholder communication strategy, Shell therefore recognises a clear split between its large institutional shareholders and the thousands of loyal private shareholders that hold its shares.

The company holds the normal regular briefings for institutional shareholders, analysts and financial journalists, and a formal AGM – as required by law – once a year. But Shell also recognises that it has a responsibility to address its private shareholders and to do so through a forum that gives them the chance to ask questions. The AGM, usually held in a large city like London, is inconvenient for many private shareholders to attend and is not geared up to address their legitimate concerns.

To give its private shareholders a better chance to know what's going on, Shell annually holds about 10 informal shareholder meetings at different locations around the country. Shareholders within a certain radius of the location are sent invitations and encouraged to attend the two-hour sessions where senior managers make presentations and a half to three-quarters of an hour is set aside to answer questions from the floor. In addition, a buffet meal is laid on and Shell managers, wearing easily recognisable badges, circulate and answer more questions.

In all, around 10,000 people attend the private shareholder meetings every year. Locations change, too, so that although shareholders are not invited every year, when they are invited it is likely to be to a nearby venue where they have the opportunity to voice their concerns.

Shell regards its annual report as being properly targeted at significant stakeholders. Shell UK, which used to produce its own report (although as a wholly owned subsidiary it was not compelled to do so) is discontinuing the practice in favour of a different approach. From May 1992 onwards, the UK company will replace its single annual report with a Business and Social Report published twice a year.

Shell reasons that in most cases the company's detailed financial performance is only of interest to City analysts. Most shareholders, it believes, hold the company more accountable for its stewardship of other resources such as people and the environment. By and large, the company feels, most of the people in the target audience for a subsidiary company like Shell UK are not interested in the financial performance of that one part of the whole organisation.

The move to a Business and Social Report reflects the company's growing awareness of the need to answer to its shareholders for its performance in areas of legitimate concern to them.

Case study: Kingfisher

Kingfisher believes in direct communications with institutional shareholders. Geoffrey Mulcahy, the Chairman and Chief Executive of Kingfisher, explains, "We try to visit all our major shareholders at least once a year – more often if they request it. We encourage our shareholders to give us a call if they have a concern or would like more information on the group's operations. They are more likely to do this if they know us personally."

Investor relations has an increasingly global dimension. The Kingfisher directors cross the Atlantic on a regular basis to update US shareholders and in addition will visit European financial centres to talk to major institutions who are taking an increasing interest in leading UK companies.

Kingfisher's investor relations programme covers a variety of different events. In addition to one-to-one meetings with major shareholders, there are presentations to groups of shareholders and potential shareholders, speeches at major retailing conferences and store visits to allow shareholders to get to grips with the "nuts and bolts" of the business. One common feature is that shareholders have direct access to the executive directors. As Mr Mulcahy explains, "We believe that fund managers need to know where businesses are being driven. And they need to hear it from those behind the wheel, rather than from the back seat."

Case study: NFC and the small shareholder

Companies with large numbers of small shareholders frequently meet the criticism that only the interests of the big institutional shareholders are properly represented on the Board. NFC, where 20% of the shares are held by 90% of the employees, tries to restore some of the balance by allowing the shareholders to appoint a director to represent the interests of the smaller shareholder. In 1992, there were 13 candidates (nine men and four women). Voting, supervised by the Electoral Reform Society, is by postal ballot, with shareholders ranking their preferences rather than simply putting a cross against one candidate.

Checklist

1. Does your company have a public statement of its responsibilities towards investors?
2. How informative is your annual report? Have you researched what shareholders think?
3. Does your company make a substantial effort to provide shareholders with information beyond legal and Stock Exchange requirements?
4. Is the AGM designed to meet top management's needs, or those of the shareholders?

Managing investor relationships

Whether they be banks, institutional investors or individual shareholders, the management objective must be to secure their trust and loyalty. The provision of information, which we have explored in this chapter, plays a strong role. But communication is two-way. It pays for top management to invest time and effort into learning what the investors think about the company and where it could improve.

While it is becoming more common for plcs to carry out surveys of City influencers, to establish attitudes towards the company and its management, very few organisations attempt to gain a broader input. Indeed, some actively discourage it, by managing their AGM in such a way that spontaneous questions from the floor are disallowed.

The more opportunities the directors have of listening to investor views, the more likely they are to understand the concerns that affect share price. That does not mean they necessarily have to follow what investors say (letting a bank set policy for the business is almost certain to lead to disaster!), but they do need to demonstrate responsiveness.

Vehicles companies could use include surveys inserted in the annual report, informal seminars around the country and simply asking people to write to the chairman expressing their concerns ahead of the AGM.

While none of this will prevent the fluctuations in share price from poor financial performance or takeover rumours, it will help stabilise them – allowing top management to focus on growing the business.

5.1 Ethical investment

The moral debate about the role of business in society is probably as old as business itself. But growing concern about corporate social responsibility issues has led in recent years to a heightened awareness of the part played by shareholders via investment.

The idea that shareholders have a more active role to play as involved owners and stakeholders in the community rather than mere speculators has been steadily gaining ground. As a result, a number of ethical investment funds have been established in Britain in recent years.

An ethical investment is one which is motivated by ethical considerations as well as by profit. For example, certain goods may be seen as inherently bad like tobacco, fur clothes, missiles and gambling. Ethical investors would normally believe production of such goods should not be encouraged through investing in companies active in those sectors. They may also view the processes of production as unacceptable: for instance, animal experimentation, or environmental damage. Ethical investors may avoid involvement in a particular country and put their money elsewhere if, for example, they believe their investment would indirectly support an immoral regime. Support by the management of a company for "wrong" social behaviour may also be a ground to disqualify companies for investment.

The Merlin Jupiter Ecology Fund, for example, deliberately invests only in the shares of companies which meet social responsibility criteria. Fund managers at Merlin Jupiter explain the rapid growth of ethical investment in this way:

"The idea of assessing the behaviour of companies before investing in them emerged in the United States in the wake of the Vietnam War. Many individuals were shocked to find that their shareholdings in chemical companies had effectively made possible an event to which they were personally opposed.... Many of us are causing, albeit unwittingly, serious damage to our planet by investing in companies which are harming the environment and failing in their responsibilities as corporate citizens. By taking care as investors to select companies with sound environmental and social management we can profit from our part in shaping a better world."

Ethical investment funds screen the companies in their portfolios using ethical criteria. In doing so, they provide investors with the opportunity to limit investment to ethically acceptable enterprises.

But as Alan Miller, Chairman of the UK Social Investment Forum, notes in his debut article as ethical investment columnist for the recently launched *Corporate Citizen* quarterly journal: "Corporate responsibility means different things to different people. To some, a good corporate citizen might be a responsible employer who takes care of its workforce and the community in which it conducts its business, to others it might mean a company's products or services are at a minimum environmentally benign or use sustainable resources."

Clearly, much depends on the social responsibility criteria used to define what counts as an ethical company. For ethical investment funds, potential problems arise, too, from the effectiveness of methods used to gather information. Simply asking companies about their activities leaves a lot of room for differences of interpretation.

David L. Owen notes in a review of recent research into ethical investment that: "In the context of information needs and sources it is interesting to note the reliance on company annual reports by ethical investors in making investment decisions, despite their awareness of major deficiencies in the provision of data on corporate social performance within such documents."

Owen also observes that a major problem in the perception of ethical funds as "involved owners" lies in their failure to play an active role in trying to change company policy. At present, they tend to simply disinvest from companies whose activities become unacceptable.

Owen's view is supported by a 1989 survey conducted among 13 UK ethical funds by the Ethical Investment Research Service (EIRIS) which found that just one fund directly attempted to influence company policies, and that only three unequivocally stated that their policy was to inform companies, from which they had disinvested, of the reasons for their decision.

Influence tends to be asserted through negative publicity. For example, EIRIS itself produced in 1992 a report, which linked 36 of the top 50 company groups with countries where human rights abuses occur.

EIRIS surveyed 590 company groups in the FT All-Share Index and compared their operations with a list of countries identified by Amnesty International with human rights abuses. Of the companies surveyed, 200 had subsidiary or associated companies in one or more of the countries identified; 180 had subsidiary or associated companies in countries where three different definitions of human rights abuses applied, and 31 had significant subsidiary or associated companies in the identified countries. EIRIS points out, however, that if an investor chose to avoid all those identified in this last case, 68% of the All-Share Index (by market value) would remain available for investment.

Peter Webster, executive secretary of EIRIS, points out: "Company groups are under no obligation to tell shareholders anything about the human rights records of the countries in which they invest. But this research provides a practical means for those concerned about human rights to reflect that concern in their investment decisions."

Mark Campanale, senior researcher at the Merlin Research Unit, comments:

"Many ethical funds currently operate on the basis of negative criteria. Not having operations in South Africa, for instance, might be one of the criteria for investment. This absolves the fund from any responsibility for establishing a dialogue with companies about social responsibility issues and reduces the ethical fund management to just another set of financial decisions. But by employing social and environmental scientists to research and monitor a range of issues, a basis for dialogue is established with companies.

"We combine buying shares in a company with buying into the values of that company. By monitoring the company's activities we act as a vital check on its assumptions concerning the environmental and social impacts of the direction it takes. It comes down to having a positive input into the evolving culture of the company to ensure it reflects social and environmental values. We still use negative screening, but we believe in a positive engagement through dialogue. Our starting position is to identify companies that are moving in the right direction and establish a base index for them with which to compare progress. By combining the research function with the investment function in this way we aim to build up a portfolio of solid long-term holdings."

As the market for ethical investment matures over the next few years, it seems likely that fund managers will apply more sophisticated research techniques to the task of tracking companies.

Where it involves a dialogue with the companies concerned, the process of ethical tracking may in time provide a valuable means for shareholders to influence company policy via ethical investment funds. To be truly effective, however, it seems likely that such moves would have to be accompanied by a greater recognition of social responsibility performance in companies' stock market valuations.

Case study: British Gas

British Gas attracted criticism in 1990 over its operations in the rainforests of Ecuador. As a potential shareholder, Merlin Jupiter Ecology Fund opened a dialogue with the company which was sustained through a series of meetings with the British Gas management team.

British Gas responded positively and has since taken a number of important steps. Most significant, according to the Merlin Research Unit, is the free release by the company of environmental impact assessments of its Equadorean operations.

While these reports are not satisfactory in every respect, say the researchers at Merlin, the company's openness is to be applauded.

Case study: The Co-operative Bank

In May 1992, the Co-operative Bank, announced that it would be asking corporate customers involved in unethical activities to change their ways or close their accounts. The announcement was timed to coincide with the bank's publication of a formal ethical policy. The policy states that the bank will not engage in business with companies involved in blood sports, the fur trade, animal experimentation, manufacturers of tobacco products promoted in the less developed world, foreign regimes in breach of human rights or arms manufacturers supplying such countries.

The bank's decision followed a market research exercise in 1991 in which it asked the views of 30,000 of its 1.5 million customers. The ethical policy is aimed at attracting new sympathetic customers rather than losing ones which do not conform. But at the time of its announcement, the Co-op said that up to five "businesses or commercial organisations" would be approached to "discuss whether it is appropriate to continue banking with us".

The Co-op and its parent, the Co-operative Wholesale Society, have long taken strong stands on ethical issues, including refusing to do business with South Africa and banning fox-hunting on their land. Of its decision to formalise its ethical policy the bank said: "We are confident our ethical policy will gain us business. This isn't a one-off campaign. It's a question of stand up and be counted."

Under the new policy, individuals will not be approached about their private activities, as the bank assumes most of them already share its values. The policy, which also commits the bank to maintain procedures and training programmes to detect illegal activities such as drug trafficking, money laundering and tax evasion, is supported by a large-scale awareness campaign both inside and outside the bank.

A series of television commercials ensured that the Co-op's ethical stand did not go unnoticed by the public, while a massive training initiative prepared 3500 bank staff for the change. "We've found our employees are right behind the policy and enthusiastic about the whole thing," says a bank spokesman.

The 360 branch and departmental managers have all attended a half-day course showing them how to keep the Co-op's business ethically sound. It will be down to them and other front-line staff to enforce the policy. More junior staff were also taught how to apply the policy at briefing sessions run by managers.

5.1.2 Managing relationships with ethical investment funds

A common way for ethical fund managers to gather information about companies is to send out written questionnaires. As a result, many companies are deluged with time-consuming requests for details of policies, practices and operational processes.

At the same time, companies may also face a barrage of questions from pressure groups and the press. Quite simply, it is not always easy to know to whom the information provided will ultimately go and companies are understandably cautious about high levels of transparency.

One solution that is gaining widespread acceptance and has much to recommend it is to produce an annual social report. The report might cover the following issues:

- the company's policy towards key stakeholder groups
- review of plans for next three years
- budgets and priorities
- examples of specific initiatives
- employee involvement
- review of press coverage
- any audits or measurements of effectiveness the company has carried out for external audiences.

Benefits of a well prepared report include:

- making it clearer to key audiences what values the company stands for

- "corporate brand" enhancement
- reduction in administrative hassle from enquiries.

There are also benefits for internal audiences, in terms of building people's pride in the organisation and helping to maintain a clear focus on social responsibility activities. In addition, moves on the part of ethical funds to standardise questionnaires would make life simpler for those who have to fill in such forms. Better still, say ethical investment practitioners, is for companies to become proactive in managing their relationships with ethical funds by inviting fund managers and researchers to attend regular face-to-face meetings.

In many cases fund managers will be sympathetic to the constraints on companies and can be reassured by strategies that undertake to improve ethical performance incrementally. Such arrangements allow a constructive dialogue and a high degree of transparency without the risk of sensitive information causing embarrassment for the company concerned.

The emergence of codes for assessing ethical performance, such as the Valdez Principles and the UK Environmental Code, which at first sight may appear threatening, may actually form the basis of progress. For example, companies may be able to say they conform with principles two, three and five and are addressing one, four and six.

With environmental liability and other ethical issues likely to become increasingly relevant to investment decisions, constructive dialogue and higher levels of transparency seem the most strategically sound way forward for enlightened organisations.

6. Responsibilities in the political arena

There are few minefields for companies as treacherous as politics, if only because there is often – by definition – no consensus on the "right": approach. To illustrate the point:

- Many companies responded to international calls to disinvest in South Africa. Others took the view, equally passionately, that they had strong responsibilities towards the black employees in their South African subsidiaries. As South Africa becomes rehabilitated, issues arise in other countries. Is it right to invest in dictatorship? What relationships should companies have with the warring factions in what was Yugoslavia? Can companies justify doing *any* business with Libya under Colonel Gaddafi?

- Horticultural companies are under attack for "stealing the genetic property" of Third World countries in the form of seeds and cuttings. Yet the companies believe they cannot create the disease-resistant, high-yield, new crops the Third World so desperately needs without access to these resources.

- Some developing nations are concerned that the dominance of the international agencies over news reporting in itself constitutes a bias towards Western, developed world values. They wish, instead, to confine local reporting to locally controlled agencies. The international news agencies and newspapers in the Western world regard this as censorship. The two views appear irreconcilable.

For the international or multinational company, wherever it is based, there will inevitably be conflicts between the demands of the host nations (including the home-base country) and those of the global organisation. The move towards glocalisation – global strategies and structures, but largely autonomous local subsidiaries able to blend in with the culture and markets of the country, in which they operate – which is now gathering pace, will help alleviate some of these stresses and strains.

The concept of concentric circles of community interests helps here. Each national community will have different priorities in the social responsibility issues it needs to address; it will also set different priorities on ethical behaviour. There may, for example, be particular tensions between rival ethnic groups (as in Belgium for example, or in Spain, where sensitivity to Catalan and Basque aspirations is essential to doing business in the industrial heartlands).

Local management needs to understand and be in control of these issues. At a regional level, management needs to develop common policies and standards, using the combined resources of several countries to enhance the impact of initiatives. One of the likely results is that the company "rounds up" on some standards, using the toughest standards within the region as the basic standard for all the national operating companies. Of course, the company has to be careful not to impose common standards for their own sake. However, in those countries where it adopts higher standards than would normally be expected, the company gains substantial benefits in image and reputation.

A similar principle should, in theory, apply at a global level. In practice, the increasing diversity of cultures and economic environment as we step out of regional geography makes it difficult to standardise at much more than the general policy level.

There are three areas of political concern, which have a strong relevance for corporate social responsibility:

- lobbying
- Third World issues
- human rights.

6.1 Lobbying

It seems ironical that the lobbying industry, which aims to influence legislation and ministerial decisions, should be faced with the threat that the parliaments of Westminster and Brussels will regulate its activities – and be unable to influence them. Unable to agree on self-regulation, the lobbyists are under increasing attack for their role in representing organisations and special interest groups.

The dilemma for companies lies in deciding when it is ethical and responsible to lobby, and when not. Clearly, any business has a responsibility to represent its shareholders' interests, and that must include attempting to persuade government not to pass legislation that will damage the company's markets, or reduce its profits, for example. But what if the interests of the shareholders are directly opposed to those of the community?

Both the Public Relations Consultancy Association and the Institute of Public Relations have codes of conduct that include references to lobbying, but there are still a great many grey areas, where managers can only be guided by what they feel to be "right".

Charles Hendry, a former political advisor to government departments and now a senior consultant with Burson-Marsteller, has observed these issues from both sides. He sees lobbying as a natural part of the marketing process and offers the following practical advice:

- Responsible corporate lobbying comes from long-term understanding. Companies, which attempt to create relationships with MPs and senior civil servants only when they perceive a threat to their business, are less likely to succeed.

Long-term relationships allow MPs to understand the company and its industry and allow managers to understand how the legislative system works. Unethical behaviour is most likely to come from organisations which do not have this understanding.

- Retaining an MP is not always the best way to influence legislation.

It is commonplace for a company to retain a member as its consultant and expect him or her to vote in the company's favour if a relevant issue arises in the House. The problem is, the retained MP often loses credibility if he has a declared interest.

However, not all members' interests are declared. If an MP is retained by a PR consultancy, for example, the public does not know which issues he is really standing for. The Register of Members' Interests will only list the consultancy and not its clients. Companies should consider whether they would be better to have an open relationship.

Another relevant issue to consider is conflict of interest. Hendry advises: "If I was an MP I would not accept payment from any company within my constituency. I should be working for them anyway. If there is a conflict of interests, an MP should ensure that the constituency comes first." He believes that select committee members should be particular who retains them, and that there should be a Register of Lobbyists, who would then have to make it clearer what they were doing.

- Lobbying is not always the appropriate way to exert influence.

A company should:

- Establish what its need is. Does it have to be done through a public affairs (lobbying) programme? Could advertising/PR achieve the same end?

"Influence the public first and then parliament," says Hendry. "The best lobbying is often good practice. For example, The Body Shop has had a huge amount of good publicity. It does not need to lobby MPs about animal testing because they are already aware of the importance of the issue thanks to media articles and consumer campaigns."

- Ensure it is not lobbying for the impossible – for example, a lowering of interest rates when high interest rates are part of the Chancellor's long term economic strategy
- If it does retain an MP, it should not concentrate its efforts on one – far better to establish a body of opinion in the House. Give those you do retain clear guidelines on behaviour, preferably in writing.
- Be careful not to ally itself with pressure groups. Says Hendry, "They often succeed by scaring people with select snippets of information and the government can be slow to check out all the facts to get the whole picture. If a company is known to take on unhelpful causes the relevant people will be less willing to talk to you. In addition, government is wary of pressure groups, because however it responds the pressure group says 'It is too little too late'."
- If the company is doing something well, write and inform MPs. Gain friends, so that in the event of a takeover bid, for example, your company is already highly regarded.
- Be open – too much secrecy and lying will destroy your case – be prepared to answer awkward questions and explain what you are doing or you will be misunderstood.
- Treat separate parties differently, but evenhandedly.

Case study: Whitehall in Industry

Whitehall in Industry aims to second senior civil servants to business and senior managers to Whitehall departments. The secondees spend a total of three weeks on attachment, joining in the activities of the host organisation and asking questions. At the end of the secondment, they may write a detailed report and present it to their hosts.

Case study: Industry and Parliament Trust

The Industry and Parliament Trust (IPT) was formed by 11 companies in 1977 to bridge the understanding gap between industry and MPs. The gap arises in part from differences in objectives, but also from the fact that very few MPs have direct experience of business management. IPT's main objectives are:

- To enable members of both houses of parliament and British members of the European parliament to widen their experience in, and increase their knowledge of, industry
- To improve the understanding of industrial managers about the problems of parliament in dealing with matters affecting industry. The trust, which is an educational charity, is strictly non-partisan. It is open to parliamentarians of all parties. It is not a lobbying organisation.

Member companies finance the trust, which runs fellowship programmes designed to give MPs an insight into industry. The MPs volunteer to spend about 25 days in one year with a major company. They get the chance to see how business functions from the inside and gain a greater understanding of the constraints business operates under.

Key points of the trust's fellowship programme are:

- To provide a bird's-eye view of the company's business objectives, its strategies for achieving them and the institutional framework for implementing those strategies
- To give an appreciation of the scope of business operations from grass-roots activities through management and functional supporting structures
- To show how a professionally managed group tackles planning, budgeting, investment appraisal, overseas expansion and other decision-making activities
- To involve MPs in the processes of management so that they can see at first hand how decisions are reached
- To create a dialogue with MPs on problems of industrial relations and employee participation and give them the opportunity to see union consultation/employee participation in action
- To improve MPs' understanding of the extent to which government strategies and legislation affect the business
- To give business a better understanding of how the parliamentary system works
- To show businessmen how MPs see companies.

Some parliamentarians enjoy the fellowship so much that they come back for another dose. In this case, the trust tries to arrange them ''postgraduate'' facilities with small businesses.

With the increase in small business activity over recent years, the trust sees it as a major objective to involve firms of all sizes in its activities. To help the politicians gain a complete perspective of British industry, the trust encourages them to take on short-term courses of four or five days with smaller companies.

Case study: Control and Readout

Control and Readout, a small business member, provided a four-day post graduate programme for one MP. This consisted of:

Day one:
am – Introduction to company organisation, management philosophy, style, history and future plans, government aids and legislation and how they affect the smaller company, effects of rapid technological change on company practices, and the personal objectives of major shareholders and directors.
pm – spent with junior directors, plus tour of the plant and confidential discussions with office and shop-floor personnel.

Day two:
Detailed session with the chairman, mainly on financial matters, but also covering relationships with the local authority. A visit to the bank for wider discussions.

Day three:
This took place a few weeks later and consisted of a session to inform employees about the workings of parliament and the legislative process, followed by a private meeting with the chairman for a frank report by the MP on his impression of the company.

Day four:
After a further interval, the MP returned for an update, and to check on projects and answer queries.

Although lobbying is usually seen as the preserve of the large organisation, or of industry federations, small firms can also exert a substantial influence. A *Financial Times* review of the topic quotes Stephen Alambritis, parliamentary officer of the Federation of Small Businesses: "Nothing carries more weight with an MP than a letter from a company in his own constituency." The article goes on to qualify that statement by pointing out that MPs' attentiveness tends to wane with the size of their majority.

It recommends that small businesses:

- establish contact with the MP before there is a problem. Invite him/her to visit the premises and gain some understanding of the business
- when a problem occurs, contact the MP either through the constituency office or the House of Commons
- via *Dod's* directory, identify and contact other MPs, who have a specific interest in the subject you want to lobby about
- seek the backing of the relevant trade association, local chamber of commerce or other business grouping
- be realistic. Changing the rules may prove too difficult for a small company, but changing how they are applied is often possible.

Checklist

1. Does your company have a clearly defined policy on lobbying?
2. Would an outside observer consider your lobbying activities as open, fair and justifiable?

6.2 Third World issues

It has to be accepted that technical skill and management skill are in short supply in many Third World countries. But to send expatriates to fill the posts only solves the short-term problem and annoys the community at the same time. It makes good business sense for companies to invest in training local people so that they can take on responsibilities including senior posts as soon as possible.

The company will probably want to include some high fliers from the Third World in its general management programme to develop managers with an international outlook and capacity. But such training has little relevance to the less-gifted managers who will have to manage the shop-floor, or the operators who need technical skills. These too have to be catered for.

Other organisations, especially retailers, go to the developing world for products and work within the confines of the training and resources available to get the best deal for both parties. Instead of training village workers in new technology and languages, they work within the traditional culture such as papermaking and wood carving, for which there is less need for locals to speak fluent English.

Developing countries often complain that multinationals (MNCs) are far too concerned with how much money they can export from their subsidiaries or sales operations. This concern frequently leads to controls over how much money the companies can take out, and of course to a resultant slow-down in investment from abroad.

The multinationals' traditional response to this issue, and the related question of transfer pricing has been that they benefit the local economy by importing advanced technology and skills into the countries where it operates. More recently, some multinationals have taken the view that the best way to prosper in a market is to demonstrate commitment to it. Among the ways they can do so are:

- make a clear policy of spending local profits locally. Where a regional economic alignment exists, the company can probably choose where it uses the money within the economic alliance, as long as it convinces the host country that it really means to reinvest its profits.
- assist in the retention of foreign currency reserves by substituting indigenous materials and products for imports. Although there are limits to how far this can be done before additional costs resulting from loss of manufacturing scale and from smaller markets make the export of end products uncompetitive, as has already happened in parts of South America, the scope for import substitution is enormous. As many less developed countries have hefty long-term debts and constantly agonise over their balance of payments problems, anything a multinational can do to reduce imports will help.
- look for opportunities to locate research and development nearer the problem. Many developing and newly industrialised countries have underutilised reserves of technical staff. India and Korea, for example, have surplus computer programmers. Some multinational computer companies have benefited from tapping this resource. Not only do these companies receive a cost benefit, but they are establishing centres of technical excellence, which they can use to grow their businesses within those countries' expanding local markets.

Unilever has for many years had a policy of conducting R&D for Third World products in the countries concerned. It finds that the research is more relevant to customers' problems if pursued by people who understand local needs. It also contributes to the local economy by identifying local materials that can be substituted for scarce or imported ingredients.

Years of lengthy and inconclusive debate in the United Nations over whether multinationals should be subject to an international code of behaviour have been inconclusive. Yet both sides have moved position considerably. On the one hand, the majority of developing nations now recognise the value of MNCs as powerful catalytic forces within local markets – because they generate an infrastructure of local suppliers – and as importers of technical and managerial skills. On the other, the vast majority of multinationals have recognised that abuse of their power – by, for example, involvement in politics or playing governments off against each other – undermines long-term trading stability. Companies which want to stay in a developing country and grow there prosper more when they are recognised as good, local corporate citizens.

As a result, many MNCs have voluntarily adopted and published international codes of practice of their own, that reflect the majority of the aims of previous attempts by Third World nations to impose obligatory standards. These companies usually find that their international codes of practice are beneficial in commercial terms, because they impose common standards of behaviour across their operations, making it easier to prevent misdemeanours by independent-minded local chief executives. None the less, one of the biggest criticisms of multinationals is that they sometimes apply different, lower standards to the Third World than to the developed world.

Cases occur commonly in the areas of:
- product safety – e.g. continued distribution in Third World countries of pharmaceutical products banned for safety reasons in the developed world; failure to provide health warnings on products such as cigarettes, when it is not required by local legislation
- employee safety – accident and fatality rates at Third World subsidiaries of manufacturing companies often exceed those at home by a considerable margin
- marketing – e.g. misleading or unsubstantiated claims about products or failing to take into account the social impact of specific marketing approaches upon unsophisticated audiences. (The dangers of inadequate attention to the potential problems of marketing in the Third World are amply borne out by the Nestlé case. More than a decade after the issue was "settled" many people still associate Nestlé primarily not with health and high quality foods, but with the death of Third World babies.)
- pollution control – some companies have taken advantage of laxer anti-pollution legislation in Third World countries to reduce production costs. However, the developing countries themselves now increasingly recognise that the environmental price they are paying to attract and keep these industries is too high. They, too, are tightening up their requirements. MNCs building new plants will therefore benefit from incorporating the most modern, effective pollution controls, on the grounds that it is cheaper to build these in at the design stage, than to add them later.

Case study: Procter and Gamble International

US-based multinational Procter and Gamble has operating companies in over 29 countries and has a clearly defined policy on how to conduct its business abroad.

The company's president, William Gurganus, discussed this policy at a conference on multinational citizenship during a convention of the National Foreign Trade Council, explaining that each time Procter and Gamble starts business in a new country it has been guided by three general objectives:

- Never to forget that Procter and Gamble is a guest of that country, is bound by its laws and is obliged to do its best to blend the company's overall policies with local customs and practices.

In practical terms, this commits the company:

- to be sensitive and responsive to the social and economic conditions in the host country.
- to employ at all levels citizens of the host country who are qualified applicants.
- to give all employees the opportunity to rise to higher positions not only in their own country, but also in other Procter and Gamble organisations around the world.
- to compete vigorously but fairly with local competitors. But to compete in ways which will lead these competitors to respect our integrity as well as our ability.
- to avoid meddling in the politics of the host country.
- to strive to achieve a reputable identity and not be looked upon as simply the branch of an American parent.
- to pay good wages in line with responsible local practices in the community in which it operates.
- to establish easy channels of communication with each community and country so that each will have a better understanding of the action or inaction of the other.

Procter and Gamble has listed its common stock on a number of foreign exchanges and regularly distributes translated versions of its annual report.

If citizens of host countries want to own part of the business, they can often do so by buying Procter and Gamble stock.

Case study: The Body Shop – First World standards in the Third World

The Body Shop has a very different philosophy from most companies. It sets out to source products in the Third World in an unpatronising and unexploitative manner, because it believes that encouraging local communities in developing countries to grow ingredients and make products for the company creates employment and trade.

The Body Shop calls its approach towards the Third World "Trade Not Aid". It recognises that projects need to be commercially viable – for both parties – while at the same time making trade with the Third World a positive force for its future.

The principles behind Trade Not Aid are:
- respect for all environments, cultures and religions

- the utilisation of traditional skills and materials
- the creation of successful and sustainable trade links
- trade in replenishable natural materials
- encouragement of small-scale projects which can easily be duplicated
- provision of long-term commitment to projects
- treating trading partners with respect.

The Footsie Roller, a smooth wooden foot massager, is a good example of the Body Shop's policy. Here the company is working alongside the Boys' Town Trust, which cares for destitute children in Southern India during their secondary school years. The boys are taught trades that enable them to earn a living when they return to their villages. This initiative has developed into a new local industry in ten very poor villages.

In order not to harm the local economy by flooding it with a mass of highly affluent teenagers, the Body Shop has arranged that the boys are paid the going rate for the local labour market and the rest (the difference between the local rate and the First World rate) is held in trust until they leave the Boys' Town Trust. When they leave, their share of the money is used to set each of them up in a trade by buying each one a lathe or a pair of oxen and plough.

The Body Shop has also set up an alternative papermaking project in Nepal, one of the poorest countries in the world. The Nepalese economy is based on fragile subsistence agriculture, now damaged by appalling deforestation.

Hand papermaking using lokta, a daphne shrub, dates from the eleventh century. Recently the industry had been stripping too much daphne bark and was beginning to destroy the forests where it thrived.

In response, the Nepalese government put a ceiling on daphne use. Papermaking declined. Whole villages were out of work. Now as part of the Body Shop project, workers are mixing alternative fibres such as banana, water hyacinth, bamboo and sugar cane with recycled daphne to make new papers, new jobs and new hopes.

Water hyacinth is a prolific weed, which chokes rivers in tropical regions. By harvesting it to make paper, you also clear the rivers. Banana trees flourish in Nepal. They grow to their full height in about 18 months and then produce fruit. The tree then collapses and the fibres rot away until a new shoot rises from the old root. Banana fibre can successfully be used with lokta, or on its own for papermaking purposes.

Mara Amats, consultant on the Body Shop's Third World projects points out: "Too much daphne bark was being stripped for paper. There was no more work for the papermakers. I simply showed them that banana was an alternative. That's my job."

The first papers arrived in the UK in early 1989. Customers can buy bags, notebooks, purses, wallets and pot pourris made from the new paper on many of Britain's high streets.

Says the Body Shop: "Trade Not Aid entails a constant search for ways in which the company can use manufactured Third World products." The company is investigating other projects in the Amazon basin with tribes living in the Xingu region. Its product development team is investigating nine materials including brazil nut, andiroba and breu branco, for a tropical rainforest range of cosmetics and toiletries. The company explains: "The Body Shop's efforts to create markets for plants from tropical forests are intended to promote the economic independence of the forest people. They are the guardians of the forest and are the primary source of ideas for regenerating areas of forest that have already been degraded or cleared. It is almost impossible to predict what effect the emerging markets will have on patterns of land use in the tropical forests of Brazil. It is also very difficult to predict what reaction there will be from wealthy landowners and businesses when they see that 'their' resource base is being spread out among a minor, under-privileged sector of the rural population.

"The Body Shop will, however, do as much as possible to ensure that markets are carefully and preferentially directed to communities of forest people."

The Body Shop policy of Trade Not Aid in India includes a specific clause to commit 20% of the money the company pays the workshops to local welfare projects. These funds, which the company regards as its social responsibility to provide, go towards healthcare, education and improving working conditions particularly in the area of health and safety.

Case study: RTZ Corporation

RTZ is a company that has received considerable criticism, particularly on environmental grounds, over the years. But the mining and manufacturing conglomerate regards itself as a caring and responsible employer and has gone to great pains to establish exemplary employment conditions in its Third World subsidiaries, such as Namibia's Rossing Uranium Ltd. When the mine began production in 1976, the company was unable to find suitably trained local labour. Most of the people in the area, seeking work at the mine, were unfamiliar with the industry. In addition, their educational levels were low and they were mainly illiterate and innumerate. So Rossing had to train employees from an elementary level before it could productively employ them.

In 1979, Rossing established formal operator training, which has now been provided to some 1200 operators. It also has a formal programme of continuous training so that people learn to do more skilled jobs, and a student programme to provide the company with future managers. Selected school leavers interested in a career with Rossing spend a year with the company, receiving bridging education in maths, science and English. During the year they also receive leadership training and broad exposure to the mine and its systems, as well as working within their chosen discipline. After completing the year they are sent to a university or technical college for degree or diploma courses in subjects such as management, engineering, accountancy and commerce. On qualifying, the graduate starts work at the mine. About 70 trainees are on the scheme at any one time.

In addition, the company constantly tests black employees with an eye to promotion. In the late eighties it promoted over 2200 blacks. Rossing teaches English literacy to its employees and encourages them to strive for a degree or a diploma on correspondence courses.

At a national level, the company established the Rossing Foundation in 1978 to concentrate on providing adult education to a wide cross-section of

Namibians. It built an adult education centre, which offers courses in literacy, sewing, and three standards of English and German. It has donated language laboratories and computers to local schools and helped to build a primary school and a secondary school in the self-contained community of Arandis. The company also sponsors Namibians to study in America and Britain on the condition that they return to their country afterwards.

Wherever possible, Rossing purchases goods and services inside Namibia. For example, it buys work clothes at the market price from a local women's co-operative.

Checklist

1. Do you have a written policy detailing standards of behaviour in host countries?

2. Do you actively reinvest profits in the host country?

3. Do you transfer technology to the developing world in line with its needs?

4. Do you place a heavy emphasis on training in Third World countries?

5. Do you attempt to work within the confines of the traditional culture?

6. Are standards of pollution control, safety, marketing and product safety common throughout your operations?

6.3 Human rights

Companies that operate in host countries with a poor human rights record have to be especially careful that they do not offend the international community to the detriment of their business.

Those US and European companies which pulled out of South Africa as a result of public pressure against apartheid took, for the most part, commercial decisions, based on the cost of loss of business elsewhere against the profits from their South African operations. Many of the multinational companies that remained have taken strong positions at the forefront of the practical fight against apartheid, providing models of how a non-discriminatory employer should behave.

These companies do not operate segregation; they pay above the supplemented living level and educate blacks in order to promote them into higher positions in the workforce. They refuse to use migrant or contract labour, give their workers fringe benefits such as pension schemes and health schemes and, in some cases, help blacks to buy their own houses or at the very least rent family homes at reasonable rates.

Some recognise the unions, if they have been set up, and encourage them by providing special training for union officials. In areas where the union movement is weak, they set up councils, which give employees an official voice.

The serious problems for these companies arise when local legislation requires them to act in ways that contradict basic standards of human rights. The experience of most companies faced with this dilemma is that they first look for ways round the legislation, then, if that is not possible, ignore it in hopes that the host government will not make it an issue if they do not. To a considerable extent, experience in South Africa has shown that this approach works. Significantly, the personnel management profession has been at the forefront of pushing the boundaries of apartheid-free practice in South Africa.

If current political trends continue in South Africa, they will presumably have an impact on companies' decisions over whether to reinvest in that country. But many of the underlying social problems will take decades (at least) to resolve and these companies must be aware that the human rights issues will remain on the agenda. Moreover, although South Africa is the country where human rights abuses have most often caused dilemmas for businesses, it is far from being the only country where companies have encountered such problems.

The value of the South African experience is that it provides useful lessons for companies in how to deal with human rights conflicts. Many companies investing in China, for example, had already been through the relevant thinking processes. As a result, their decisions to withdraw, either permanently or temporarily, were made rapidly, without lengthy public pressure.

A clear statement of company ethics – i.e. a code of international practice – is a key starting point for making judgements about appropriate behaviour. It not only gives local managers a touchstone, but allows the company to put its behaviour into an ethical or moral context to concerned audiences in other countries. The statement should examine, among other things, the conditions under which the company would no longer find it tenable to continue business operations within a country and how it would alleviate the human problems, such as job losses, which would result from a withdrawal under those circumstances.

Checklist

1. Does your company have a policy of equal employment opportunity, wherever it operates? Is it implemented?

2. Does your company have clear guidelines on how to react to human rights problems?

7. Responsibilities towards the broader community

One of the clear signs of the maturing of social responsibility practice in the UK is the gradual replacement of the concept of corporate philanthropy, first with community investment, then additionally with community partnerships. Instead of operating autonomously, at arm's length and sometimes suspicious of each other's motives, companies and not-for-profit organisations are collaborating in far more supportive ways. Companies recognise that, to change public perceptions, they must gain insights into the ambitions, prejudices and motivations of communities of interest that only the voluntary sector can tap effectively. The voluntary sector, on the other hand, has learned the value of tapping not just the corporate purse, but the skills, expertise and commitment of its employees. There has also been a growing understanding of the mutual benefits that come from combining resources and expertise from the private and voluntary sector.

It has taken a long time to evolve to this stage.

The concept that companies have responsibilities towards the community at large is far from new. Corporate philanthropy was a burning issue for the Victorian entrepreneurs, for example. In his book *Enlightened Entrepreneurs*, Ian Campbell Bradley explores the lives of ten Victorian businessmen. Although many of their policies on community care might now be regarded as paternalistic, they were the forerunners of today's social responsibility movement.

In the 1800s, the Nonconformist Colmans, still famous today for their mustard, established provident funds, clothing funds and compulsory accident insurance. Colman's wife Caroline launched a works kitchen which provided cheap food and drink. Prices covered the cost of raw materials. Preparation and cooking costs were met by the company. Caroline herself acted as "lady superintendent" and specified that they should open at 5.45 am in the morning for tea and coffee for workers who had a long walk to work.

Boots is to the retail trade what Colmans is to mustard. Jesse Boot's attitude to the workforce was autocratic but beneficent. Boot was involved with several philanthropic projects in Nottingham, where the chain first started in the mid-1800s.

In 1908 he established 11 homes, in memory of his daughter Dorothy, for veterans of the Crimean War and the Indian Mutiny. In the same year he gave much of the money to rebuild the Albert Hall, a centre for temperance meetings and Wesleyan Methodist services in Nottingham. He also gave £5000 for an organ in the hall, provided that popular recitals would be held there every Saturday afternoon with cheap seats so all could attend.

Quakers George and Richard Cadbury, founders of the chocolate manufacturers, built a model village in Bournville, Birmingham, for staff and the local community. They bought the land because they were determined to prevent speculators moving into the area and putting up cramped sub-quality houses for their workers.

In their village, a pedestrian could walk from one end of the estate to the other without leaving parkland and each house had a large garden.

Bournville was used as a showplace and helped create a much greater interest in town planning. George Cadbury continued his interest in the issue by establishing a lectureship in civic design and town planning at Birmingham University.

Why should today's companies exhibit this concern?

The most forceful arguments come from the companies themselves. Thorn-EMI has a well-established giving policy and involves itself in everything from charitable donations through to educational sponsorship and training, giving over 0.5% of UK pre-tax profits through its corporate responsibility programme. Explains chairman Colin Southgate:

"No business exists in a vacuum. At Thorn-EMI we are conscious of the influence our businesses have on communities throughout the UK both locally and nationally. We recognise that 'business' is not only a matter of serving our customers well – it brings with it responsibilities to the communities where Thorn-EMI businesses operate.

"If a community as a whole flourishes, the individual members of that community tend to flourish too. A flourishing community is one which is prosperous, healthy, educated, inventive and which cares for the less fortunate. All these aspects are related and any company which wishes to make a meaningful contribution to the community, as Thorn-EMI does, will try to address these aspects.

"It is in Thorn-EMI's interests to be part of a flourishing community. The more prosperous a community, the more it will buy our goods and services. This is mutually beneficial, since the more we can improve our financial performance, the more we can give back to the community."

IBM's community investment policy states three clear reasons for its detailed strategy:

- to contribute to the economic and social well-being of the communities in which we operate, thereby helping to make them better places for us to do business
- to be recognised by government, customers, business partners and our own employees as a leader in effective and enlightened corporate community involvement
- to improve morale and motivation of our employees through their awareness of, support for and involvement in the company's activities.

A strong common theme running through many of these corporate statements is that involvement in community affairs is of mutual benefit to both the company and the community. It is not enough for a company to exist in harmony with the community – it must also have a strong interest in its development. Having made the philosophical commitment to community involvement, there is no shortage of opportunities – quite the opposite. The problem comes in finding a structured approach for both the community and the long-term shareholders.

A good starting point is to classify activities into broad categories upon which the organisation can make decisions about the extent to which it should become involved. It can then subdivide these categories where it believes it should become involved into areas, upon which it can make more specific decisions.

We suggest here four such broad categories:

- corporate and staff giving
- secondment
- education and schools liaison

- small business development

As with most classifications of social responsibility issues, there may be overlap between these categories.

In the previous edition of this book, we included sponsorship as an element of responsibility towards the broader community. The argument was that, if all social responsibility was of benefit to the organisation, then the distinction between contributing, say, to a local hospice appeal and sponsoring a theatrical event to achieve publicity is at best grey. There is, however, an alternative view, based on management practice. Most companies with clear policies in this area make a distinction between community activities, which are increasingly frequently run by a community affairs professional; and commercial sponsorship, which tends to be the responsibility of the marketing department. Undoubtedly, there are areas where the two sets of responsibilities overlap, but best practice appears to be that the two departments meet regularly to discuss actual and potential projects and to agree where responsibility should lie. Techniques such as The Giving Matrix (see page 172) often help. Frequently, a sponsorship arrangement will throw up opportunities for more specific community activities and vice versa.

In this edition, we have opted to separate the two approaches, to bring the organisation of the book more into line with accepted management practice. The issue of sponsorship is therefore dealt with in a chapter of its own (see page 202).

7.1 A helping hand

Evidence suggests that, in general, companies' commitment to charities has remained strong in the last few years despite recessionary pressures in the economy. In 1991, British companies gave an estimated £190 million to charitable causes – compared with £135 million in 1988. National Westminster Bank topped the league chart of charity contributors, according to the *Daily Telegraph*, with donations of around £13,710,000. British Petroleum and British Telecom came second and third with £13,500,000 and £13,090,000 respectively.

Figures for the top 100 corporate donors compiled by the quarterly journal *Corporate Citizen* show that average donations in 1990-91 were 2% of pre-tax profits, compared with 1% for 1989-90. The ranks of frequent givers also include a growing number of small and medium-sized companies.

But why do companies give? According to *A Guide to Company Giving*, published by the Directory of Social Change, keeping up with similar businesses is a common reason. Other companies like to give to charities whose activities will benefit their business sector – for example, pharmaceutical companies sponsoring cancer research, computer companies helping spread computer literacy, or retail businesses sponsoring crime prevention projects.

Some companies simply want to be seen as good neighbours and will support charities where they have branches – banks, retail chains and building societies are especially fond of this form of giving. The pay-offs come in improved recruitment and, for service businesses such as hotels, enhanced market awareness.

In addition, a lot of companies believe that employee fund-raising initiatives encourage team-work that benefits the business. Others have schemes to donate money to charities that employees are involved in, thereby encouraging good relations between staff and management.

There is evidence, too, that charitable giving may be a factor in the way companies are perceived by those outside the organisation. For example, of the top ten most admired managements in Britain identified by *The Economist* and Loughborough University in 1991, only Greycoat plc – whose community programme has been squeezed by the property slump – does not appear in *Corporate Citizen*'s top 100 ranking of charitable contributors. And all of the top ten companies seen as most able to attract, retain and develop top talent appear in the ranking.

As the benefits become clearer, so companies are taking more steps to ensure that they receive the credit due for their good works. A community affairs director from a major bank said: "In recent years the government has been demanding that we take a more responsible role in the community. We have always taken on that role but now we are publicising it more."

Case study: The Per Cent Club

The Per Cent Club is a group of some 200 leading companies, which are committed to making a significant contribution to the communities in which they operate. More than half the members are in *The Times'* Top 500.

Launched in 1986, the qualification for membership is the contribution of no less than half a per cent of pre-tax (UK) profits to the community. Companies may donate to charitable organisations, job creation initiatives, training schemes, local economic development as well as education, the arts or music.

7.1.1 A helping cheque

High profile companies receive hundreds of requests for donations every year. A filtering and decision-making system is therefore essential. Typical systems involve the following:

1. A written document stating priorities gives the company a formal reason for accepting or rejecting requests. The giving policy document should also specify the sort of funding you are going to undertake. Many corporate donors will not give money towards core funding. Others prefer to give money to a small project that can be closely monitored. Others, such as Allied Dunbar, are willing to hand over large sums of money to help set up charity organisations in the hope that once the charity is successful, other companies will take over the funding.

2. A vetting system. Once a company has decided on the type of funding it will give, it must then work out a way of deciding whether candidate charities are going to be able to use donations effectively. In early 1990, many large and experienced corporate donors got their fingers burnt when the organisation War on Want went bankrupt.

Some companies send their employees to the charity in question to vet it. Other firms audit the accounts and study how much money is going to the people the charity is supposed to help before making a decision. Other companies just opt for large charities, safe in the knowledge that their money is in professional hands.

Some corporate donors demand that the organisation is not an enabling charity, like the Worldwide Fund for Nature, but actually does the work.

In picking a charity, donors usually like to ensure that they have not chosen a similar cause to their competitors, otherwise the business value of the philanthropy will be reduced. So, for example, each bank has its own preferences. National Westminster supports the Worldwide Fund for Nature, while Barclays supports the Royal Society for the Protection of Birds.

Once you have selected and vetted a charity, it is important to allocate responsibility for keeping up to date with what it is doing. You should also let your employees know you are supporting it and why – for example through articles in the company newsletter.

Case study: British Telecom

BT is one of the most generous corporate donors in the UK. It has developed a strong and structured community policy since it became a public limited company in 1984.

The logic of its policy is that since its business takes it into every community in the country, it has an obligation to play a wide role in the health of those communities. It's a policy that is enshrined in the company's mission statement which states the company's intention: "To make a fitting contribution to the community in which we conduct our business".

In 1992, the BT community programme was restructured to make it clearer to its customers and the wider public. There are now six areas BT aims to support as follows:

- people with disabilities
- people in need
- economic regeneration
- education
- the environment
- the arts.

During the current recession, BT has been overwhelmed with calls for community and charitable help. It has had to say no to many of them. But BT believes that specifying the areas it actively seeks to support will help to channel its giving more effectively. The new areas go hand-in-hand with a number of new initiatives the company has undertaken. One of these – in the area of economic regeneration – is Futurestart, BT's community venture fund.

Futurestart represents a fresh variant on BT's existing support to help the regeneration of less prosperous areas. It has involved BT in an injection of £3 million into what is a pure venture capital fund with no connection with BT's own operations or telecommunications in general.

The criterion for Futurestart is simple: companies that apply should be in deprived city areas or in areas of rural poverty.

The fund is managed at arm's length – both for legal reasons and to ensure there are no conflicts of interest – by a firm of venture capital specialists.

Grants range from £50,000 to £150,000 and take the form of share investments in newly started companies which show evidence of their potential and managerial competence. Futurestart made its first investments in 1992 with grants given to a lighting company in Birmingham and a steel door manufacturer in Northern Ireland.

Disability causes have long been close to BT's corporate heart. The company's ongoing concern was a natural consequence of its decision in 1984 to set up Action for Disabled Customers – a special unit to serve customers with disabilities.

That concern has led to BT's continuing involvement through a number of sponsorship events, training programmes and the BT Kielder Challenge. In the Challenge, mixed teams of youngsters, able-bodied and disabled, compete in outdoor problem-solving activities in a nationwide series of heats, leading to the final at Kielder Water in Northumberland.

Case study: Allied Dunbar Assurance plc

Allied Dunbar is a founder member of the Per Cent Club, annually donating 1.25% of pre-tax profits to charity – over twice the qualifying amount. It also has one of the biggest staff charity pay-roll schemes in the country.

A leader in the field of managing community involvement, the company has defined a set of principles which underlie its giving policies. Its overall aim is to support practical social welfare projects, but it has five guiding principles which help it decide which causes to help.

1. Allied Dunbar focuses on defined geographical areas -usually local to its own operations.
2. It aims to support projects where its own donation will produce a knock-on effect, i.e. where a grant will help an organisation create a model which can be replicated elsewhere or will help it attract funds from statutory organisations.
3. The company prefers to back people rather than causes in the belief that success depends on the effectiveness of the people involved.
4. Allied Dunbar tends to give larger grants to fewer organisations rather than spray money around without having a significant effect. That way chosen projects are better able to concentrate on development and consolidation.
5. The community affairs department tries to remain flexible to changes in society and to help charities that tackle emerging issues.

The aim is to develop policies and procedures which meet the charities' priorities and perception of needs rather than the company's. Allied Dunbar particularly recognises that it is often necessary to guarantee core costs such as salaries.

Des Palmer, community affairs manager, points out: "The intention here was never to link charity work with company business. The Allied Dunbar Charitable Trust was established to ensure that independence."

In line with the corporate giving policy, about one-fifth of Allied Dunbar's donations are concentrated around Swindon where the company has its head office.

Allied Dunbar was one of the first companies in Britain to inaugurate a professionally staffed community affairs department. The department has a staff of nine and produces an annual business plan like every other department detailing its objectives, policies and budgets for the coming year. The benefits of a cohesive, professionally managed social responsibility policy are reflected in the number of requests the community affairs staff receive to speak at national and international conferences on the subject. Allied Dunbar is also frequently positioned on corporate donor lists alongside companies which are 20 or 30 times its size.

As part of its community strategy, the company tries to avoid taking over responsibilities relinquished by the state, although Palmer admits this is an increasingly grey area. The company also has a policy of promoting more effective management of charities. As part of this, it has established an Open University diploma course, Managing Voluntary and Non-profit Enterprises.

Case study: Midas Construction Ltd

Midas Construction, part of Devon-based Midas Construction Group, found an innovative way of combining business with giving to help a local school.

The story starts when Devon County Council awarded this medium-sized company the contract to carry out alterations and extensions to Honiton Littletown Primary School. Because of the alterations, the pre-school nursery, which had originally been housed in the school, had to be re-sited.

To solve the problem, Devon County Council agreed to give the school a mobile classroom as a nursery as long as the school paid for preparing the site. Midas Construction responded flexibly when the governors approached it for the necessary work. The company agreed to do the additional labour, crane in the new building and contribute £500 towards funds.

Mr Roy Cook, headmaster of the school said: "Midas have kept the cost down to a minimum. We have worked together on the school site in harmony. And then to find that the directors of Midas responded to my request for financial assistance with a cheque for £500 was overwhelming."

Case study: Forte plc

Forte plc, one of the UK's largest hotel and catering companies, provides financial help to groups within a community that are improving, conserving and preserving the environment.

The Community Chest launched by Forte in 1984 and organised by the Conservation Foundation, awards monthly grants of between £200 and £2000 to local environmental projects throughout the UK. Since 1984, the Community Chest has helped restore a vintage double-decker bus, re-seed village greens, create school wildlife gardens, plant trees, restore church steeples and transform acres of wasteland into community gardens.

Groups who apply are judged by an independent panel of judges, headed by TV presenter and naturalist, David Bellamy. Once a group is awarded a grant, the Conservation Foundation puts it in touch with a local Forte hotel or restaurant to organise a cheque presentation.

Checklist

1. Does your company have a clear, written policy on corporate giving, setting out key priorities?
2. Do you vet charities against clear criteria?
3. Do you have both national and local budgets?
4. Do you monitor how the charity applies your donation?
5. Do you seek out charities which meet your community objectives, rather than wait for them to come to you?

6. Is your company a member of the Per Cent Club?

7.1.2 Giving in kind

Cash is only one of the resources a company can provide to help community initiatives.

Within the corporate environment are vast stores of equipment and technical know-how, from word-processing, desk-top publishing and printing equipment, to jobbing workshops for maintenance. There may also be buildings which can be loaned to the community outside working hours for social functions, training or exhibitions. Almost every facility a company has could potentially be of value in the community, at very little cost or risk – if only someone takes the trouble to seek appropriate opportunities.

Some companies, which produce and sell office equipment, loan, give or – more frequently – sell it at reduced rates to bona fide voluntary organisations or to schools.

One of the first steps companies can take is to conduct a regular survey of corporate resources. Among the questions to ask are:

- What machinery or office equipment do we have that is no longer used?
- What machinery or scientific instrumentation do we use, but could make available on a temporary basis to voluntary organisations? (For example, small businesses often have contracts with photocopier suppliers, based on minimum monthly volume. Giving any spare volume to a local charity costs nothing except paper, which the charity itself can supply.)
- Do we have spare office space/premises we no longer use, but don't want to rent out/sell?

All these questions the company ought to be asking for its own benefit anyway. Usage of equipment is important in determining the degree of waste in capital resources, and may lead to the hiring out of spare capacity in some cases. The storage of unwanted equipment may be tying up capital in the most unproductive way and using valuable space as well.

A resources survey may also point out poor usage of office or workshop space. If this can neither be used to good effect nor let to an outside organisation, it is likely to be an invaluable gift to a charity even on a temporary basis. The biggest fixed overhead of many charities is space for chairs and filing cabinets.

It can also be helpful to request all managers to check with the appeals committee before throwing out any obsolete equipment, or even partially damaged equipment that could be repaired by someone with the time. A desk minus a leg, an ancient manual typewriter, or a pile of paper with an outdated letter-heading are all likely to be of use to some voluntary organisation. For example, when communications company, The ITEM Group, replaced its computer systems, it donated some of the outdated computers to a charity. The cost to the company was nil; the value to the charity considerable.

Case study: British Rail

British Rail gave 11 building units to new firms in a disused train crew depot as part of Lincoln Enterprise Agency's innovation centre. This was a partnership between the City and the County Council, the Manpower Services Commission and the local enterprise agency.

Case study: IBM

During 1989 IBM offered 100 fully configured personal computer systems to charities and community organisations nominated by employees. Successful charities were chosen on the basis of their relevance to IBM's community investment priorities, the length and extent of the employees' involvement and the charities' ability to use the system effectively and advantageously.

IBM has also given equipment to the United Kingdom Support Centre for People with Disabilities, established at IBM Warwick in late 1988. This is the flagship of IBM's UK's information technology (IT) and disability activities. The centre gives specialist and technical advice on how IT can meet the needs of the disabled.

Other projects involving equipment donation include one at the Open University, which uses IBM PS/2 screen readers to support blind students, speech viewer trials at the National Hospitals Centre for Speech Sciences in London, a PS/2 project to develop software for people with head injuries at the ACE Centre in Oxford and a PC-based note-taking and transcription system for the deaf at Bristol University.

In addition, IBM offers a special price scheme to people with disabilities and non-profit making or government organisations established to work on their behalf.

Charity customers can buy equipment at 40% discount from IBM list prices. The scheme covers the complete Personal System/2 range, including a selection of accessories and attachments, software and networking and communications equipment. It also covers post-warranty maintenance agreements.

Case study: Allied Dunbar Assurance plc

The Allied Dunbar Charitable Trust recognises that money is rarely the only commodity a charity needs. Wherever possible, it seeks to work with charities to provide a package of support which will help them make more effective use of the finance they receive. This can include technical advice, management support, equipment, access to company premises and publicity.

Under the ALPHA Scheme (Allied Professional Help and Advice), the company loans out people from its accounts, premises, systems, personnel and marketing departments to help charities. For example, training staff from the personnel department have established a management training and development consultancy programme with five major charities in Swindon where the company is based.

Allied Dunbar also offers a free design and printing service to Swindon charities and regularly allows them access to its offices to hold special meetings, seminars and AGMs. Those who have made use of the facilities include Drug Link, the Samaritans and Wiltshire County Education Department.

The staff of nine in Allied Dunbar's community affairs department give advice and information on fund-raising for charities and companies and maintain a community affairs library. They also sit on charity appeal committees, produce regular bulletins and write, print and distribute free of charge, publications such as "Pennies from Heaven" – a guide to sources of funds for small and medium-sized charities – and "Dos and Don'ts of Applying to Charitable Trusts".

Case study: Radio Rentals

Oxfam celebrated its 50th anniversary in 1992. To mark the event the charity conducted a campaign to persuade UK companies to commit A Million Days for a Fairer World by donating their time, services or cash equivalent.

To support the campaign, Radio Rentals lent a free TV and video package to each of Oxfam's 850 shops across the UK for one week in 1991. This allowed Oxfam shops to screen a special video for their volunteers explaining the campaign and the important role they would have to play in its success.

Case study: Coverdale Organisation

Smaller companies sometimes lead the field in finding new methods of giving.

The Coverdale Organisation is a management consultancy and training service employing about 100 people. It runs subsidised consultancy and training courses for worthwhile causes in the community.

The programme is run by Coverdale in the Community, Coverdale's community affairs agency, and is an extension of its policy "contribution in action". Rather than donate sums of money to charity, it prefers to donate skills.

The Leadership Development Programme is Coverdale's newest and most ambitious scheme. A bursary programme, it helps disabled people develop management skills through training over a year. The content of the training is determined by the bursary winners in partnership with Coverdale's consultants. Teamwork, leadership and negotiation form the core framework. Midland Bank is supporting the scheme by offering access to its own in-house training programmes.

The scheme is a prime example of how businesses can work together for the benefit of each other and the community at large.

The programme is unusual, because it gives skills directly to disabled people rather than to the charities that represent them.

In the first year, three people were offered a place on the programme. Midland Bank was so impressed by one candidate that it created a fourth place for her, on a Midland bursary.

The Coverdale places are called the Brisenden Bursaries, in memory of Simon Brisenden, a writer on disability issues, who died in May 1989. Simon was one of the first disabled people to attend a Coverdale course.

The managing director of Disability Matters Ltd attended a managers' and professionals' course in September 1989 as part of Coverdale in the Community programme. He explains in the June 1990 edition of the *Coverdale Review* that he has been able to pass on what he has learnt to other disabled people and incorporate many of the ideas into his own work. In addition, other team members, who had often had very little contact with disabled people, had the chance to learn more about disability.

Case study: Price Waterhouse

The South-east office of accountants Price Waterhouse identified a novel way of attracting custom while helping the local hospital in Redhill, Surrey. It held a number of business briefings for local businessmen, but instead of charging a fee to attend, it invited delegates to donate towards the cost of diagnostic equipment for neurological investigations. Together with a top-up by Price Waterhouse itself, the hospital received £1500 from the events.

Case study: Waterstones Booksellers

Since 1990, Waterstones has developed a close relationship with Shelter – the National Campaign for Homeless People – partly as a result of the personal interest in the plight of the homeless taken by the company's chief executive, Tim Waterstone.

Waterstone, who also acts as chairman of Shelter's 25th Anniversary Appeal, manages the relationship himself, delegating to Waterstones' staff where appropriate. According to the charity, his enthusiastic support has enabled it to introduce the issue of homelessness to many key decision-makers.

In addition, a number of initiatives organised through the company's book shops have raised awareness among members of the public. In December 1991, for example, Waterstones sold an exclusive range of 100,000 Shelter Christmas cards through its 70 branches. The promotion sold out, prompting a projected increase of 50 per cent in volume for Christmas 1992 and plans to involve children in local schools through a competition to design a bookmark. Winners will receive Waterstones' book tokens.

Checklist

1. Do you do a resources audit regularly?
2. What do you do with spare equipment/space/premises? Could you give them to a needy charity in the area?
3. Have you allocated somebody to monitor resources and suggest recipient charities?
4. Could you loan equipment to a charity to help it with essentials such as publicity or accounts?

7.1.3 Employee giving

Companies that encourage their staff to raise money for their favourite charities through raffles, sponsored walks or sponsored diets reap the rewards in improved motivation, team spirit and local reputation.

Some companies run "Give as You Earn" schemes to help employees make giving to charity part of their regular expenditure. According to the *Daily Telegraph*, 3% of all charitable giving in 1991 was by pay-roll deductions. Employees merely sign an agreement assigning a proportion of salary to a charity. But this type of scheme has its disadvantages, as a major retailer explains, "It is not very popular. It does not encourage team spirit. The money is just taken from your wage packet and you don't see anything tangible. It is much better to do raffles or sponsored events, which involve staff getting to know people from other sections of the business."

Companies can also show their encouragement for employee involvement in charity initiatives by pinning requests for volunteers on the notice-board. Staff who volunteer to work at a charity in their spare time will have an inside knowledge of its activities. When the company is looking for worthy causes to support, employees can then put their charity forward.

Another way of ensuring employee involvement is to ask staff to nominate the charities they would like the company to support on the grounds that they are more likely to put more effort into fund-raising activities for these charities.

Similarly, some companies have found they can achieve objectives such as quality improvement or workplace safety by donating incentive payments to employee-chosen charities instead of to individuals.

Case study: Barclays Bank

Barclays Bank has over 3000 branches and outlets all over the British Isles and staff at these outposts make a major contribution to local and national charities through their own fund-raising activities. The bank matches staff fund-raising pound for pound which gives fund raisers an added incentive to organise fancy dress days and sponsored darts events.

Case study: ICI

When ICI Pharmaceuticals, Macclesfield, had won major awards in the past, it usually recognised employees' efforts by presenting them with a token, such as an inscribed pen. More recently, however, it celebrated receiving the Queen's Award for Industry by asking employees how they would like to use the money. They suggested donating two ambulances, costing £28,000, to Community Transport Macclesfield Borough, a charity that operates transport services for elderly and disabled people.

Plant management had looked for a project that was related to health care and was visible so everybody could feel proud of the gift.

The retired employee who suggested the idea is now treasurer of the charity. He originally approached ICI for £1000 towards running the fleet.

ICI gained coverage in the national press, and a more motivated workforce. The ICI venture is the first time any of the 2688 winners have put the award to such imaginative use.

Case study: Kingfisher plc

Kingfisher's Helping Hands Awards are designed to recognise employees who spend their own time putting something back into the communities in which they live and work.

The award, which was created in 1992, is open to all employees within Kingfisher Group companies, with a separate award for the best entry from each operating company. Each winning entry is awarded a cheque for £500 to go to the named charity or project.

A panel of judges, comprising representatives from across the group and invited celebrities, selects an overall winner to receive a top prize of £1000. The winners, who may be individuals, teams or a whole store, then receive their awards at a special presentation dinner in November.

Entries are encouraged from projects working with children, community safety, environmental issues, the homeless and people with disabilities as well as helping to build educational links between schools and the community. Each entry is evaluated on demonstrated commitment to the chosen charity or project, details of the work done and the results achieved.

Details of the award are communicated through an in-store poster campaign with entry forms available from the stores, regional and personnel managers and on request from the Helping Hands award office.

Case study: John Laing

Construction company John Laing became convinced of the potential in employee fund-raising in 1984, the centenary year of the NSPCC (National

Society for the Prevention of Cruelty to Children). In deciding to support the centenary appeal, the company felt it appropriate to gain as much employee backing as possible and so agreed to match whatever the employees raised £1 for £1. It set a budget of £100,000, on the assumption that employees would raise between £50,000 and £100,000. It also established a structure that has formed the bedrock of its employee volunteering programme till now.

The structure involved:

- a steering committee comprising the chairman, two other main board directors, the wives of two other directors, an administrative secretary and the chief accountant
- a co-ordinator, John Farrow, then personnel director of the construction business
- 25 identifiable fund-raising units, each under the responsibility of a line manager.

To launch the appeal, the chairman wrote to each of the 25 line managers, exhorting them to demonstrate their commitment and to appoint a liaison person to be the main contact with head office for the duration of the appeal. Each unit set up its own fund-raising committee, with the line manager acting as chairperson in about half of them, and set its own fund-raising targets.

The campaign was supported by suggestions from the centre, by letters to some 300 senior staff suggesting they support the appeal through a covenant (about one-third agreed) and by promotion through the company newspaper. The press office helped by arranging local and national publicity, and other parts of the company assisted with loans of equipment (including a crane for a sponsored "jailbreak").

The net result of all this organisation was that the employees raised nearly four times the expected maximum.

A second campaign during 1988 in support of 20 children's hospitals was even more successful with the employees raising £625,000.

Checklist

1. Do you allow staff time off each year to help their charity?
2. Have you got a "Give as You Earn" scheme?
3. Do you consult your staff about what charities you donate to?
4. Do you hold sponsorship events to raise funds for charity?
5. Did your company have a collecting box for any of the major recent national appeals? Was somebody nominated to take it around for a week?
6. Does your company match employee giving?

7.1.4 Employee volunteering

Every year millions of people give up some of their free time to improve the quality of the communities in which they live and work. The majority of these people are also working full time for companies and other organisations but get little or no recognition for their voluntary work.

However, a growing number of enlightened companies are now starting to recognise formally the valuable contribution their employees make to local communities. These companies realise that they have an important responsibility to create a climate which actively encourages employee volunteering.

To foster understanding, Whitbread and Company plc commissioned a best practice brochure called "A Guide to Employee Volunteering" and a MORI survey. Conducted in 1990, the survey showed that:

- three in four employees have taken part in some form of volunteer activity
- only 20% considered they had the support of their place of work
- one in four people who had never volunteered would be more inclined to become involved if they had the support of their company
- a similar proportion of active volunteers replied that their level of involvement would increase if they had the support of their place of work.

In the United States there are estimated to be around 800 formal company-based volunteering schemes. Many of these include mechanisms to recognise employee volunteer effort through awards and certificates. Yet in the UK such programmes have been much slower to get off the ground. One explanation could be that, in general, British companies have traditionally tended to pay less attention to what their employees do outside of work hours. In so doing they have often missed out on valuable information about employees' talents.

These days, employee volunteering schemes are to be found in a wide cross-section of companies in the UK. By supporting their employees in their commitment to helping local communities, these companies not only help good causes, but also benefit from the knock-on effects.

For example, studies of volunteer motivation and recruitment clearly show that people are driven to volunteer by more complex forces than the simple altruistic urge to help people. Frequently, there is a range of personal reasons which include the desire to increase personal esteem, raise confidence and face new challenges. Sometimes the motivation is more specific such as wanting to work with a particular group of people or to obtain general managerial experience. Creating a climate which encourages employee volunteering increases the stature of the company in employees' eyes. In many cases it also leads to those participating developing new skills which are directly or indirectly useful to their jobs.

The employee volunteer programmes already underway in the UK differ greatly in scope and nature. All, however, are managed according to the business principles which are standard practice for the organisations operating them. From these it is possible to extract the essential elements required to make an employee volunteering scheme work. Typically they have:

- clear policy guidelines with objectives expressed as goals that are attainable, relevant to the organisation and its employees, and integrated with the needs of the community
- targeted programmes with a defined format and shape, giving a clear policy focus, guidelines on staff eligibility (if not open to all employees) and the specific area or areas to be tackled
- a broad platform of internal support, including senior management, middle management, staff groups and representatives and employees
- administration that ensures the programme runs smoothly, pools information in an accurate database, is capable of providing information requested quickly, keeps accurate financial records and is able to handle feedback from all sources
- a communication strategy which brings the existence and details of the programme to the notice of key audiences inside and outside the organisation, and is targeted, frequent and purposeful
- mechanisms to recognise employee contributions such as direct incentives, status rewards, awards and organised events attended by senior managers
- regular monitoring procedures to evaluate the success of the programme in meeting objectives, and to ensure it remains relevant, cost effective and enjoyable for those participating.

Case study: Lawyers in the Community

Lawyers in the Community is run by the national charity Action Resource Centre. The scheme matches volunteers from London law firms with voluntary organisations in inner city boroughs.

The project aims to recruit practising solicitors in City and West End law firms, and place them with voluntary organisations requiring an injection of management skills in the inner London boroughs of Hackney, Southwark and Tower Hamlets.

As management committee members, volunteers may give general advice but are not permitted to represent the group or act purely as a fund-raiser.

Ten firms are currently members of the project and 55 volunteers are working with local organisations on a regular basis. Each member firm contributes £2000 per annum to establish a working budget on top of a £15,000 grant earmarked by the London Docklands Development Corporation in 1989 to be provided over three years.

The project's stated objective is "to place volunteers from member firms onto the management committees of inner city community organisations, thereby enhancing their effectiveness and widening their skill base".

Case study: Honeywell

Honeywell's Community Service Award is a company-wide volunteering recognition scheme run annually and open to all 2600 UK employees. Introduced in Scotland in 1982 and extended to England two years later, the awards are presented to employees who have made a substantial voluntary contribution to an organisation that helps people or enriches the community.

The work in question will normally be undertaken on a regular basis, and must be performed in the employees' free time. Employees can nominate themselves or a colleague, although previous winners cannot be renominated for three years and then only for a different activity.

An additional award for consistent voluntary service in the community introduced in 1989 is also open to all UK employees and is not subject to any nomination restrictions.

The stated objectives of the award scheme are to recognise the voluntary efforts of Honeywell employees and demonstrate support for them in accordance with the Honeywell principle of good citizenship. Award costs are met from within the overall human resources department budget and administration is handled by human resources staff.

Information and nomination forms are circulated to all employees in June, to be returned by the end of August. Candidates are then judged in September or October by a panel which includes the managing director. The staff magazine gives details of the scheme and the results, with a feature article on the winners. In addition, individual managers publicise the scheme to their staff by memo.

The award is presented in October at a designated ceremony by a senior manager, usually the director of human resources and community relations, and the winner's divisional director. Each winner receives a specially made pin, a certificate of merit and a cheque for £200 made out to their chosen charity.

Allen Sparks won a Honeywell community award in 1991 for his voluntary work over the last 11 years organising and orchestrating a Christmas food parcel programme in conjunction with Age Concern. Sparks was responsible for persuading individuals and local companies to subscribe to the scheme, which in 1991 delivered over 1000 parcels, and arranging for food to go inside them to be purchased at preferential prices. He also arranged for Honeywell warehousing people to pack the parcels and for Honeywell car owners to deliver them.

Says Richard Potter, assistant human resources officer at Honeywell: ''The Community Service Award helps illustrate the importance the company places on encouraging members of staff who are giving their time and talent to the benefit of the local community. It also helps build a good community image of the company with the outside world.''

7.1.5 Managing community investment

''A corporate community affairs programme is not a distraction from the serious business of running a commercial enterprise. It is actually part of the enterprise and is as important as other ancillary service areas, such as public relations departments. If it is well managed, it will not only make a real contribution to the community but will in the process enhance the reputation of the enterprise.'' Joel Joffe, former deputy chairman of Allied Dunbar, told *Business in the Community Magazine* in Spring 1989.

But to have a successful community involvement policy, a company must:

- decide primary aims of policy
- select areas it is going to support and formulate a written policy
- decide on criteria for beneficiary organisations
- state clearly what it will *not* support
- allocate a person/set up a department responsible for giving
- ensure the community involvement department reports regularly to the board.

In addition as Joffe points out, a company should be:

- defining objectives – clear objectives must be agreed reflecting exactly what the company hopes to achieve from the programme
- fixing budgets – a decision on the amount of the budget, preferably for an ongoing amount determined without

annual reference to the board. A measure satisfactory to many companies is a fixed percentage of the profits
- delegating – delegate responsibility and accountability away from the board. The board should be informed periodically of progress, as in other areas of the company.

Joffe also suggests that grants to voluntary organisations are formalised into negotiated agreements so that reasons for support are clear and the objectives and targets of the organisation are also stated.

Identifying and categorising potential recipients of donations can be a time-consuming task, fraught with value judgements. Although value judgements will always be present, it is possible to reduce their impact by imposing formal methods of analysis. One proposed some years ago by one of the authors is the Giving Matrix, see below.

The axes of the matrix are:
- value/benefit to the company
- value/benefit to the community.

Using Delphi techniques, simple questionnaires, or preset criteria developed from the overall giving objectives, the company can fairly rapidly identify those opportunities which will be of significant mutual benefit.

A low score for the company, but high for the community will trigger the question "Is this something we should support just because no one else will?"

A high score for the company but not for the community indicates that this is something for a different budget – probably marketing.

A low score on both axes automatically rules a project out.

The Giving Matrix: 1

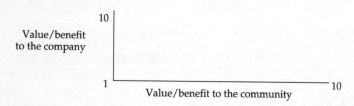

A high score on both counts means that the project should move to the next stage. Here the two axes of the matrix become overall benefit and cost.

The Giving Matrix: 2

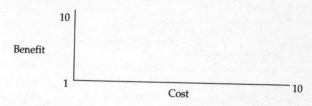

Clearly, the lower the cost and the higher the benefit, the more attractive the project will be.

Additional questions you might ask in evaluating a proposal to donate to a charity, would be:

1. Does the proposal fit within our guidelines?
2. Is it original, or does it duplicate existing activities?
3. Will it have a significant impact on the recipient charity?
   - will it enable the charity to carry out an activity that would otherwise not be possible?
   - will it have a one-off or a lasting impact?
4. Will there be a significant benefit for the company?
5. Will the money be used efficiently?
   - how much will be used for administration?
   - can the recipient realistically resource its part of the deal?
6. Would all or part of our help be better given as goods or time?
7. Would our employees/shareholders/other stakeholders feel this was a good use of our resources?
8. Are we the right donor or would this be better supported by someone else (e.g. should this really be a government responsibility)?
9. Can we publicise this effectively?
10. Are there any hidden costs for the company? For the charity?

Key steps

1. Select areas in which to solicit proposals
2. Evaluate proposals against preset criteria
   - relevance
   - clarity
   - originality
   - etc
3. Check the charity for:
   - quality of previous projects (ask previous sponsors if possible)
   - financial accounts
   - background and qualifications of the project team
4. Agree responsibilities, budgets, project milestones (review dates) reporting format, what control the company will exercise and how the project will be evaluated
5. Agree communications plan
6. Pilot, where possible
7. Monitor and review.

Monitoring and reviewing a community initiative

1. What objectives/measurements did we set?

   For the company   For the charity
   - ●   - ●
   - ●   - ●
   - ●   - ●
   - ●   - ●

2. To what extent has each been achieved?

   For the company   For the charity
   - ●   - ●
   - ●   - ●
   - ●   - ●
   - ●   - ●

   How do we know?
   - ●   - ●
   - ●   - ●
   - ●   - ●
   - ●   - ●

3. What lessons can we extract from our successes and failures?

For the company
-
-
-
-

For the charity
-
-
-
-

Of course, these broad-brush evaluation techniques cannot give the whole picture and the organisation will normally wish to take into account other factors, such as implementability, whether the project is local or not, and timing. Nonetheless, the disciplined approach is a useful means of filtering out the mass of requests in a fair and logical manner.

Case study: Marks and Spencer

The company commits over £4 million every year to its community involvement programme. This includes cash contributions and over 20 members of staff who are seconded to a wide range of charitable organisations, job creation and youth training schemes.

The community affairs department has ten employees who handle over 8000 requests a year. The team also assists many organisations by giving them guidance on fund-raising and management techniques.

Stores are encouraged to help decide which local charities to give money to. Each store manager has funds to available to support local appeals. In addition, staff often raise considerable sums for their favourite charities. Marks and Spencer supports those charities which do not usually generate major public support but which reflect the needs of the communities where it has stores. Often it hands over seed-corn money to help a deserving project get started.

Job creation, youth training, education, health and projects for the disabled and elderly are included in the brief. The company also sponsors the arts and local events.

It does not support overseas projects, political organisations, animal welfare charities, individuals, sports (except for the disabled), capital and endowment funding, third party funding or major national charities except in special circumstances.

Case study: Barclays Bank

Barclays receives over 40,000 requests for money a year. From a position of reacting to requests from charities, Barclays is increasingly moving towards approaching target charities and requesting them to come up with suitable projects. Brian Carr, head of Barclays Community Enterprise, and his 12-

strong team shortlist charities that fall within their brief. The department has built up a large database on charities within its target area and monitors them continuously. One beneficiary of this approach has been Riding for the Disabled, which Barclays asked to nominate one or more projects in 1990. One of the two selected was to build a complete new equestrian centre at Guildford.

They research the charity's effectiveness by looking at the administration and balance sheets over a period of years as well as statistical analysis of how many people the charity has actually helped. If the charity passes the test, Carr approaches it and asks if there are any projects that the bank can sponsor.

In 1991 Barclays ranked fourth in the league table for overall community support given by the top 400 corporate donors. Carr says: "These days it is not enough just to do good, you have to be seen to be doing good in the community and that is what we try to achieve."

Among Barclays' policy decisions are to give where the benefits can be clearly seen and to avoid political issues. Carr explains: "We would rather give money to people to make things happen than to campaigning-type organisations. For instance, we would not give to a local action group campaigning against putting effluent in a river because they could be protesting against the activities of one of our customers."

Neither will Barclays fund individuals or certain charities which already have strong support. Carr says "We focus our support on those charities meeting the needs of young people and those who are elderly, disabled or disadvantaged. Other specific areas supported are the environment, education and medical research. We try to stick closely within those categories.

"Detailed guidelines go out to the regional offices for them to adapt to local conditions. Under the heading of young people, for example, we refine the guidelines to focus on organisations that help young people to learn self-reliance, leadership and so on. So we wouldn't normally support a sports charity, unless it had a strong emphasis on leadership development, or was aimed at, say, the disabled.

"National charities we support from group headquarters; regional and local initiatives from the regions. This means that we have to redirect a lot of requests that come here to the centre.

"As members of the Per Cent Club, we aim to spend 1% of our UK pre-tax profits on the community. We adopt a flexible approach, however, especially in times of low profitability, so as not to cut back our level of support too drastically.

"We have a series of budgets, approved by the board, under a number of specific headings:

- charitable donations
- sponsorships – where the primary beneficiary is the community rather than the company (where there is significant promotional payback for the bank, sponsorship must come from the marketing budget)
- UK-based overseas charities (i.e. for Third World projects)

- the environment
- the arts
- employment initiatives
- secondments of bank staff.

"Branches occasionally make small donations from their own budgets. Anything bigger they have to request from the regional office. Regional offices operate within guidelines from Barclays Community Enterprise. They also have their own small budgets for community sponsorships, such as a centenary match for the local cricket club.

"At all levels, the decisions on which requests to respond to positively are made on the basis of an analysis along the following lines:

- Does it fit in with the guidelines?
- Does it overlap with any existing project we are supporting?
- Have we supported it in the past and what was our experience then?
- How effective are they? (Typically, an efficient charity might spend 10% of income on administration.)"

7.2 Secondment

Seconding employees is an accepted way for companies to loan charities their most valuable resources – people, and their management skills. As the concept grew in the early 1970s, a number of businesses came together to form the Action Resource Centre (ARC) to help and advise companies in making secondment work. ARC is now the main clearing house for secondment, although many companies organise their own schemes. More recently companies have recognised the value of secondment as a means of developing management trainees.

Secondment has a number of advantages. The secondee gains an opportunity to:

1. Develop previously unused skills
2. Cultivate an interest in social issues
3. Come into contact with a different way of life, organisation structure, values and ideals and learn to get the best out of it
4. Use their initiative.

The charity gains:

1. A professional it could not otherwise afford
2. The chance to learn new business techniques
3. A contact that may be useful later
4. Extra manpower.

The company gets:

1. Fast and challenging development of management or the opportunity to ease valued employees into retirement
2. General approval from employees and the broader community
3. An opportunity to influence community planning
4. Understanding of the community through direct contact of secondees.

The amount of time spent on secondment varies. Some secondees have acted as advisors to charities on an ad hoc basis, some have spent a two-year stint working with a voluntary organisation before retiring; some have worked with a charity on long-term secondment in mid-career; and some companies, such as major accountancy firms, use secondment as a means of broadening the knowledge and scope of trainees.

ARC also encourages companies to allow voluntary staff from charities on internal training courses. Community organisations are often so desperately short of professional and management skills that ARC advocates that firms second people with training skills, who can pass on their knowledge and have a lasting effect on their placement organisation.

The secondee's return to the company must be handled with care. Early experience with secondment found that instead of increasing employee motivation as the companies had expected, in many cases it increased the secondees' dissatisfaction with their jobs and their employers. After working in a broader environment, where they can make decisions on their own initiative, and from having a project of their own, they found it hard to readjust to an organised, disciplined and bureaucratic atmosphere. Other secondees have come back to find there was no longer a meaningful job waiting for them. They had little choice but to look for alternative employment.

Still others have enjoyed their secondment so much that they decided not to return. Marks and Spencer lost a personnel officer a few years ago after she did a stint for Oxfam, and IBM in the UK had to relinquish a senior manager who was so taken with a secondment project that he stayed on as director at one-third of his previous pay.

These companies learnt that the secondee needed to be kept in touch with his or her former department throughout their absence and that secondment should be viewed on all sides as a significant opportunity to gain subsequent promotion.

Case study: IBM

IBM UK has run a secondment programme since 1970. To date nearly 200 employees have been loaned out for periods ranging from one month to three years. The objective of the programme is to make a contribution to the community through the transfer of skills, while at the same time contributing to the career development of IBM employees.

The programme is open to employees from all levels of the company who have three years' service. Although the majority of secondments have been to traditional charities, a growing number have been to enterprise agencies, which help establish small businesses. Attachments have also been arranged to universities and government departments. More recently, some 50 civil servants and academics have joined IBM on inward secondments, bringing different skills, expertise and perspective.

Among typical secondments, an IBM technical support manager joined the Coventry Enterprise Agency as its director for two years, helping the growth of self-employment and small businesses in the city. After doubling the clientele and income of the agency, he returned to IBM as an agent manager drawing directly on his newly acquired experience of small firms.

IBM's director of personnel, Len Peach, joined the Health Service, initially as its director of personnel. Within a year he was promoted to chief executive. During his three-year secondment, he helped improve the management systems and practices within the service. He has now returned to his former position with IBM.

A junior IBM personnel officer spent six months handling recruitment for Save the Children. The experience she gained meant she could return to a more responsible post at IBM.

A chief inspector from Chiswick police station undertook a three-month study on workload for an IBM regional group. He returned to a post in Scotland Yard, where he is now concerned with the career development of police officers.

Case Study: Boots plc

During 1991 Boots Community Relations Department (with the help of the Nottinghamshire branch of the Action Resource Centre) managed a pilot scheme involving short-term project-linked assignments within the voluntary sector. Known as Development Assignments, these short periods of secondment – lasting not more than 100 hours – were offered as part of the year's graduate development programme.

Six trainees were nominated. Their specific training requirements were identified and each individual was carefully matched with a project to meet his or her development needs and to provide a challenging and demanding new experience. The following are just two examples of assignments successfully completed:

- Peter Exley, Operation Improvements, undertook a recycling research project for Broxtowe Borough Council, which culminated in a formal presentation to a full meeting of the Council. It was agreed that recommendations in Peter's report will form the basis of the Borough's environmental policy.

Peter is currently involved in package recycling for Boots and apart from successfully meeting his personal skills training and development needs, this assignment substantially contributed to his knowledge of recycling practices and current legislation on the subject.

- Jane Murray, BTC Finance, produced a business plan for the Indian Community Centre at Basford, to be used as a strategy for development of the Centre. Jane also established effective accounting and budgeting systems, and recruited and trained an accounting clerk under the Employment Training Scheme.

  The Manager of the Centre said that Jane's assignment "significantly enhanced Boots' image amongst the local Indian community, and is a substantial step forward in race relations".

All six trainees maintained that the experience had shaped them into more confident, adaptable and competent people and felt that their experience would benefit them in their work for the company.

Following the success of the pilot scheme, all graduates who have completed the company's graduate development programmes will in future be offered an opportunity to undertake an assignment.

These short-term secondments are an exciting and significant development in the community support programme, but have also been promoted as important and innovative training opportunities. Consequently, the trainees have taken their projects very seriously, working conscientiously to complete their assignments to the best of their ability, and contributing a significant amount of personal time. Their diligence and commitment have gained the respect of their voluntary sector hosts and resulted in significant benefit to the wider community.

Case study: Marks and Spencer

Janet Walton and Gill Henderson from Marks and Spencer in Leicester took on an assignment through ARC's Compass scheme, a pilot project that ran for a year using assignments for development of management staff. They spent 50 hours each on a part-time basis at Sofa, a community project recycling second-hand furniture to people on low incomes. After a period of research they were able to recommend ways of increasing donations and putting together mailing lists to target publicity. They also ran training sessions in customer care for staff and volunteers.

The results – increased income and greater awareness of Sofa in the surrounding area.

As for the two secondees, they were able to test new skills such as team working, planning, information analysis and general communication and negotiation skills. The assignment also gave them a broader social awareness and extended their outlook as well as their skills.

Case study: Nationwide

Nationwide was one of the first to pilot short-term secondments to develop and challenge management trainees. The building society wanted to practise secondment but did not want to lose staff for long periods of time. ARC and Nationwide developed 100-hour secondments with a specific project. Secondees are usually released for one day a week for a couple of months.

The scheme was feasible because it released staff for one or two days at a time. It helped a number of voluntary organisations and lifted the society's profile in the community while it widened the horizons of some of the employees.

ARC identified six projects in the London area and worked out with the organisations what skills were needed by the secondees who were to complete the projects. ARC matched seven management trainees with the projects on an induction day. The company also set up pilot projects that weren't restricted to management trainees, in Northamptonshire, where the society has a large administrative base.

Two trainees did a survey on the effectiveness of Hampden Community Centre, London. The trainee managers drew up a questionnaire which they sent to over 2500 homes. The response was so low that they spent much of their secondment going to interview local residents on foot. During the survey they spoke to over 2200 people including a high proportion of Bengali speakers and residents of a large council estate. Both felt the project had been very successful. They identified over 40 new facilities that people wanted and managed to find over 25 people who said they were willing to help out at the Centre. The project increased the trainees' self-confidence because they felt they had managed it from beginning to end. One of the trainees also stated that the data-handling techniques he had learned could be used to fine-tune marketing for individual branches and increase sales turnover.

Sam Walker was seconded to Choice, an advisory centre for disabled people. The two research workers from Choice needed guidance on recruitment of extra employees and some general advice. Walker provided them with a checklist to use while they were interviewing and left them with their own tailor-made personnel manual. Walker used his personnel department and ACAS to help. He also says that this practical experience of background personnel work will stand him in good stead when managing staff.

The scheme was referred to in *Personnel Management*, in January 1990: "These projects called for a different approach to working within the secure confines of the Nationwide Building Society. Trainees have to demonstrate initiative, creativity and a fair amount of planning, and they have to go out and execute their plan."

Secondment by smaller companies tends to be concentrated among agencies and consultancies. London-based management and training consultancy, Linley-Norman, for example, seconds director Harry Bunkell to the Multiple Sclerosis Society. Bunkell spends one and a half days a week as Appeals Co-ordinator for The Horley Project, raising funds to build a rest-care hotel for MS sufferers in his home town. Other examples of small company secondments from the files of Action Resource Centre include:

- Profile Corporate Communications, a London-based PR company, which contributed five executive days per month over three months to NCVO's Charities for Change campaign. Seconded employees handled media counselling, contact-building and copy-writing for the charity.
- Five Lamps Group donated £1500 worth of assistance in kind to ARC Derby for a promotional event, producing slides, rehearsing speakers and providing an audio-visual technician on the day.
- Thomas-Zedora Associates, a Derby management consultancy, loaned staff to Derby People's Housing Association over six months to help draw up a business plan.

Many small companies can't spare the manpower for community work, but they can make employees aware of the possibilities available. Some companies list appeals for volunteers in their employee newsletter or magazine, others pin them to the company noticeboard.

Companies can also make their employees aware that almost everybody has something to offer in the way of ability that a charity can make use of. It is helpful to appoint someone in the company, who is responsible for finding out what skills community groups require and for ensuring that employees hear about the openings. The appointee can arrange for charities to send representatives to talk to the employees about their work.

Lending people is clearly a lot more trouble than giving money, but the pay-offs are potentially much higher.

7.3 Partnerships in education

One of the most rapidly evolving areas of community involvement is the relationship between businesses and the world of education. From an arm's-length relationship, where businesses felt they had a duty to do something for local schools, or saw the production of education packs as either a form of marketing or a philanthropic gesture, there has developed in the 1990s a strong sense of mutually beneficial partnership.

This flavour of shared concerns permeates the revised policy statements of many companies and industry bodies. For example, the Education Liaison Group of the British Retail Consortium aims:

- to assist the education system in preparing young people to contribute to the economy and to the life of their communities
- to encourage lifelong learning and the updating of skills.

The rationale for this investment by companies which make up the consortium has several levels. At the broadest, the companies depend for their prosperity on the performance of the economy as a whole. A well-educated workforce, constantly improving its skills – and hence its earning power – is an essential element in achieving prosperity, especially when the UK's major international competitors are investing so heavily in education.

By making education more enjoyable, more accessible and more relevant to the world of work, companies also stand to reap the benefit of new recruits who are already motivated towards continued learning. By contrast, many major UK companies are presently having to invest considerable sums in reintroducing employees (some as young as 21) to the idea of learning as a useful activity.

Michael Heron, a director of Unilever, expresses the point forcefully in an article in *The Evening Standard*:

"This is not just an option for companies committed to education for corporate reputation reasons; it is a must for every company recruiting and training staff for the new technologies.

"It should also be a must for every company concerned with the stability and integration of society when the chances of being employed depend on education and training... The current skills shortage and the need for broadly based, high education standards show that the UK can no longer rely on educating the able few but must maximise the contribution of all."

A useful summary of the benefits on each side comes from Business in the Community. It states in a booklet on education/business partnerships that a schools involvement policy will benefit:

Young people
- through better motivation, attainment and qualifications
- through greater self-confidence and having more to offer to society
- through a greater understanding of what business, work and enterprise are all about

- through vocational training that is more closely linked to education in school and is relevant to available jobs
- through better chances of a worthwhile job, combined with training.

Schools and colleges will benefit from:
- a richer curriculum and greater capacity for developing it through wider contacts with industry
- improved management skills at a time when head teachers and principals are being given financial control of schools and colleges
- new resources for learning including local employers, workplace environments and materials
- access to equipment and other material resources.

Employers will gain from:
- a potentially better qualified and well-motivated workforce
- an opportunity to influence the curriculum of schools and colleges
- development of staff through contact with education and the community
- a range of services which schools and colleges can offer to improve the effectiveness of local employers
- a more stable and prosperous local environment in which to trade
- an opportunity to enhance their reputation in the local community.

The range of activities a company can involve itself in to develop partnerships with education is wide and growing. BP categorises them as follows:

Work related: work experience, business simulations and vocational training.

Work experience is an obvious means of shaping young people's perceptions about career opportunities. It can begin at a very early age – one region of the Co-op created a store management team of five-year-olds. The youngsters not only learnt about trade, through projects such as tracing food products back to their source, but gained some understanding of complex issues such as economics and teamwork.

Work experience might also involve a 16- or 17-year old shadowing a manager for a period; or simply providing holiday working opportunities.

Business simulations come in a variety of forms, with Young Enterprise being among the longest established. Another, supported by BP, is a business game competition between schools from different countries which simulates problem-solving associated with international trade.

Vocational training covers areas such as careers information, helping with the transition from school to work.

Learning enrichment: curriculum development, developing teaching resource materials, opening up company resources.

The opportunity to influence curriculum content has not been taken away by the National Curriculum. If anything, it has been enhanced.

The Curriculum has three levels of subjects – core and foundation subjects, cross-curricular skills and dimensions (e.g. numeracy or problem-solving) and cross-curricular themes (broad topics that should be reflected in the other levels, but will not necessarily be taught as subjects in their own right). Among the skills and dimensions are many themes which form the focus of management training and could readily be adapted for use by a younger audience. Among the cross-curricular themes are five particular areas, where companies can also draw on their own expertise, or where there are strong business reasons to promote knowledge within children. These areas are:

- economic and industrial understanding
- health education
- careers education and guidance
- environmental education
- citizenship.

BP has found opportunities to fund a teacher training programme to promote economic awareness in schools and for its engineers to work with teachers to develop technology projects.

Learning materials can be closely business related (for example, B&Q has helped develop a maths project based on bar codes) or associated with one of a company's core community themes (for example, British Gas was able to adapt an environmental video originally aimed at staff, and make it suitable for use in schools).

The Past Speaks Out was a national competition organised by the Worldwide Fund for Nature and BBC Regional Broadcasting which encouraged schoolchildren to identify a current environmental problem and then try to discover its historical roots. Entries were presented in the unusual form of a ten-minute audio programme. The best entries were also published as part of a teachers' resource pack aimed at developing a cross-curricular approach to the study of history incorporating the environmental, social and economic aspects that have influenced decision-makers.

An important resource within a company is management expertise. The general shortage of school governors led to a government campaign in mid-1992, aimed at stimulating businesses to encourage managers to join governing bodies. The benefit is far from one-way; while the school gains the benefit of business expertise in financial management, recruitment processes and so on, the managers have an opportunity to practise at what is, in effect, a board-level position (rather like being a non-executive director of a small company). Indeed, there is considerable scope for companies to include school governor positions in their management development programmes.

Companies can also make resources available simply by opening their doors to school visits, or by providing real life examples to illustrate projects or theory. For example, BP makes staff and documents available to students carrying out business studies projects and encourages 17- and 18-year olds to visit BP sites as part of their field study work in another country. The company also organised a study tour for a group of teachers to examine BP sites as a potential learning resource for physics teaching.

Attachments: either from the company into education, or vice versa.

Teachers from local schools have been invited to participate in company management training programmes or been seconded to a department to carry out a project for several months. On the other side of the coin, a senior BP manager has work-shadowed a head teacher.

Carol Kay, a head teacher, spent a year at Kingfisher as part of the University of Warwick's Head Teachers into Industry programme. During her time at the company she conducted a review of the retail group's business-education links.

David Hicklenton of the Biology Department at Gosforth High School spent a week's work placement with Northumbrian Water plc. He used his experience there to match sixth form syllabus work on health and disease with practical sessions at the company, and to set up school visits to the company's site at Howden.

Donations: Financial support for institutions and individuals.

There is a variety of ways in which donations can be directed for the mutual benefit of companies and schools. In some US cities, for example, shoppers are encouraged to keep their supermarket checkout tape and hand it in to their local school. At the end of the year the school will redeem its collected checkout tapes with the participating supermarket chain in return for computer hardware and software. In 1990, an average-sized school in Pittsburgh picked up half a dozen AppleMac PC's and 20 software packages. The supermarket chain met the cost out of its profits. The managing director says it's hard to imagine a better $3 million PR campaign. In the UK, Tesco has already given away over £3 million in a similar scheme entitled Computers for Schools.

Services from education: research support, expertise and consultancy, training and gaining access to potential recruits.

A growing number of companies now recognise the direct benefits they can gain through partnerships with education. Schools and colleges offer an excellent source of bright and enthusiastic individuals. As part of the Shell UK sponsored Science and Technology Education Project (STEP) award scheme, final year students are matched with companies to work on specified projects. For example, Mark Howson, a French and Communications Arts student from Huddersfield University, was given a project with Design Fabrique looking at market research and development of fleecy-lined mountain jackets. As well as establishing contact with a number of European specialist magazines, Mark came up with the idea that Design Fabrique should move into the workwear market. He set in train discussions which led to Design Fabrique designing a garment for Norweb.

In another case, a business economics and marketing student from Paisley College in Ayrshire, Rosemary Stewart, carried out a market research study for the double-glazing firm, Prestige Windows. She looked at why approximately 40% of people who contacted the company bought from it, and more importantly, why 60% didn't.

In addition to a whole range of individual partnerships between a school and a local employer, there are some 50 Compacts and 120 Education-Business Partnerships operating across the UK.

Education-Business Partnerships go beyond individual initiatives by companies, bringing together a number of companies in an area, alongside Training and Education Councils, local authorities, schools, colleges and members of the community to develop a much wider programme of activities. One of the advantages of this approach, which is funded initially by the Department of Employment, is that it is a large enough umbrella to draw in small businesses, too.

For companies taking the first step towards developing partnerships with educational bodies, advice and assistance are available from a number of organisations, some of which are given in Appendix 3.

The Gardner Merchant Award for Excellence in Education-Business Partnerships is co-sponsored by the CBI and catering firm Gardner Merchant. It seeks to recognise outstanding examples of business and education working together to prepare young people for a career after school. An important element of the award is to encourage partnerships of all sizes to report their experiences, methods and successes so that others may learn from them.

Winner of the 1991 Gardner Merchant Award was the Clydebank Compact from Scotland whose work brought together a total of 150 firms and schools in the Glasgow area. The Compact enables hundreds of pupils to gain work experience with local employers, while giving company managers a valuable insight into educational methods and needs. Following its success, Clydebank has received requests for advice from all over the country, and Scottish Enterprise now refers enquiries to Clydebank from as far afield as Pakistan, Eastern Europe and the Middle East as an example of good British practice.

Case study: Superdrug

Superdrug's published policy on Educational Partnerships is an explicit statement of their value to the company. Derived from a corporate policy from its parent company, Kingfisher, the policy states:

- education partnerships form a significant part of Superdrug's strong social responsibility and employment policy and is a means by which commitment to the company's values can be demonstrated
- partnerships with education are a crucial aspect of good management and commercial success by which Superdrug can enhance local communities and promote the company
- the company can use its position as a leading retailer as well as its influence with policy-making bodies to enhance the status and quality of education and training

- Superdrug believes in the value of education as a national resource for the successful provision of its future workforce and citizens and actively will seek to participate in the process by means of its education partnership policy
- the potential for the success of its education partnership policy lies in its nationwide network of local stores and the strength this brings to the national education business partnership movement
- Superdrug believes in being a "preferred employer" and recognises the legitimate interest that others have in its performance and will, therefore, communicate openly about education partnership policy and activities
- partnerships with education will provide opportunities for recruitment, staff development and job satisfaction for employees
- Superdrug believes that customers and potential employees will increasingly look to the company's values and philosophy – particularly its record on supporting education – when determining where they wish to shop or work.

Some other examples of policies in this area are reproduced in Appendix 2.

Case study: Pilkington

Pilkington initiated STEP, the Science and Technology Education Project, in November 1990. STEP aims to provide primary schools in St Helens, where the company is based, with teaching equipment, teacher training and school back-up to support the new science and technology curriculum.

The project was initiated in response to Pilkington's desire to help the UK education system. The company's research revealed there was little involvement of industry in primary schools, with lack of equipment to teach the new National Curriculum in science and technology a particular problem.

Says education support consultant, Tony Chaplin: "Pilkington considers that school pupils are potential employees and they need better preparation for the working environment.

"It was discovered that a certain amount of practical help was needed in primary schools to support teachers providing basic science and basic technology. So STEP was born."

A small team of teachers were asked what equipment they wanted to enable them to teach the new curriculum to their pupils. No constraints of cost or scope were placed on the team. The specified equipment was assembled into a prototype teaching pack which included work stations designed and built by Pilkington's own Community Project. The work stations are easily wheeled from classroom to classroom and include useful features such as built-in tool racks and storage bins.

A pilot system was set up in September 1991 at Grange Valley School in Haydock where it was enthusiastically tested. Following the successful trial, phase two of the programme's introduction was completed with the assembly and distribution of the teaching packs to a selection of schools in the area.

"To complement these packs we are working closely with the local authorities, head teachers and a local college to give teachers confidence and skills to make the best use of the equipment supplied," Tony says.

"In addition to providing equipment and training, the project plans to set up and run a resource centre to act like a supermarket for science and technology teaching equipment and materials for primary schools. The centre will be able to provide spare parts for the equipment, with the more expensive items available for hire and consumable items such as cardboard, wool and wire on sale."

The first two phases of the STEP initiative have been funded by Pilkington, St Helens Community Education Authority and Qualitec. However, the plan is to involve the whole St Helens community in the funding of the third phase which includes raising £130,000 to set up the resource centre.

Case study: IBM

IBM UK, the British subsidiary of IBM, the world's largest computer company, gives just over £2 million a year to educational activities, one of its five select priorities. Its overall aim is to build educational partnerships with an emphasis on growing teachers' management skills, encouraging students to continue in higher education and helping them to prepare for working with information technology.

As part of the programme, IBM staff are allowed to spend up to 10% of their working time on approved community activities and they are actively encouraged to take on posts such as school governorships. The company's four main educational priorities are schools, education and training for 16- to 19-year olds, higher education and adult education. These four activities are plotted against five key IBM operational interests:

- development of its market
- influencing the public policy debate
- recruiting and training
- investment in the community
- research.

For example, the company sees a link with a school not as a community investment but as a marketing strategy. The company does not like giving straight donations of computers to schools and educational institutions, although it does offer personal computing equipment plus software and support, often at 60% of retail price. Instead, it uses IBM's expertise to offer free management training to teachers. Two-day teacher management workshops for deputy heads and heads of departments are run at IBM locations around the UK and were attended in 1989 by more than 225 senior teachers representing 187 schools. One reason for the strong interest in these courses is the government thrust for schools to run themselves more as businesses.

IBM's manufacturing and development centres at Havant, Greenock and Hursley ran lectures for the Institute of Mechanical Engineers. Called the Leonardo Da Vinci Lectures, they were aimed at encouraging young people towards careers in information technology. More than 20,000 students attended the roadshow at 52 locations in the UK and Ireland.

In addition, the IBM Institute backs the use of information technology in teaching through projects with schools, polytechnics and colleges. IBM also backs training initiatives through a number of associations including the Foundation for Education–Business Partnerships and Business in the Arts.

IBM desk-top publishing systems have been donated to 19 university subject centres established in 1989 under a joint initiative of the Computer Board for Universities and Research Councils and the University Funding Committee.

The St Paul's Open Learning Technology centre in Bristol opened its doors in November 1989. Its aim is to help the unemployed in inner city areas find jobs by offering them free computer courses. IBM employees are helping out and the company has donated its machines.

7.3.1 What kinds of involvement can companies undertake?

Companies can increase the volume of school leaver applicants they receive by providing more opportunities for the number of local school children to receive short periods of work experience. However, these opportunities need to be planned and managed to give the young people an understanding of how rewarding work can be. All too many employers simply give them a routine, mundane job such as photocopying all day – and are subsequently surprised that the youngsters emerge with a negative view of working for that organisation. Companies can also open their doors for open days, parents' evenings, career talks and pupil visits, and use educational links to sponsor careers fairs, school teams, clubs, trips and award schemes. The community becomes aware of the company's presence in a positive fashion. These regular, co-ordinated links with schools can give a company a distinct competitive edge over rivals in the local employment market.

Companies can also get involved in the local community through government-funded Compacts. There are over 50 of these formal partnerships between inner-city schools and business. The Compacts are designed to meet local educational and recruitment needs and involve pupils, parents and employers. The original aims were to raise standards of performance and attendance at school, to encourage more young people to continue their education after 16; and to influence employers, especially those in the inner-city areas, to change their attitudes towards educational links. The first Compact, which was modelled on an original in Boston, Massachusetts, was run by the Inner London Education Authority and local employers including Whitbread.

Young people work with their school and parents towards a set of measurable personal goals and standards. These include academic progress and personal and social development. Schools and colleges commit themselves to work towards specific targets for their students as they progress through education and training to take their place in the workforce. Finally, the employer's part of the deal is to agree to give jobs with training, or training leading to a job, to the youngsters who manage to achieve their targets. Firms can therefore recruit from well-motivated achievers.

If there are no Compacts in your area, you can always set up an "education/business partnership" promoted by Business in the Community. Trade unions, voluntary groups, small employers, education officials and other interested parties are encouraged to set up a steering group, make a joint statement of policy and outline a programme of action with a time scale and performance review.

Companies can also get involved in Training and Enterprise Councils, which were designed to take over from the Training Agency which ran large national training programmes. The TECs offer a more localised opportunity for education action. Directors of local companies sit on the board alongside academics and advisors. The TECs are financed mainly by government money but, according to James Jolly at Business in the Community, the government hopes that employer participation on TECs will encourage businesses, too, to invest in training youngsters in their communities.

Universities and polytechnics also offer endless possibilities to companies which are willing to exploit them. Larger companies like to sponsor either posts or courses at educational institutions. This is a good way of getting the company's name known in a particular area.

As grants decrease in real terms, more and more employers are realising the advantages of subsidising a student through college or university. With, for example, science and computer graduates in short supply and an expected eventual shortfall of graduates in all disciplines, this is a practical way of laying claim to high-calibre graduate employees.

Another popular and less-expensive method is to open your doors to undergraduates for work experience. The company can spot talent early and make an offer well before the student graduates.

Case study: British Gas

British Gas's educational policy covers almost the whole spectrum of education, from universities to primary schools. At a higher education level it funds academic posts, ranging from a British Gas lecturer in energy and buildings at Oxford Polytechnic through to a fellowship for women returners into science and engineering at the University of Surrey and research study into gerontology at the University of Birmingham.

It also sponsors Sci-Tech, an international scientific film and television festival held every two years in Bristol. Says Tony Wyatt, head of the social policy unity at British Gas, "Bristol stages this festival partly to boost the city for visitors from the rest of Britain and abroad. We sponsor it partly as a demonstration of support for the Bristol community, partly to support this particular art form, partly to increase awareness of the importance of science and technology to all our lives, and partly to allow us the facility to contribute to extra-curricular activities at universities by running a university roadshow of the winning entries."

British Gas higher education sponsorships are limited to its own employees. It funds, among others, an annual MA in Business Information at the University of Edinburgh, two scholarships a year at the Guildhall School of Music and Drama, support for mature female students at graduate and post graduate level at the Lucy Cavendish College, Cambridge, and six scholarships at the University of Strathclyde every year for students from developing countries.

At the other end of the educational spectrum, the company is also backing research into how primary teachers process scientific information and a doctoral thesis on children's understanding of energy-related software at the Institute of Education at London University.

Schools involvement

Wyatt explained at a conference on social responsibility that the company maintains a warehouse in West London where users can obtain free or heavily subsidised educational materials. The catalogue alone runs to 60 pages. Schools and the general public can also use the company's film and video library. All publications are drawn up along guidelines suggested by the National Consumer Council's "Guidelines for business sponsors of educational material". Many of the materials are designed by teachers for teachers and evaluation is invited by those who use them, and by Her Majesty's Inspectors.

Schools and teachers need much more than materials. So British Gas sends out over 200 staff to visit schools regularly and give presentations on a range of energy-related topics. A Science of the Flame lecture is popular with 12- to 14-year olds, for example.

In addition, staff in the regions hire out gas cookers so that pupils can gain practical experience on modern appliances. The company also supports two theatre companies, Molecule and Floating Point, that use drama to show the young how exciting maths and science can be. Other exciting activities have included a Treasure Trail competition for schools to back up the sponsorship of the National Heritage Memorial Fund's exhibition, Treasures for the Nation, at the British Museum.

Recently, British Gas has helped develop the new National Curriculum and supported the design and technology work at the University of Salford and through the National Business and Information Studies Centre. It also funds

Leeds University's Learning in Science Project, which explores how young people can be challenged and motivated to take a greater interest in science and technology, and a bus to tour girls schools for the Women into Science and Engineering campaign (WISE). The vehicle is equipped with work stations with microelectronics, pneumatics, computer-aided design.

None the less, British Gas has taken a cautious attitude towards government initiatives in education and schools liaison. Says Wyatt: "The considerable ramifications of our liaison service and the extensive other linkages that we have developed have tended to make us cautious in recent times in embracing the numerous voluntary and government initiatives with which we have all been faced over the last 10 or 15 years. While we are strong supporters of Business in the Community we have not been in the van of developing education-business partnerships, at least not in the sense of 'local' partnerships. My company is so far only involved in a handful of Compacts and only three TECs and we shall want to see how universally they develop before we adapt our traditional links dramatically.

"In the meantime, our intention is to develop mutual experience. On the one hand, to encourage more of our employees to become more involved with the work of the schools by becoming school governors, for example. And on the other, by encouraging more of the school population, undergraduates and teachers, to come into our company to experience for themselves the world of industry and commerce. In this respect, we are developing arrangements with the organisation Understanding British Industry to give senior teachers the opportunity of benefitting from our Management Development and Training programme."

Other organisations the company has supported include the Association for Science Education, the National Association of Environmental Education, the Centre for the Study of Comprehensive Schools, and Education 2000, a teaching experiment based in Milton Keynes, which investigates modern technology teaching and methods.

7.3.2 How to organise educational activities

Business in the Community, (BiC) in its booklet "Writing a Boardroom Policy" outlines the importance of a written company document for companies that want a co-ordinated, effective educational policy. It emphasises that written guidelines ensure support is concentrated on those educational activities which have been identified as beneficial to the company. They give justification to the expenditure of management time and resources by identifying clear commercial benefits to the company.

The booklet states that in a recent survey involving managers from Marks and Spencer and Royal Mail Parcels the most commonly expressed incentive to take action was the publication of a policy statement endorsed by the board. However, this may still not be enough and BiC suggests other ways to encourage action:

- include educational responsibility in appropriate job descriptions
- set job targets and include in annual appraisals
- give the local manager a small budget to spend on school links activities
- give personal recognition from the chief executive or senior manager
- nominate a person in each location to be expert on the various government initiatives and on what other independent link bodies can contribute and who can co-ordinate the company's local activities.

Checklist

A. Schools liaison
1. Do your local managers have a budget for educational activities? Are they assessed on their achievements in this field?
2. Do you offer access to your company through work experience and/or pupil visits?
3. Do you have a planned strategy for involvement in local educational activities?
4. Have you developed a close partnership with at least one local school?
5. Do you have a system for identifying any surplus material you could give to schools?
6. Could you fund any prizes for achievement on certain parts of the curriculum?
7. Do you encourage employees to become school governors?
8. Could your company provide any of the following to local schools?
   - career talks and counselling
   - explanatory leaflets and videos
   - holiday jobs
   - interview training
   - joint work projects
   - teacher secondment
   - inclusion of teachers on company training courses.

B. University liaison
1. Could you fund a university post?
2. Could you fund any courses ?
3. Could you subsidise a student through a degree course?
4. Could you sponsor a university road show or careers fair?

7.4 Small business development

Businesses cannot live in isolation from the broader community any more than they can live in isolation from their markets. They rely on those communities for staff and customers as well as shareholders and the support of opinion leaders. The belief that a company's community contribution was to run an efficient, profitable company has become increasingly untenable. For many companies, the watershed came in July 1981 with the Toxteth and Brixton riots. Part of the solution, according to Michael Heseltine, then Environment Secretary, was business involvement in the community, through enlightened self-interest.

In response to this, Business in the Community (BiC) was formed as an umbrella organisation to bring the voluntary sector, trade unions and local and central government together. To date it has over 300 members. Enterprise agencies are the building blocks of the organisation. There were only 28 when the organisation was formed in 1982; now there are over 314.

But what are enterprise agencies and what do they do?

These organisations are operated as limited companies. They offer help and advice to people running small businesses as well as those hoping to start one up. Many run for their clients small business clubs, which meet regularly to swap experiences and learn about new management techniques or regulations. The agencies often organise training courses or "meet the buyer" sessions to introduce small businesses to potential big customers.

Money comes from the government, but is dependent on equal or greater sums from the private sector. A host of companies regularly second highly qualified people to help run enterprise agencies across England and Wales.

There were, of course, a number of enterprise agencies, even before the formation of BiC. For example, in 1979, Lenta (the London Enterprise Agency) was created because a group of major companies felt that they should play a significant role in tackling inner-city dereliction in London. According to Lenta's 1989 annual report, they also wished to encourage other companies to follow suit in other cities. This role was later passed onto BiC after it was created in 1981. Since 1979, Lenta has provided business counselling to over 50,000 people and provided entrepreneurial training to over 14,000.

BAT Industries helped launch the Southampton Enterprise Agency in 1981 with a guarantee of full funding for the first two years. This enabled a supporters' club to be developed in parallel, whose members eventually became contributors to expenses. BAT continued its support with secondees from its member companies, while National Westminster and Barclays provided one secondee each on a two-year basis from 1983. In its first five years the agency handled over 5000 inquiries and conducted over 2000 counselling sessions, leading to almost 600 business start-ups or expansions. During this time there were only 24 known failures – a rate of only 4%.

Case study: Royal Dutch/Shell Group of Companies

Shell is one of the leaders in the field, setting up first a small business unit and now operating its community activities through the Shell Enterprise Unit. As a founder member of Lenta, The London Enterprise Agency, Shell has regularly seconded staff to the organisation. Experience taught the company that there were several key areas where it could be most effective. These included running training courses for would-be entrepreneurs, providing counselling and advice and developing small industrial and commercial units for embryo businesses.

In the mid-eighties the company wholly funded several ventures of this kind. Two examples are the Broad Oak Enterprise Village at Sittingbourne, Kent and Carrington Business Park near Manchester. At Sittingbourne, Shell paid for the £400,000 conversion of its laboratories into an enterprise village. It undertook a similar scheme in a redundant cluster of buildings on 17 acres within the 300-acre Shell Chemicals Carrington plant. Over 50 companies established themselves at Carrington in the first phase of the project. As other companies became interested in the area, they brought with them new jobs and prospects for the locals.

BiC draws together a host of other initiatives promoting business involvement in the community. These include Young Enterprise, a national charity that gives young people the chance to run a scaled-down version of a company, through to Project Fullemploy, which brings together public and private bodies dedicated to helping young people of mainly ethnic minority origin fulfil their potential through training. Shell guaranteed funds until 1991 for one of these initiatives, Livewire, an organisation formed to help 18- to 25-year olds create their own work.

Case study: BP Innovation-LINC

As a test of organisational skills, BP's Innovation Link scheme is considerable. Its aim is to provide strong regional and national networks of advice and expertise to inventors, via local enterprise agencies.

The need for specialist advisors to support the Prince of Wales' Award for Innovation and to help enterprise agencies with their daily work stimulated Dr Hilary Trudeau, on secondment from BP, to develop an organisation where inventors could have access to the best advice, wherever in the country they were located. There are currently 22 innovation advisors across the UK, liaising with BP and their own local enterprise agency. Through a directory and other forms of communication, including a newsletter and twice annual conference, each advisor has access to the specialist contacts of his/her colleagues.

In the first development phase, during 1991, BP invested £250,000 to set up the initial network and to promote the concept to inventors. Further stages will enhance the effectiveness of the networks and tap the piloting and testing expertise of other large companies.

BP expects to measure the success of the scheme in three main ways:

- how quickly an inventor gets to the right source of advice. The two-telephone call test is being applied to measure how many people callers have to contact before they reach someone who can really help.
- the amount of additional help given to the scheme by other companies, including lawyers, patent experts and R&D facilities
- the amount of new local investment attracted to innovations in the network.

Case study: Barclays Bank

Barclays has worked hard to help people hit by unemployment. Back in 1989 the government closed the Sunderland shipyard. More than 6000 people were forced onto the dole. Brian Carr, head of Barclays Community Enterprise at Fleetway House, London, acted quickly: "We have always been a strong bank in Sunderland, so after a few phone calls and arm twisting in certain quarters we put together a loan fund with soft capital repayment to help the redundant start up small businesses on their own."

By the end of 1989, 12 small businesses had taken advantage of the scheme. Brian said: "People set up businesses in design and manufacture of furnishings and desk-top publishing. When you are loaning to small operations you have to make sure that you are giving to organisations that can operate successfully without buying expensive equipment."

Over the last two years Barclays has given over £400,000 to establish loan funds to help set up small companies in areas such as Cleveland, Newcastle, Manchester, Greater London and Devon and Cornwall.

Carr also seized the chance to use some of the experience he gained as deputy of the bank's agricultural team for ten years.

"Northumberland was suffering a serious decline in the agricultural and mining industries. I realised that tourism could take up some of the slack. So I set up a Tourism Development Project to encourage people to take holidays in the area, which has a rich Roman and Christian heritage. We aimed to educate the farmers and small shopkeepers to provide a better service, so we set up an award scheme, which has successfully made these small concerns aware of tourists' needs."

Companies can also make a significant contribution to the establishment and growth of small businesses by making specialist expertise available, either through development/enterprise agencies or schemes set up by professional bodies. For example, the Teesside branch of the Chartered Institute of Marketing set up a Marketing Advice Centre, aimed at helping small businesses apply effective marketing to their activities.

Checklist

1. Is your company actively involved in local enterprise agencies?
2. Do you create opportunities to get to know local small businesses and their problems?
3. Do you have unused premises that could make useful starter units for small companies?
4. Do you have an active policy to reduce the impact of downsizing in your organisation, by helping people start new businesses?

Social responsibility issues

In the wider sphere of social responsibility, there are a number of emerging issues – including crime prevention, road safety, and public health – that contribute to the general well-being of our society. These issues are likely to become increasingly important in the future, with a range of activities seen as the legitimate domain of companies acting in the best interests of their stakeholders.

In the area of crime prevention, for example, public concern over figures showing an increase in criminal activities – from burglary to joy-riding – makes this an area of growing interest for corporate involvement. Companies can approach crime prevention from a number of directions. For instance:

- sponsoring youth initiatives in high crime areas to prevent teenagers drifting into trouble
- supporting safety training schemes to help young children avoid becoming victims of bullying or harassment
- replicating the Co-op scheme which helps parents respond to the early symptoms of drug abuse
- working with the police and local authorities to improve city centre environments to reduce fear of crime.

One of the reasons for Kingfisher's interest is that the company feels it has a duty to protect its 61,000 staff, who are often the victims of crime. In 1988, over 75 people working for Kingfisher companies were assaulted and needed hospital treatment. Many others suffered minor attacks, which still caused distress and shock. One manager at B&Q was stabbed in the neck as he chased a thief out of a store.

The financial costs of crime to business are easy to quantify. The retail industry loses over £2 billion a year through crime, a high proportion of this due to shoplifting and other forms of theft. Security costs are inevitably reflected in prices.

Among the most active of umbrella organisations in this area is Crime Concern. Says Nigel Whiskin, chief executive of the Swindon based charity:

"A safe community is good for business and companies can play an important part in tackling the crimes which affect their customers, staff and premises. We have been very impressed by the willingness of some 2000 major companies to support practical action at national and local levels in partnership with the police and the official agencies. Business sponsorship can help us to develop innovative approaches . Experienced executives can contribute management skills to help projects take shape. Support for this work gives a good public profile for the sponsor."

Case study: Legal & General's Kickstart Clubs

Legal & General introduced its Kickstart programme as a response to the high crime rates among 7- to 15-year olds in inner-city areas. Much of the crime by youngsters is the result of boredom, so L&G piloted four schemes in different regions to establish local clubs, which will offer youngsters a range of challenging and exciting activities for 10 to 20 hours a week outside school hours.

The programme organisers have the task of liaising with the local community and other agencies to identify what kind of activities would be worthwhile, and to attract volunteer leaders. Where appropriate, they also arrange activity leadership training.

Case study: Kingfisher and Crucial Crew

Children often become victims of crime out of ignorance. To help educate them in how to deal with dangerous situations – both crime and other forms of crisis, such as a fire in the home – Kingfisher helped Crime Concern launch Crucial Crew.

The concept behind Crucial Crew is quite simple: children set out in pairs on a pre-arranged course around their home town, where they meet a variety of perils, organised by their teachers, local crime prevention officers and the emergency services. These simulated dangers are then used as the basis for discussing what they should do. The scheme not only helps them deal with dangers such as strangers who want to entice them away by offering "sweets", but develops good citizenship and understanding of the role of the police and emergency services.

The initial costs to Kingfisher included the national launch and contributing to the funding of some ten pilot programmes. The company has now published a full do-it-yourself guide and a growing number of locally funded schemes are taking place.

At a national level, the scheme has contributed to Kingfisher's general reputation for community concern. At a local level, B&Q, Superdrug and Woolworths stores provide prizes and help cement their overall community relationships.

Case study: Crime Concern and the Daily Express

Crime Concern and the *Daily Express* have joined forces to produce an entertaining newspaper each school term in which young people write about their successes in tackling crime. Personal safety is a major consideration for them and practical action is being taken up by an increasing number of Crime Prevention panels in schools. *Youth Express* – the voice of young Britain – encourages these initiatives and also contains upbeat articles on fashion and entertainment. The print run for each edition is 800,000 copies.

8. Creating partnerships through sponsorship

The argument about when community investment should come out of a company's marketing budget or from a social budget inevitably has its grey areas. It is not uncommon, for example, for a company to have a straight commercial, public relations deal with a charity under its sponsorship programme and to have a number of other relationships, such as secondment or fund-raising by employees, for the same cause.

In a sense, sponsorship is the purest form of enlightened self-interest. There is (usually) little or no confusion about the motives and intentions of either party and the mutuality of benefit is usually high. Like most other aspects of social responsibility, however, the bottom line benefits of sponsorship are not always easy to measure (the exceptions being campaigns tied directly to product purchases).

However, the increasing volume of sponsorship activity in the UK and Europe is a testament to the growing conviction that real returns do accrue to the sponsoring company.

One of the core benefits appears to lie in the maintenance or building of the corporate reputation. To be perceived as a caring, responsible organisation has commercial value (as we discussed in Chapter 1). According to its proponents, sponsorship is significantly more cost-effective than advertising in building empathy, confidence and brand recognition – particularly in market sectors where there are numerous players with relatively undifferentiated products.

Case study: British Telecom

British Telecom, struggling to break free from years as a monopoly, has a clear business objective: to improve its overall public image. It is doing so in part through PR, partly through radical programmes to improve service quality and through rapidly rising expenditure on sponsorship.

A senior executive at BT explained: "We're in danger of being seen as bureaucratic, faceless and sometimes apparently uncaring. I hope to see that image dead and buried. Our sponsorship budget may be small compared to our annual promotional spend, but we are now one of the largest corporate sponsors of the arts and environmental projects in the UK. It's a fine balance between philanthropy and enlightened self-interest, but we are looking for recognition for our not inconsiderable efforts.''

From a standing start four years ago, BT now puts £1 million a year into the medium across three areas: the arts, the environment and the disabled. These range from travelling exhibitions to high profile involvements with the Royal Philharmonic Orchestra and the Royal Shakespeare Company. BT wants to be seen as improving the quality of life in the community.

Case study: W.H. Smith

W.H. Smith wished to build its reputation for supporting education. Says sponsorship manager Michael Mackenzie, ''The Arts Programme is an excellent way of making a statement about what we stand for.'' Over two decades, the group's arts sponsorship programme – which is based largely on practical workshops connected with the written word and music, and involves schools and colleges around the country – has become well established.

An indirect benefit of this reputation building, says Richard Busby from the agency Strategic Sponsorship, is that it provides mitigation against times when something happens to put the company's reputation at risk. He explains: "Shell recently benefited substantially from its past sponsorship record. As the judge implied very strongly in a recent environmental court case, he would have fined Shell far more than the £1 million, but for their record in both environmental and community sponsorship."

Another strong motivation is direct product promotion. Tying sales of a product to donations to specific charities benefits both organisations, if the project is well managed. Many of the most successful cases of this kind of sponsorship are from the United States. Specialist consultant Dragon International calls it public purpose marketing and extracts from its files the following illustrative examples:

- *American Express*
  In possibly the first example of public purpose marketing, American Express approached the committee in charge of the restoration of the Statue of Liberty in 1984. American Express agreed to give $1 of each purchase made with an American Express card and $5 with each new card application to the Statue's restoration fund. During the campaign, the company raised $1.7 million for the Statue and American Express card use rose 17%.

Amex has continued to develop public purpose marketing programmes, the latest one of which is in association with COTA (the Children's Organ Transplant Association) and Best Western Hotels. Every time an American Express card is used at any of the 1800 Best Western Hotels, a donation will be made to COTA. In 1992, it operated a similar scheme in the UK, where 1p was put aside for every transaction on the card in February. £25,000 was raised for a variety of charities.

- *Thrifty Car Rental*
  This innovative scheme is aimed at consumers over 55. For every 25,000 car rentals to members of the American Association of Retired Persons, the company donates a van to a senior citizen centre. In research, 40% of older adults said that this would now make them choose Thrifty.

- *B. Dalton Bookseller*
  A major bookseller in the USA, wanting to encourage people to buy more books, helped reduce adult illiteracy by financing a special TV series for adults with reading difficulties, and providing special books and worksheets in their shops.

- *Ben & Jerry's*
  Ben & Jerry's is a company built on the principles of public purpose marketing. One of its first initiatives was the Peace Pop – a chocolate product, the wrapping of which invites consumers to join a movement called 1% for Peace, which advocates the reallocation of America's defence budget to the funding of "alternative to war" projects.

- A more recent initiative has been the *Giraffe* project, an American national not-for-profit organisation that encourages people to "stick their necks out" to make a difference to society. Aimed at increasing sales and traffic through stores, Ben & Jerry's new shops are now Giraffe headquarters where customers can read about current Giraffe activities, pick up membership applications and submit nominations.

UK companies have linked sales of (largely consumer) products to a wide range of good causes, from preservation of tropical rain forests to national children's charities. For example:

- *McDonald's*, the fast food chain, holds a bi-annual McHappy Day, when 50% of the proceeds from each Big Mac sold go to Ronald McDonald Children's Charities (RMCC), a foundation specialising in giving grants to charities that help children, and in particular, to children's homes. As a regular event, with staff directly involved, there are strong motivational benefits and, of course, the company increases sales overall for that day.

- Supermarket chain *Tesco* developed a campaign to help schools buy computers and software. Each £25 spent at the checkout earned a voucher which parents, teachers and relatives could give to the school, and which the school could eventually exchange for computer goods; 200 vouchers obtained a software package and 4000 a top-of-the-range computer.

- *London Broadcasting Company* (LBC) introduced its Public Affairs Forum as a quarterly update on community issues. Each programme focuses on a different theme and invites listeners to write and telephone with their opinions. Some themes, such as The Homeless in London, are accompanied by special appeals. Sponsoring companies receive commercial air time during the seven hours of each Forum programme and during the two weeks around it. They also have the opportunity to include their message about community involvement in a programme booklet, sent to MPs and other opinion-formers.

LBC gains from having programming costs underwritten and from a powerful boost to audience figures during the period.

The Co-op, which has experimented with this form of marketing from time to time, now views it with some caution, however. It is concerned that, if the benefits become too heavily weighted towards the Society, or seen as insufficiently relevant, people will actually feel less goodwill towards it.

Among other common reasons for embarking on sponsorship deals, says Busby, are:

1. *Increased awareness*. The public is made generally aware that the company exists.
2. *Corporate hospitality*. This is the traditional form of sponsorship. Though still important, it is now heading down the list of priorities.
3. *Image enhancement*. Increasingly companies use sponsorship as part of a bigger overall campaign.
4. *Attitudinal reinforcement or shift*. For instance, when a company wants to emphasise its stability and size, it may sponsor traditional upmarket activities such as cricket and opera.

5. *Direct acquisition of new customers* – if the firm has a stand where the event is being held.
6. *Staff relations and recruitment*. To enhance the company's image to would-be employees. Dull companies can seem exciting if they are associated with glamorous sports.
7. *Investor and government relations*. Istel, the Information and Technology Services Company, sponsored the first ever outdoor performance of the Royal Opera at Kenwood to attract the attention of opinion-formers, when it was contemplating a flotation.

In terms of value for money, it is hard to make exact comparisons with other forms of promotion. However, insists Caroline Kay of the Association for Business Sponsorship of the Arts (ABSA):

"Smaller companies and local branches of large companies in particular are starting to compare the benefits of advertising in the local paper, where the message may be diffused among a lot of people they don't want to target, against sponsorship, where they can reach individual customers very precisely."

On the negative side, sponsorship, like advertising, is sometimes extremely difficult to measure in terms of impact. While broad measurements of public awareness and goodwill can be made through surveys, any changes for better or worse are likely to be the result of a mix of factors, including the other ways in which the company tries to enhance its reputation. The most easily measured type of sponsorship is product sponsorship, where specific campaigns can be assessed against actual increases in sales over the period.

None the less, some research has been done. This suggests that sponsorship scores over other advertising media by the length of people's memory. Mars' sponsorship of the London Marathon was still strong in people's memory 15 months afterwards – in a survey, 43% of the population associated it with the sport. Other very high recollections include Embassy and snooker (42% of the population), cycling and milk (26%), Barclays and soccer (21%).

A survey carried out in 1991 by AGB research investigated what the guests attending sponsored arts events felt about the experience and about their hosts. The interviewees were all senior managers.

The survey found that:

- the managers generally preferred to be invited to the theatre, rather than to a sporting event
- the most common invitations were to the opera or a classical concert, followed closely by a sports event
- they considered that arts sponsorship was a good thing for the company to undertake
- most people would not have attended the event if not invited by their host
- the main impact of the event was to reinforce rather than improve their perception of the host company. Says AGB: "What seems to impress is the fact that, if an event in itself is well-organised and co-ordinated, this must be a reflection of the capabilities of the host company."

A strong argument against sponsorship used to be that national media were reluctant to credit sponsors when they reported events. A determined campaign by ABSA has largely removed that impediment, pushing up the number of reviews, in which the sponsor gains a mention, from one in three to three in four.

A sponsorship programme cannot make a company something it is not. A food company may look to sponsor a sports event to give it a healthy image, but if doubts are cast about the validity of the product's health claims or associations, neither the sponsor nor the charity will benefit. If the sponsorship has to be withdrawn (for example, the British Heart Foundation will not renew its sponsorship with Van den Bergh, the makers of Flora margarine, a policy that it plans to extend to all food sponsors), the resultant bad publicity can be even worse for the sponsor.

According to ABSA's Caroline Kay:

"Most problems in sponsorship occur through lack of communications between the sponsor and the organisation receiving help. The problem was often exacerbated by reluctance on the part of the charities to argue their case with managers giving their organisations large sums of money. We are gradually seeing an increased confidence among arts organisations, in approaching companies. Now they know they have something to sell that the companies want, and they are becoming more professional in presenting their own propositions, rather than just saying yes to what companies offer.

Sometimes problems also occur if the sponsoring company wishes to capitalise on its investment in ways that the voluntary body had not considered. Caroline Kay again: "The most visible problems tend to arise through insensitive handling of entertaining on the part of the sponsoring company. In one well-publicised incident, a company made a point of bringing hordes of middle managers to the opening night of a performance by the National Theatre. Many of the managers, not being regular London theatre-goers, turned up in black tie and DJs. This was also press night and what should have been a positive occasion was ridiculed by the press."

Mutuality of benefit occurs most often when both sides manage the process of sponsorship effectively, recognising what the commitments they are making really mean and planning meticulously.

The process, once again, involves the key steps of setting clear, focused objectives; selecting the right opportunities; controlling implementation; and measuring success in a way that allows for improvements in the management of the next involvement.

8.1 The management process

In practice, most companies with a developed sponsorship activity have fairly clear guidelines that help them distinguish whether an initiative should come under the community involvement or the marketing/sponsorship budget. For example, Barclays Bank is clear: "If it has our name on it, it's sponsorship".

John Laing uses the trustees of its charitable trust as a sounding board if it has any doubts. Group director of community affairs John Farrow applies a number of basic criteria, including:

- is the receiving organisation a registered charity?
- does the activity fall within our key areas of community action (i.e. does it represent people who are disadvantaged)?

In most cases, he finds, the distinction between projects that potentially fall within his budget and those which belong to marketing are quite easy to identify, because the commercial benefits are easier to define in the latter case. The pay-offs of commercial sponsorship may not be short term, however – one of Laing's sponsorships via the marketing department, is a group of young tennis players, who may take years to make a significant public impact (if at all).

Most experienced companies also have a strong focus on a small number of sponsorship areas. They select these on the basis of:

- *cost:* often negligible if the company simply guarantees any shortfall in income from an event, but equally can be very high (Blue Arrow's support for the British attempt on the Americas Cup involved several millions and may have been an element in investor concern at how the company was managed)
- *location:* many companies prefer to focus on local events, where they can achieve greatest promotional impact
- *the size and nature of the audience:* how many of them will watch the event, or read the account in the press?
- *prestige:* is this an event that will enhance our reputation by association? (Not many companies openly sponsor fox hunting, for example.)
- *potential:* will this activity grow in importance? Minority sports can grow to become prime time television events (e.g. snooker was a forgotten activity 15 years ago); companies that provide support in the early years can benefit substantially as the sport takes off.
- *need:* how important will our involvement be to this event or organisation? There are often more benefits from being the sole sponsor than from being just one of many.

While sensible, these criteria give rise to a potential problem. To obtain the maximum leverage from a sponsorship, it makes sense to be in at the start and to be there alone. Inevitably, this can predispose companies against existing projects, where someone else has had the best of the glory, and against joining forces except on big national showcase projects. On the other hand, it also helps limit the number of me-too projects (although there are still a good many of these).

Before choosing events to sponsor, however, one of the keys to good management of sponsorship, says Ken Parker, director of Agency Research Services Ltd, is to understand your customers. In a report of a speech he gave to the Incorporated Society of British Advertisers, he explained that analysing their motivations and aspirations is essential in deciding where sponsorship money will have most benefit for the company. In particular, it is important, where large sums of money are involved, to research adequately how it will affect a brand to be associated with a specific activity.

When it comes to choosing between specific projects, the same criteria apply, but are supplemented by other considerations, such as:

- the reputation and management capability of the voluntary organisation
- to what extent can we link this initiative with others already in our portfolio, or being pursued by other subsidiaries of our company in other countries? For example, credit card company Visa joined other Visa operations in Europe to sponsor an artist each to attend the 1992 Barcelona Olympics. The artist selected from the UK was a photographer, David Hiscock. The combined muscle of a multi-country approach provided much greater impact than would have been gained from a Visa UK initiative alone.
- how big a difference will our involvement make?

The more that both the company and the voluntary organisation can apply marketing techniques and disciplines, the closer both will come to meeting the needs of their target audiences. This means in both cases establishing very strong profiles of their target audiences and the best way to serve them.

An increasingly common practice is to request potential sponsor partners to produce their own business plans for a project. On the one hand, this provides a useful insight into their management competence; on the other, it helps ensure that they understand the company's objectives (and their own). Key questions to ask at this stage are:

- is the project realistic?
- will it achieve the objectives we have both set?
- what negative effects might our participation here have?
- have we budgeted sufficient to cover the promotion costs as well? (A good working figure suggested by the Sports Council is that the promotion budget should at least equal the operational budget.)
- are we providing the right balance of resources (cash, people, goods in kind)?
- who else could and should we involve?

Once the project is under way, the sponsoring company has to exercise a balance between making sure that its money and/or resources are being used effectively, and not interfering with the voluntary organisation's work. Too great an attention to the implementation process can waste a lot of company time and breed resentment in the sponsorship recipients.

Good management processes suggest that there should be:

- a clear and fully understood contract outlining what each party expects of the other. A legal agreement may be appropriate, but more valuable will be a simpler document spelling out to everyone who may become involved what the various responsibilities are
- preset milestones to examine progress against agreed criteria (e.g. number of attendances at sponsored theatre events; quality of a sponsored production; completion of a defined stage in a construction project)
- a contingency plan (and budget) to cater for the unforeseen
- regular review meetings and progress reports
- where appropriate, access to external advice
- a formal post-project review, to assess the lessons.

A communication plan is as essential a part of the sponsorship as the event itself. All the experts we spoke to were concerned that many companies became so wrapped up in the delivery of the project that they paid little or no attention to how they would publicise the sponsorship and which target groups they wanted to reach with publicity. A good working rule appears to be that the time, effort and money spent on the event should be equalled by that spent on the promotion.

Communication needs to aim at internal as well as external audiences – employees are likely to promote the event, if they feel proud of their employer's involvement. Among innovative ways of raising employee awareness was BT Scotland's competition for employees to win tickets to performances by the Scottish Chamber Orchestra.

Not all attempts at evaluation are successful, however. One company reportedly had researchers quizzing the person in the street over a campaign that had been aimed at key influencers in the City.

The range of areas, where companies can apply sponsorship is growing rapidly. However, the dominant recipients are undoubtedly sport and the arts. Significant emerging areas include the environment and general leisure amenities (such as footpaths or gardens).

The range of companies which can make use of sponsorship is also wide. Small companies can obtain significant benefits from investments of £1000 or less, if they focus their giving on specific projects with high visibility rather than on simply handing out a few pounds whenever asked. Some of the cases in this chapter deal with smaller companies' experience.

8.2 Sports sponsorship

Sponsoring televised sports such as football, horse jumping, golf or cricket reaches a wide audience and provides many additional opportunities to promote the company. But sponsoring small local events, such as a disabled sports day, can be equally effective in value for money terms.

Unusual or growing sports are also a lucrative area for sponsorship. Baseball, softball and Japanese wrestling are all increasing in popularity. Companies whose name is linked with them now will reap the benefits if these sports follow the example of snooker or darts and become regular television events.

Sports sponsorship benefits from the strength of sports coverage on TV and in newspapers. According to Research Services Ltd, 60% of newspaper readers turn to the sports pages every day, and 75% of men read them at weekends.

Alan Pascoe of the eponymous sports sponsorship promotion agency emphasises that the benefits of sports sponsorship depend heavily on the objectives you set. The more specific a company can be about what it wants to achieve, the greater the benefits – on both sides. In his experience, sports sponsorships work best when they:

- start with a very clear brief, outlining objectives and how broadly they will be measured
- involve some initial feasibility research, including detailed responses from target charities
- involve more substantial research subsequently to test the concept in practice and to establish specific benchmarks, against which to judge the sponsorship
- have a detailed implementation plan, where both sides know what is expected of them and where adequate budgets are assigned to both the event and its promotion.

"Sport sponsorship tends to take place at two levels," says Bob Peach of the Sports Council. "At a national level, companies are looking for major events with a strong national profile. Their main objective is image building." Funding tends to come from advertising and promotion budgets and can therefore be more severely hit by downturns in trade than local events, which tend to be funded out of the community investment budgets of these same companies' regional or local branches. Sponsorship by locally based companies tends again to come from the advertising and promotional budget – these companies are often much more hard-nosed about gaining a direct return, in terms of customer goodwill, from their sponsorship expenditure.

Peach estimates that there are up to 150 sports which receive sufficient national coverage to attract large company sponsors. That leaves about 250 sports which have to rely on regional sponsorship for smaller scale, local events. The Council has a grants scheme, to support both individual events and capital investment. Private company sponsorship tops up this spending by about 20%.

The limiting factor, says Peach, is often the availability of professional help. He advises companies not to try to develop events themselves without expert advice – not least on how the proposed investment will be seen by people connected with the sport, and how to extract the most value for both parties. The Sports Council has a number of development officers, part of whose jobs is to advise on event management and to help companies and sports organisations develop partnerships. However, they are thin on the ground. Commercial sports sponsorship agencies tend to concentrate on large national events.

Case study: British Telecom

BT sponsors the Kielder Challenge, where teams of disabled and able bodied take part in outdoor events. The aim of the challenge is to promote teamwork, build self-confidence and to open up a challenging environment the youngsters would not normally encounter.

Thanks to BT support, the British Sports Association for the Disabled has enlarged its swimming championships and run a National Swimming Development programme. Among the skills the participants learnt were basic water safety techniques, which are vital if a disabled person is to enjoy water sports regularly.

Case study: Alliance with smaller companies

A number of smaller sports companies collaborated with Barclays Bank in sponsoring an aerobic "Workout with the stars" in aid of the mental health charity, MIND. Participants who raised £100 received a leotard or other item of sportswear; those who raised £250 or more received a pair of Avia sports shoes; and the top fund-raiser received a weekend for two at a health hydro. For Avia and for Inglewood Hydro the promotional benefits of being advertised through leaflets and posters in Barclays' premises and elsewhere, substantially outweighed the cost of providing prizes.

The costs of sports sponsorships vary considerably. At the one extreme, an entry in the Americas Cup can costs £10 million to sponsor. At the other, small local sports events can be sponsored for as little as £100. For the large sports sponsorships, the Sports Council operates a matchmaking service; the regional sports councils handle smaller, local events. Some of the regions publish detailed lists of sponsorships. The Scottish Sports Council, for example, has a newsletter entitled "Leads", which regularly lists opportunities for sponsorship, ranging from £200 to sponsor the Scottish Junior Dinghy Sailing Championships to £100,000+ for the Women's World Bowls.

8.3 The arts

Annual spending on the arts by national and local government in the UK is much lower than in most of the other major nations of Europe, totalling only around £700 million, compared with £2800 million in Germany and over £4 billion in France. Business sponsorship is also lower in the UK, at £30 million, compared with around £50 million by France and Germany; and nearly £150 million in Italy, according to Arts Council figures. So the potential for companies to exploit the possibilities of arts sponsorship is still relatively untapped.

Part of the problem, says ABSA's Kay, is that "The arts sometimes fall into the grey area between community and charitable activities and high-profile logo recognition. By and large, sports sponsorship tends to do better in terms of profile. Unfortunately, the arts do not necessarily do so well out of community investment budgets either, because the very phrase often has the wrong image, suggesting something that is a luxury compared to other community issues, such as homelessness or disadvantaged children." On the other hand, ABSA boasts it can match almost any set of corporate objectives against an appropriate arts programme.

Most arts sponsorship is in cash, but an increasing amount is in goods in kind (for example, using company facilities to produce programmes) or secondment of staff. ICI is one of a number of companies that has made effective use of goods-in-kind sponsorship. Although the Bolshoi Theatre Grigorovich company has a number of sponsors, ICI Tactel achieved lead sponsor status by providing 10,000 litres of Dulux paint and 25,000 metres of fabric.

Alliances between sponsors are becoming more common, too. Among interesting combinations of interest are:

- sponsor + newspaper + event (e.g. *The Times* and Shell promoting Museums year; Mercury and *The Independent* developing a Pop Art programme)
- sponsor + charity + arts organisation (e.g. Natwest and Save the Children Fund working with the National Children's Opera)
- "designed sponsorships" (e.g. management consultancy KPMG has teamed up with the National Theatre, the Tate Gallery and the English National Opera to promote new artistic work).

Case study: Barclays and arts sponsorship

Explains Ros Frost, Barclays sponsorship manager: "We treat the arts somewhat differently. Until 1986, our support used to be for lots of small, usually one-off events here and there. When we took a step back and looked into the policy, we saw it wasn't working for us or for the community. Now we look for projects that will have:

- national recognition
- a flagship event at the top
- geographical spread (i.e. preferably a touring event or one that involves communities across the UK).

"Some of these programmes are aimed specifically at youth. For example, the Youth Music Theatre auditions school orchestras and provides professional feedback to the entrants. The best orchestras compete at a well-publicised national event.

"Other projects involve touring companies, which will reach a large number of communities over the course of a year. As major sponsors, we can help direct them to communities we think would benefit from their presence. Most touring companies visit six or seven locations. We chose to sponsor London City Ballet because they visit 40-plus locations. At each venue, regional and branch staff can use the visit to entertain key customers. There is often a free ticket competition and an opportunity for local managers to make a photocall with the cast. Sometimes, we arrange for the local football team to train with the cast. It all helps to build our profile in the area.

"Our flagship project is Barclays New Stages which, like the Youth Music Theatre, we created. Companies don't usually fund the experimental end of theatre, so we saw here an opportunity to avoid me-too sponsorship. New Stages is an award scheme aimed at independent theatre companies, both amateur and professional. They can include the disabled, mime or prison troupes, for example. The theatre companies can apply for grants of up to £10,000 for new productions – sufficient for them to be able to go to the Regional Arts Board with a good chance of getting more. Usually, they tour, with short stays around the country and there is additional money available to help them advertise the performances locally. Each year the director of the Royal Court Theatre in London will select four or five to appear on his stage – often the first time these companies will have played in London. It gives the companies real status.

"One of the objectives of our arts sponsorship is to gain standing for Barclays among our peers and in the arts world. We get positive feedback, for example, when our schemes are mentioned in the House of Commons."

Case study: Henley Management College

Henley Management College uses sponsorship as an effective, low-cost method of building bridges with the local community. With the appointment of a new principal, Ray Wild, the college began to look at its use of space. Among the most wasted (and drabbest) areas was a broad hallway and corridor. For the past two years this area has been the site of a continuous stream of four to six week exhibitions of paintings, craftwork and photography by local artists.

Each exhibition is opened with a reception, for which Henley pays and to which both the college and the artists invite guests. Most of the exhibits are for sale and many are acquired by staff or visitors. The gallery is open to the public as well. The costs, says marketing manager Michael Pitfield, are marginal, but the benefits, in terms of familiarising local people with the college and its activities, and in providing an informal atmosphere to meet clients, have been substantial.

Henley has since extended the concept to monthly musical evenings where young local musicians are invited to give concerts to an audience of participants on Henley courses and invited guests.

Case study: Eurocharing

Eurocharing is a local Audi dealer in Charing, Kent. Introduced to the concept of sponsorship by Audi, which sponsors the Young Musician of the Year Award, general manager Brian Phillips and his colleagues decided to launch out on their own. The venture they chose to support was Primera Trust, one of the county's leading chamber orchestras, in putting on a performance at Wye Parish Church. Eurocharing took 80 of the 400 seats and invited customers and potential customers to join them at the concert.

The cost to Eurocharing (who took over sponsorship from Eurotunnel) was £2000. Because the company was a first-time sponsor, its contribution was matched by ABSA. "I'd rather spend money on this than advertising," says Phillips, "because it's more effective, more fun and more targeted on the people we want to reach. We gained local publicity anyway, not least because we attended an ABSA award ceremony."

Case study: Armstrong Watson

Armstrong Watson is a firm of solicitors based in Carlisle and employing a total of 300 people in 21 offices around the North-West. Marketing manager Robert Ghey had experienced sponsorship operations in a previous job and felt they had not been managed well. In particular, he had observed that the selection of events had placed that company in the position of being just one sponsor of one event in a string of orchestra visits to the region – there was little opportunity to differentiate its contribution in public eyes.

The opportunity to sponsor the Royal Shakespeare Company's visit to Carlisle met Ghey's criteria more closely. Although five separate companies were sponsoring each of the five evening performances, the uniqueness of the event gave it a higher profile. Moreover, Ghey was able to exert a fair degree of control by bringing in his own public relations supplier to handle the press and promotion work. A cash sponsorship of £1000, backed up with additional grants by ABSA and Northern Arts, made up half the total cost to Armstrong Watson, with PR and hospitality making up the rest.

Ghey was also very focused in the selection of the guests invited to the performance, concentrating on intermediaries such as bank managers and solicitors, rather than individual customers. "At the end of the day," he explains, "I am looking to get the most effective promotion I can. Introducing new business is our main goal but, if we are seen to be putting something back into the community, then so much the better."

Encouraged by the success of this venture, Ghey subsequently sponsored a visit by the Moscow City Ballet. Again, using his own PR resources, he was able to extract considerable promotional value. Bringing 50 local young ballet students into the theatre on the second morning for a workout with the ballet company provided a great deal of extra press and TV coverage. "From someone who was fairly cynical before, I have become so taken by sponsorship that I have budgeted for two major events in 1992-3. The key for us is to have as much control as possible over our involvement."

One of the interesting benefits of arts sponsorship for the arts organisations is that it frequently widens their audience. Many junior and middle managers, for example, first experience opera courtesy of sponsorship by their companies. Some arts institutions have responded to this realisation by holding "corporate evenings" – special events to introduce business people to performances.

Company-sponsored events often prove remarkably popular with employees, too. Reportedly, when Brother offered employees tickets to a sponsored concert by the Hallé orchestra, the demand was significantly greater than for free tickets to a Manchester City football match.

Peter Walshe, director of Millward Brown International Market Research, is one of the few specialists in sponsorship measurement. He makes the point that it is relatively easy to compare who received the message against who it was aimed at –

if the measurement approach is built into the project from the start. He recommends a two-stage approach, as follows:

First, an accurate profile measure is taken of the attenders at a sample of performances/visiting days. It is important that this is carried out properly, giving everyone an equal chance of responding, so that the profile is not biased because of poor research and sampling. The favoured method involves giving out questionnaires, or placing them on selected seats, for the head of each party to self-complete at the venue. This has the benefit of covering the entire audience with fewer questionnaires because the head of the party also fills in the details of the others with him or her (someone alone counts as a party of one). Getting a good response is also vital to the success of the measure and the incentive of a prize draw, notices about the survey, prominent return boxes, pens, nicely laid-out short questionnaires have been well documented. This first stage gets the information on exactly who the visitors are (i.e. a definition of the sponsorship target).

The second stage is a follow-up among a representative sample of the audience by telephone (their permission and telephone numbers obtained during the first stage). This usually takes place within a week of the performance and covers the awareness of the sponsor, whether those aware were different in profile from those who were unaware, attitudes towards the sponsor and sponsorship in general, how the sponsorship was noticed, what message was conveyed and so on.

Measurements may be aimed at elucidating who noticed the sponsorship, how suitable they felt the company's involvement to be, how accurately they absorbed the intended message and how they got the message (i.e. through what medium). "Understanding what people infer from the message is vastly improved by comparing the results from other similar events," says Walshe, who has been compiling a database of normative data in this area since 1989. Even if companies do not use professional services to test the assumptions from their surveys, it would seem to make a great deal of sense to exchange data with other companies, so the results are not simply taken in isolation.

Among other points made by Walshe are that:

- Results in the UK have often shown that arts sponsorship is underpromoted, both at the event itself and around the event.

- When the purpose of the sponsorship has been clearly and interestingly explained to audiences, the recall has been better and attitudes more favourable.
- The research so far indicates that the arts need to be less precious about the sanctity of their "product" and to be more open to finding creative ways of enabling sponsors to get their message across. Sponsors, in turn, need to define, integrate and support their messages within the total context of their brand or service to get maximum benefit (much as they would do with the rest of their marketing spend).
- Creating effective arts sponsorship seems to be at a relatively early stage of learning and development. The danger is that the arts could lose out if the effectiveness is not more extensively researched and proven.

8.4 Other areas of sponsorship

Almost anything outside the commercial and governmental sectors is a potential target for sponsorship. The following examples give some idea of the scope within general leisure and local community initiatives.

Case study: Coutts & Company

In celebrating its tercentenary in 1992, Coutts & Co wanted to address three audiences – its customers, its employees and the community at large. Management decided that the community should be the main beneficiary. It chose one key charity project itself and asked staff to suggest others. One of the suggestions, from staff who were keen gardening enthusiasts, was to sponsor a garden for the disabled in the Royal Horticultural Society's gardens at Wisley. Staff also contributed to the costs of the venture, through their own fund-raising.

Says Julian Marczak, of Coutts' marketing department:

"For a number of years, the bank has endeavoured to present opportunities to young talent, namely by allowing young, highly talented musicians to perform at Coutts' unusual Garden Court Banking Hall at 440 Strand. This is something we are continuing throughout our tercentenary, with a series of concerts involving students of the Royal College of Music playing with leading artists, such as guitarist John Williams. To further this theme, the bank put forward the suggestion to the RHS that a nationwide competition be held, with the prize money to be given by Coutts, to attract a suitable design of the garden by a young student of horticulture. The competition was in fact won jointly and it is the design of Jonathan Selman and Rosalind Haddrill which has been adopted.

"Throughout the planning of this project, regular meetings have been held between representatives of Coutts and the RHS in order that the two could work in close partnership and all concerned could feel they had achieved something of benefit.

"Our view is that it is extremely difficult to reach a bottom line; the aims must be to ensure all aspects of the sponsorship have a synergy with the marketing and business aims of the sponsor and, indeed, those of the party being sponsored."

Communication is often an undeveloped discipline among charitable organisations. Opportunities to sponsor newsletters and other forms of promotion for a charity abound. For example, Barclays recently sponsored a newsletter for the Countryside Commission to promote the Thames Path, a newly opened trail from the river's source in Gloucestershire to the Thames Barrier below London.

Case study: Rover Group

Rover sponsors a school libraries programme so that school leavers will be aware of the company name and will perhaps think of the company when they choose a career and an employer.

Local authorities are a relatively recent, but increasingly active partner in this kind of sponsorship. As a result, there are special opportunities for smaller, community-based companies. Colin Graham runs a small florist shop and landscape gardening business in Maidenhead, Berkshire. The opportunity to sponsor the landscaping of one of the town's main traffic roundabouts provided an ideal marketing medium for him.

Graham had already had some exposure to sponsorship as a supplier to major events, such as the Stella Artois Tournament, but had not actually participated as a sponsor before. The roundabout in question, on one of the main routes into the town, lies opposite Northern Telecom, a major client, which agreed to co-sponsor the project. Graham explains that he has maximised the benefits by "making sure it looks different and keeping it at a very high standard of maintenance. The district council has had a lot of congratulations. It's a shop window for our contract business." Like many other small companies, Graham diverted money from his advertising budget to cover the £3000 cost.

Other local sponsors of roundabouts within the same district include the Princess Margaret Hospital.

Tony Gunning, the promotions consultant behind these two roundabout sponsorships, is an enthusiast for this kind of involvement. Provided the company is not simply substituting for activities which should properly be publicly funded, he explains, the returns to the sponsoring company can be substantial. "Increased awareness comes from signs on the roundabout and from publicity when the Mayor dedicates the landscaping. As long as they see it as a genuine community activity, the press usually provide good coverage. The sponsors also receive invites to civic events, where they meet other influential people.

"Part of the problem for the small business is that it is often very difficult to find ways to promote trade. Sponsorship can provide a cost-effective way for them to reach the right audience. It has an additional benefit in that it emphasises to employees that the company is wedded to the community, so they feel more secure."

Among other local sponsorships targeted at small businesses is a scheme to convert a disused railway line into a cycle and walking track. Local pubs, sports shops and businesses, whose employees may use the facility, are being asked to sponsor 0.25 kilometres of track each.

Says Gunning: "Roadside verges, sports facilities, nature centres, park benches, cricket teams, flower troughs, hanging baskets, concerts, waterway locks, library exhibitions, cemetery facilities, children's play areas, council employee uniforms, school lectures and medical units are all capable of attracting sponsorship provided potential patrons are presented with a credible proposition against which their marketing funds can be applied."

Sponsored research

Sponsored research has become an increasing proportion of the revenue of Britain's universities and polytechnics over the past decade. Company sponsorship of research extends from the technical to pure science, from social science to strategic management. 3i, for example, sponsors the Cranfield European Centre for Enterprise, aimed at promoting the economic significance and role of small and medium-sized enterprises in Europe.

Although a high proportion of this activity is directly related to commercial benefit, much is also of more general benefit. Companies gain a reputation for involvement in innovation and special relationships with polytechnics and universities. Bright post graduate students, for example, can be directed by their tutors towards the company for employment.

Case study: Lloyds Bank

Lloyds Bank provides the core funding and operational costs of Oxford University's Environmental Change Unit, set up in the early 1990s to investigate the impact of global warming, deforestation and pollution on the environment.

Case study: BP and sponsored research

The *Financial Times* bills BP's Venture Research as "one of the world's most imaginative corporate research programmes". For the past ten years BP has funded speculative science in a wide field from advanced mathematics to biology. The research does not need to have any relation to BP's oil, energy and chemical businesses – or any foreseeable industrial application at all. The fund supports scientists who are researching ideas considered too unorthodox to be funded by corporate R&D departments or public agencies.

BP transferred its portfolio of research and intellectual property rights to Venture Research International in 1990. It has become a corporate shareholder along with a number of major corporations, such as Sony, whose interests together span the industrial spectrum.

Among the projects sponsored is an investigation by two botanists on the three-dimensional structure of the genetic material (chromosomes) in cells.

The research was important because, although thousands of scientists worldwide were unravelling the chemical sequence of DNA within chromosomes, no one had looked at the arrangement of chromosomes within the cell nucleus. The two botanists received £100,000 a year, which enabled them to develop new techniques for investigating the structure of cell nuclei and start to apply them to human genes.

While many of these "pump-priming" activities have led to nothing, others have stimulated advances of substantial commercial value. One project, for example, subsequently received over £7 million of government money, because it had great significance for the pharmaceutical industry.

The degree to which sponsorship continues to grow during the 1990s and beyond, will depend to a large extent on its reputation. That, in turn, depends increasingly on how adept companies become at managing the conflict between the need to separate overt, short-term sales activities from longer-term community investment, and the need to ensure consistency between social responsibility and marketing objectives in sponsorship. The greater the respect afforded by the public to sponsorship activities, the greater the value to both the community and the company. That respect depends heavily on how well the company thinks through and communicates what it is doing and why.

Checklist

1. Do you have clear objectives for your sponsorship activities?
2. How will you measure success?
3. Do you have policies to guide local managers in the selection of sponsorship projects?
4. Do you provide adequate resources to communicate your sponsorship activities effectively?

9. Responsibilities towards the environment

"The environment will be one of the most important political issues of the 1990s, notwithstanding events in Eastern Europe", claims the CBI in a 1991 report on a survey conducted jointly with the leading international management and technology consultancy, PA Consulting Group.

Entitled "Waking up to a better environment", the report goes on to state that one of the key areas for debate will be the tensions between pressures for a tougher regulatory regime and the need to allow corporate social responsibility and market pressure to generate environmentally beneficial policies.

Part of the problem will be defining exactly where companies' environmental responsibilities begin and end. Certainly any organisation that assumes it will have a good environmental record simply by not emitting any dangerous or noxious waste products from manufacture is living in a fool's paradise. Increasingly, a company's environmental performance is also measured by how proactive it is in areas such as:

- reducing noise pollution
- demanding that its suppliers do not use environmentally harmful products
- energy efficiency
- active participation in improving the environment, for example through inner city development
- encouragement of environmental initiatives.

As the *Financial Times* expressed it (21 June 1990): "Saatchi's research shows that people now expect companies to be environmentally aware in every area of their activities. Companies cannot expect people to be impressed by their new green product or by their advertisement – if they do not take a responsible attitude to the environment in areas such as corporate strategy or production planning."

The CBI report points out that penalties for non-compliance will increase at the same time: "A shift towards polluter-pays taxation, ultimately to be manifested through a carbon tax, for example, will be matched by a growth in environmentally based litigation. The lessons of the *Exxon Valdez* oil spill have spread further than the problems of the clean-up operation."

Public concern about green issues and the existence of well-organised environmental pressure groups, make remedial legal action against companies and individual directors all the more likely in the future. Indeed, according to the CBI, recent legislation reflects a change in the climate towards stricter enforcement of environmental standards. The Home Office White Paper, "Crime, Justice and Protecting the Public" confirms the government's view that criminal law is the appropriate medium to protect the public from actions which are either a risk to public health and safety or which cause harm to the environment.

For example, companies and directors now face unlimited fines if they fail to comply with the latest rules governing the disposal of waste. Duty of care regulations under the 1990 Environment Protection Act are now in force, making firms responsible for: the safe disposal of their waste even if they are paying someone else to do it, checking that the person taking waste away is fully authorised, packing it safely and keeping proper records.

That they can be held responsible as individuals for their company's transgressions is an additional spur for directors to become environmentally aware. And while the concept of personal liability for directors is not new, the increasing trend for civil and criminal litigation to be brought against both company and director means that they neglect statutory responsibilities at their peril.

The pressure for stricter environmental regulations, both at home and from Europe, also makes it likely that environmental goal posts will continue to move. A major problem for companies in the future will be staying abreast of developments to ensure compliance with new regulations within the given time-scales.

Evidence of investor concern over companies' environmental records comes from an agreement in May 1992 from a consortium of banks from 23 countries. Meeting at the United Nations, the banks, which included Natwest and the Royal Bank of Scotland, established common principles of taking environmental issues into account in both their lending and their internal operations. All the signatories committed themselves to ensure "the best practices in environmental management, including energy efficiency, recycling and waste minimisation". Natwest was reported as emphasising that environmental risk is now an important element of credit risk.

Already many companies are setting themselves tough environmental guidelines in the belief that self-regulation is preferable to imposed government regulation.

These companies have found that good environmental management is also an investment. It can:

- improve the company's reputation
- boost employee morale
- help attract high calibre recruits
- increase efficiency and cut costs by eliminating avoidable waste
- improve profits, by turning waste into marketable by-products
- provide competitive advantage, through market positioning.

The CBI report maintains that failing to adopt environmentally responsible policies and behaviour can lead to:

- fines
- higher costs
- lost profits
- a sullied reputation
- as well as the possibility of stricter legislation and higher penalties.

However, a 1992 survey by Trudy Coe for the British Institute of Management , entitled "Managing the Environment", found that less than half of organisations studied had an overall strategy for managing environmental issues. Where they did have a strategy, it would most likely concentrate on obvious areas of business return, such as energy conservation and recycling. And of those companies which did have a corporate policy, less than half had the confidence to make it public.

Among other disturbing findings of the report were:

- few organisations gave any priority to environmental training
- only just over one in three had allocated specific management responsibility for environmental issues

- only half the managers who had been given environmental responsibilities had relevant qualifications or training
- less than a quarter had undertaken environmental audits.

Says the report:

"An holistic approach to environmental management allows organisations to respond to rapid changes on the environmental agenda in ways which maximise benefit to the company as well as to the environment. It does require major changes in the way environmental issues are handled and changes in the organisation of business functions. It does require the time and commitment of senior management and will need personnel and financial resources. The benefits though are significant:

- Gaining competitive edge: a business with a sound environmental management will have an improved customer image and will be better placed to identify and respond to green opportunities.
- A better profile with investors, staff and the public: increasingly, investors and their advisors are avoiding companies with poor environmental records. Staff and new recruits are concerned about the environmental performance of employers. A good environmental record boosts the company's public image.
- Avoidance of liability and risk; environmental management allows businesses to choose when and how to invest in better environmental performance, rather than reacting at the last minute to new legislation or consumer pressure.

"Investment in effective environmental management can thus turn environmental issues from threats and costs into profits and opportunities. It requires:

- Setting goals and objectives based on a thorough understanding of the environmental impacts of the business (environment policy).
- Reviewing current environmental performance against the objectives and identifying options for improvement (environmental audit).
- Developing a programme to implement change throughout the business (environment strategy)."

Until quite recently, most of the debate about companies' environmental responsibilities tended to focus on larger organisations. The emphasis was very much on the damage caused to the environment by nameless, faceless representatives of "Big Business". As larger companies have begun to address their responsibilities through environmental audits, however, attention has started to shift onto the smaller companies.

Unfortunately, many small firms simply cannot apply the same approaches to environmental issues as larger organisations. For example, creating a specialist environmental department or investing large sums of money in new environmentally friendly technology is likely to be a luxury a small or medium-sized enterprise cannot afford. In recognition of the realities facing smaller companies a number of initiatives are currently in train to assist them in addressing their environmental responsibilities.

However, in spite of the difficulties facing them, a number of smaller companies have won awards for good environmental management. In many instances it is less the environmental policies and procedures that small companies have in place that bring innovations and more the flexibility of smaller operations to react quickly to a changing business climate.

For example, PA Consulting's Golden Leaf Awards, which are presented annually for "responsible environmental action resulting in demonstrable business advantage and the achievement of a stated business goal", have shown what smaller companies can achieve. The PA awards are made by a panel of judges that includes botanist David Bellamy. Winners of these awards include the following smaller and medium-sized companies.

Case study: Appleby cheese factory in Cumbria

Express Foods Group won the PA Golden Leaf Award in 1991 for a series of environmental initiatives instigated by its 106 employees at Appleby cheese factory.

Appleby is a small market town in the Eden Valley in Cumbria. With the existence of a cheese factory, while creating employment, there was also the possibility of environmental problems. In 1987 there was a leak of ammonia from one of the factory's cooling towers, killing fish in the local river.

The incident drew criticism from the local community, but also raised environmental awareness among the factory's employees. As a result, John Williams, the factory manager at the time, instigated the creation of an internal environmental awareness committee with the help of Gordon Bell, the production services manager. The purpose of the cross-functional committee was to examine the vulnerability of the factory's systems and procedures to risks from pollution. It also aimed to make staff more environmentally aware.

As a result of the activities of the committee a graduate trainee was taken on to conduct an environmental survey of the factory. The survey led to the appointment in 1988 of David Barker as a full-time effluent control manager. Barker's role was seen as liaising between the factory, the local water company, the National Rivers Authority and the local community to monitor effluent disposal.

By then, too, the environmental awareness initiative had really begun to take off among employees. As a result of initiatives introduced by Barker to make production processes more environmentally efficient, and general enthusiasm within the factory, Appleby saved £85,000 in the first year from reduced wastage.

Since then, further savings of £250,000 in recoverable product that could be reprocessed have also been identified and Barker, now the environmental control officer, is currently looking at energy conservation within the factory.

Today, Appleby cheese factory also enjoys good relationships with the water authorities and the local community thanks to a well-executed communication campaign. John Bolton, factory manager at Appleby, explains that the changes that have occurred were sparked off initially by the effects of the pollution incident on the factory's workforce.

"We put the changes down to a total change of emphasis on environmental issues which started with the spillage. The impact that the pollution incident had, has become known here as the 'Appleby experience'."

Since then, says Bolton, the company has spent more than £200,000 on environmental improvements. For example, the unloading of caustic substances is now carried out in bonded areas where a spillage could be contained.

But, although the company restocked the river with fish, to begin with the stigma remained. What made the difference in the end was the decision to become proactive by sending representatives from the factory down to the town. A team of five – Barker, two production supervisors and two production managers, stopped people in the street with a questionnaire, went into the local bank and visited between 30 and 40 private homes.

In addition, local people were invited to a questions and answers session at the town hall. "We expected to be shot down in flames", says Bolton, "but people were so pleased we were concerned that they were nothing but positive."

Since then the factory at Appleby has hosted a series of open days at which local farmers and others are invited to inspect the plant's safety procedures.

As a result of its environmental awareness campaign, Appleby now has a thriving suggestion scheme, with employees rewarded with cheques up to 10% of the first year's savings for green money-saving ideas.

According to Bolton the "Appleby experience" is a prime example of what can happen when a workforce goes through an environmental culture change. Winning the PA Golden Leaf Award gave the factory local newspaper and TV coverage, too, which has helped cement its new found popularity within the local community.

Case study: Heatwise, Glasgow

Heatwise, part of the Wise Group, has provided home insulation and advice since 1983. In 1990, the company, which employs a full-time staff of 20, was involved in a project to refurbish a number of council flats in the Easthall area of Glasgow.

Through a package of innovative energy conservation measures, including solar design features, cavity wall insulation and external and internal wall cladding, the company has pioneered energy conservation techniques in council flats in Glasgow.

The potential savings of the project are still being monitored but results so far indicate that the company's approach makes it possible to keep an entire two-bedroom flat warm for less than it previously cost to heat one room.

As well as providing benefits for tenants, Heatwise has created business advantages for the local authority. By offering higher-quality accommodation, Glasgow District Council was able to cease payment to tenants for the effects of damp and secure full occupancy and satisfied tenants.

The project has improved the local environment, created jobs and demonstrated that it is possible for people in the coldest housing in Glasgow to have warm, dry homes at an affordable cost.

As a result, European and local authority funding was agreed to refurbish a further 36 flats to the same high standards.

Case study: J. McIntyre (Non Ferrous) Ltd, Nottingham

J. McIntyre (Non Ferrous) Ltd has been in the metal recycling business for many years. In the 1970s the company, which has 70 employees, decided to replace seven old open-well furnaces used in aluminium recycling with new "environmentally friendly" equipment.

At that time there was no suitable furnace in existence, so the company's chairman, Michael Pownall, collaborated with Dutchman Adri Hengolmolen to design and build one. The furnace had to be capable of recycling the most abused aluminium such as soft drink cans (covered in paint) or discarded aluminium window frames (coated in plastic). In fact it had to have the versatility to melt all kinds of aluminium in order to save money on sorting and pre-processing.

They designed a recycling furnace that was sealed, thus reducing air pollution. In addition the doors were designed as ventilators to enable pressure to be released if necessary to prevent an explosion. Another key feature of the new furnace was its process control which monitors and co-ordinates the hot gas recirculation system, ensuring pressures are kept uniform. Process control also allows the operator to programme the most efficient temperatures and melting times for different types of material.

In commercial terms the spin-offs from developing the new furnace have been considerable. It allows J. McIntyre to process metal at 35% of the standard industrial cost. It can cope with any kind of scrap which means in turn that the company can afford to pay more for its feedstock material. This has led to the recycling of materials which would previously have been uneconomical to process.

Other benefits include a better working environment, reduced absenteeism and worker illness because no heat is emitted until the furnace is opened. Downtime and breakdowns have also been reduced because the furnace is process controlled to a level which minimises wear and tear on parts.

Among larger winners is Manchester Airport.

Case study: Manchester Airport

Manchester Airport has developed a structured approach to managing its environmental facilities – so much so that it was one of the first winners of the PA Golden Leaf Awards for environmental management. It organises its environmental management activities through an 18-staff environmental and human health department which reports to the airport's senior management.

Also reporting to the airport's senior management are a number of technical tasks forces, focusing on different environmental issues, for example, an energy group is tasked with saving energy costs. Among its accomplishments is an £8.5 million sound-proofed heat and power station, designed to operate at twice the efficiency of a normal generator. Another task force – the landscape working group – looks after the visual impact of the airport. Similarly, the noise technical working group has been instrumental in developing a noise contour model and reducing noise pollution.

Liaison with the community is through a consultative committee comprising 35 representatives from a number of different areas. These include local councillors, members of the local business community and representatives of amenities groups close to the airport, as well as representatives from the airlines and tour operators that use the airport. The committee is chaired by a local councillor and its secretariat is run by Cheshire County Council. The only airport employees on the committee are those in non-managerial positions.

An important part of Manchester Airport's approach is the involvement of staff. The Ideas for Life programme is part of an employee suggestion scheme organised through the staff newspaper. The suggestion scheme works at two levels, with staff encouraged to send in general suggestions on any environmentally related subject, as well as competitions targeted at specific environmental issues. One suggestion regarding the procedures used by the airport fire service led to substantial reductions in CFC propellants associated with the use of fire retarding foam.

Environmental issues also pay a part in the airport's sponsorship activities. For example, money raised via paper recycling programmes and as fines imposed on airlines for aircraft which exceed the permitted noise levels, is used to sponsor activities including a wildlife ranger in the nearby Bollin River Valley, and a scheme to transplant orchids growing at the airport to local parks prior to the construction of a new terminal. £1 million is also allocated each year via grants to local householders in the immediate area of the airport to allow them to fit secondary sound-proofing insulation to their homes.

Among possible future developments on the environmental issue, the authors of "Waking up to a better environment" (see page 225) predict: "Insurance companies will be more thorough in their investigation before issuing cover. Other institutional investors will be more vigilant before subscribing funds. Customers and suppliers will seek evidence of a compatible code of conduct". Research has already identified a number of companies which are scrutinising their suppliers' green record with a view to ceasing business with those who do not meet specifications of environmental responsibility. The evidence suggest that investors, too, are becoming more conscious of environmental risk.

9.1 Pollution control

What are the key issues on a socially responsible company's green agenda? The CBI/PA survey discovered that companies perceived air pollution to be a high priority. The disposal of solid waste and effluent also featured as major issues for concern. So we start with these issues, all of which belong under the general heading of pollution prevention.

Case study: 3M

3M, a diversified manufacturing company which employs 88,000 people in 57 countries, was one of the first to implement an environmental programme. The UK subsidiary, which employs over 4800 people at 17 locations, started the successful Pollution Prevention Pays (3P) programme in 1977.

Up to 1990, the UK programme had saved the company over £8,042,000 with 104 projects. It has reduced air emissions by 5013 tonnes annually, solid waste by 2358 tonnes per year and water effluent by 34.3 million gallons per year. The savings are always calculated in the first year only of the projects, so the real figures are a lot higher than this. Worldwide, it is calculated that the 3P policy has saved the company over £537 million, from 3007 projects.

Explains Dr Richard Smith, environment, safety and security manager: "In 1975 we realised it was to our advantage to look at waste minimisation technology. We decided to improve existing processes."

In addition to 3M's global environmental policy, the UK company has its own vision and strategy. This includes a six point programme:

- to develop closer working relationships between its manufacturing, engineering, research and development, technical and marketing employees on environmental issues
- to develop less environmentally harmful products and processes that meet or anticipate the needs of the marketplace
- to develop internal awareness of 3M's environmental policies and build environmental responsibility into all aspects of 3M's UK operations

- to develop links with relevant governmental, industrial, professional, community and education groups, keeping them informed of 3M's environmental interests
- to work with suppliers and contractors to ensure that they provide products and services that do not transmit environmental problems to 3M or its customers
- to encourage and support employee initiatives that contribute to an improved environment at work, at home and in the local community.

The company has published a series of booklets which outline its activities in the environmental field. These include an environmental policy document, brochures introducing 3M's environmental policy to its customers, suppliers and other interested parties, and a "Guide to Environmental Policy Making and Implementation". The latter was produced in conjunction with the Environment Council's Business in the Environment Programme.

The "Guide to Environmental Policy Making and Implementation" aims to help steer companies through the process of deciding that they need a policy, designing an appropriate and workable plan, and implementing and auditing activities that are undertaken.

3M's most recent environmental publication, "Meeting the Environmental Challenge: 3M Policies in Action", describes 3M's philosophy, policies and programme in more detail, and particularly in relation to Europe. It outlines the goals that form the basis of "3P Plus", 3M's stringent expansion to the 3P environmental programme.

Since the announcement of 3P Plus, the company has gone even further, declaring its intention to reduce all hazardous and non-hazardous releases to air, land and water by 90%, and to reduce the generation of hazardous waste 50% by the year 2000.

In addition to its environmental goals, 3M has a corporate goal that 25% of income must be generated by products less than five years old. In order to achieve this, the company invests heavily in R&D; currently at a rate of over 6% of turnover. By preventing pollution at source wherever possible, products are brought to market with minimal environmental effects, and considerable financial resources that would otherwise have been spent on pollution control and waste disposal later in the product's life cycle are saved.

Checklist

1. Does your company have an environmental policy encompassing a wide range of issues?
2. Does it have a system to monitor each of these issues and alert it to new issues?
3. Is someone responsible for monitoring performance and reporting to the board and to shareholders?

9.1.1 Water pollution

The government is about to bring in stringent new environmental guidelines on water pollution. Self-regulation with the help of experts in the industry is better than imposed regulation. The water industry is at present engaged in a massive investment programme to improve the quality of Britain's bathing beaches. The oil industry, too, continues to invest considerable sums in marine research, helping to improve our knowledge base and so define appropriate environmental control strategies for the North Sea in particular.

However, all companies should be examining their effluent emissions. It not only makes economic sense to minimise this waste, it also shows environmental acumen.

What can you do? Among obvious steps:

- Any pollution programme must have the support of the board to succeed. This support should be enshrined in an environmental policy statement with specific reference to water pollution.
- Companies should maintain close contact with their water authority, which will be glad to give advice. Ideally, an organisation should ensure that it has regular contact with a relevant specialist at the authority. Frank discussions with a person you can trust can help resolve problems at an early stage.
- Make sure your company is monitoring effluent emissions and is up to date on current anti-pollution technology in your field.
- Ensure that the relevant staff are familiar with the nature of your discharge. Ensure that they are committed to any pollution prevention programme by informing them of its importance through training sessions, booklets and the company newsletter.
- Either employ a water pollution specialist or environmental expert, or assign the responsibility to an existing member of staff. Part of his or her task will be to keep up with current and proposed legislation and ensure that the company remains well within prescribed discharge limits. To be caught unawares, if stringent new regulations are enacted, could mean costly expenditure on new equipment, at short notice and at worst, large fines.

Case study: ICI and the North Sea

ICI is planning a multi-million pound investment to completely eliminate, by the mid 1990s, the disposal in the North Sea of chemical waste arising from its methyl methacrylate (MMA) manufacturing operations at Billingham on

Teesside. MMA is a key raw material, which is used to supply ICI's growing business in acrylic polymers, which in turn form the basis for products such as Perspex sheet for baths and shop signs.

Most of the expenditure will be on a sulphuric acid recovery plant to process the large volume of acidic ammonium sulphate effluent from the MMA operation. At the moment, this is shipped out and dumped in the North Sea under licence from the Ministry of Agriculture, Fisheries and Food.

Although extensive research over the past ten years by both government and ICI scientists continues to indicate that sea disposal does not significantly harm marine life, ICI has decided to stop its river and sea programme entirely, on the grounds that public concern is an important consideration in its own right.

The decision has been taken within ICI's overall corporate commitment to improving the environmental performance of its plants. The new investment will secure the existing MMA operation at Billingham for the foreseeable future.

Case study: ICI, Teesside

"Over the centuries, the Tees estuary has been a focal point for tens of thousands of migrating birds. In more recent times, it has become a Mecca for a number of international industries and the birthplace of ICI, one of the world's leading chemical companies. The river itself became a victim of industrial success and was becoming one of the most polluted stretches in the world by the 1960s," says David Bellamy in a booklet "The Tees: The Living River".

Now ICI and all the large companies which use the river are cleaning up their act. ICI has assigned laboratory facilities to monitor effluents and staff to investigate ways of reducing pollution.

Discharges have been reduced fourfold so far. This is reflected in an increase in species found by ICI's Brixham laboratory, from 33 to 81 since 1978. ICI has achieved the reduction in effluent discharge by measures such as installing a new £6 million ammonium sulphate plant, which converts waste into low grade fertiliser.

Case study: J. Sainsbury

Sainsbury's Greencare range of household cleaning products has been formulated with the environment in mind. The seven products are free from additives that cause pollution and are formulated whenever possible from vegetable-based ingredients that are renewable and biodegradable. None of the products has been tested on animals.

Sainsbury's was the first UK supermarket to stock products from Ecover, the company that specialises in environmentally friendly cleaning products.

9.1.2 Air pollution

Wise manufacturing companies, recognising the trend towards tighter and tighter air pollution controls at both national and supranational levels, are taking early preventive action.

Precedent has already been set by the CFC issue, which highlighted the importance of monitoring and controlling dangerous atmospheric emissions. Some companies predicted the problems and acted quickly to get rid of CFCs in their manufacturing process. These later had the advantage of being able to claim that they had been in the vanguard of any environmental movement. Moreover, as public interest and media attention in the issue increased and the government started to look at the problem, these companies did not lose sales and could claim to be greener than slower-moving competitors.

So what can concerned organisations do to improve their clean air image? The CBI suggests that companies should:

- monitor and audit air emissions. This can help improve profit margins and will provide factual data to tackle complaints
- keep abreast of changing technologies. Timing change for the most opportune time can save costs and avoid unnecessary disruption of production
- look out for environmental pressure and legislative change. Early signals can help influence decisions or help you prepare for the change
- record all wastes, the improvements achieved and the responsibilities of company personnel.

However, companies have to make sure that they get their research right. After all, it would defeat the object if a company introduced an alternative chemical which was later found also to be environmentally unsound.

Companies that don't cause atmospheric pollutants directly can still benefit from an environmental audit that focuses on these areas. They can, for example, ensure that the products they buy or stock are themselves produced by environmentally friendly processes. They can, for example, ensure that the polystyrene cups they buy for coffee machines are not made with processes that use CFCs. They can also keep abreast of new developments on the use of "greenhouse gases" in fire extinguishers and other products.

Case study: 3M

Central to 3M's latest comprehensive pollution prevention programme, 3P Plus, is a £150 million investment in air pollution control equipment to reduce the company's annual worldwide solvent emissions by more than 55,000 tonnes. The ultimate goal of the programme is an 80% reduction of all 3M manufacturing air emissions by 1993.

In addition to the introduction of air pollution control equipment, 3M has accelerated scientific research to eliminate sources of pollution in its manufacturing processes and to place greater emphasis on recovery and recycling of waste materials. Pollution prevention requires the manufacturing process to be scrutinised. It also necessitates a close examination of the formulation of 3M products. 3M's goal of removing all volatile fully halogenated chlorofluorocarbons (CFCs) from 3M products and processes by the end of 1990 was achieved with only a few exceptions. These were notably health care products, for which an alternative date for elimination has been set.

Dr Richard Smith, environmental, safety and security manager, says of 3P Plus: ''There are four key points to emphasise. Firstly, the effort is entirely voluntary. Secondly, the reductions are beyond any necessary to ensure regulatory compliance. Thirdly, there is little or no economic benefit to 3M; and fourthly, it reflects 3M's commitment to improving the environment.''

Of the total 3P Plus investment in air pollution control equipment, most will be spent in the US. There, 3M has 90 plants in 40 states, many of them built in the early twentieth century.

The results of 3M's drive to develop new technologies to reduce or eliminate pollution at source are already making themselves felt.

For example, traditional methods of making adhesive paper used chemical solvents, which emitted toxic substances into the atmosphere as they passed through the drying chamber. 3M developed a water-based solvent for the coating process, and this was then applied in the manufacture of abrasive paper, with substantial reductions in air pollution. Another relevant technology, a hot-melt process used to apply adhesive to abrasive discs, replaced the traditional process where adhesive was applied from a solution containing a volatile, toxic hydrocarbon solvent. This could not be recovered because of the large air dilution of the exhaust system and eventually escaped into the atmosphere. Installation of the hot-melt process has resulted in savings of £150,000 a year, while reducing the amount of solvent released into the atmosphere by over 75 tonnes. This hot-melt process has now been extended to water-based treatments following the installation of a curing oven.

Case study: LINPAC Plastics International

LINPAC Plastics International, one of Europe's biggest producers of expanded polystyrene, had been entirely dependent on CFCs until late 1988. According to the Industrial Society magazine in December 1989, it cost LINPAC a six-figure sum, a total rearrangement of 30,000 square feet of factory space and the re-training of 360 staff to stop using the ozone depletant.

The move followed intergovernmental discussions in early 1987. These proposed a 50% reduction by 1997 of CFC 11/12, which LINPAC used as a blowing agent for trays and boxes, and an eventual total ban on the substances.

Although packaging companies which used CFCs as a blowing agent only took up 2% of the world's CFC use, this 2% is still important. LINPAC literature states: "If the packaging industry... uses CFCs of any grade, it is most definitely contributing to ozone depletion and the greenhouse effect."

Some companies replaced CFCs with HCFC materials, which are similar to CFCs, but have much lower ozone depletion potential. LINPAC felt this was not enough. Managing director Peter O'Shea and his researchers looked at alternative blowing agents and settled on pentane, a hydrocarbon that the company had stopped using in 1987. Pentane was chosen because it did not harm the ozone layer, is not a greenhouse gas and breaks down rapidly at low atmospheric levels. Pentane is a low-level pollutant, but according to LINPAC "the environmental impact of expanded polystyrene production is regarded by experts as infinitesimally small compared to other sources such as emissions from motor vehicles. The switch to pentane had no significant impact on product performance."

By March 1989 – way ahead of any international directives and before most companies had even thought about changing their processes to tackle the problem – LINPAC was able to stamp its meat trays, fast food boxes and egg boxes with the slogan "CFC FREE".

Case study: Friends of the Earth

Friends of the Earth (FOE) took a leading role in the global campaign to force manufacturers to reduce their use of ozone-depleting chemicals. The pressure group compiled a list of all companies known to be using CFCs and announced that it intended to make the list public. FOE claims that the threat made seven aerosol manufacturers agree to look for alternatives.

As part of the campaign, the group also organised an influential international conference on ozone depletion, attended by some of the world's leading scientists, in November 1988. This was followed by the launch of a campaign against the use of CFCs in the construction industry with the publication of the reports "Safe as Houses" and "Uses of CFCs in Buildings". These reports were welcomed by the Royal Institute of British Architects and others within the industry. The pressure group was also influential in the development of environmental policing.

Pippa Hyam, FOE's senior information officer, explains that although the campaign had been highly successful, the organisation's next goal is for aerosols to be banned altogether: "Aerosols are energy-intensive and you can't throw them away. Alternative propellants also damage the atmosphere, albeit to a lesser extent."

Friends of the Earth succeeded in keeping the issue of ozone depletion firmly in the public eye throughout 1990 and 1991 by exposing green cons and false labelling of ozone-damaging products. In the face of what it sees as a failure of the government's voluntary approach, Friends of the Earth continues to press for tough legislative action to phase out industrial use of ozone-destroying chemicals.

Case study: 3M

Programmes introduced with the intention of reducing or preventing pollution can be both simple and inexpensive to implement. For example, at 3M's Gorseinon-based magnetic media plant, a quantity of "special" waste is produced during the video tape manufacturing process. This includes mop heads, rags, pressurised aerosol cans, other waste with a high concentration of flammable material as well as a considerable quantity of volatile solvents. The "special", unstable waste was previously contained in drums, and could only be disposed of by incineration.

An economic and straightforward engineering solution was developed by the warehouse manager, working with 3M's waste disposal engineer and a waste disposal contractor. Within each production area, solid wastes are suspended on a well-ventilated grille over a drum and are drained until they are completely dry. They are then landfilled in polybags. Solvents are sent for recovery to a specialist company. The cost of the drum grid and stand systems came to less than £500, and the benefits are significant. Non-pulpable waste from the plant has been reduced by 75%, 15 tonnes of solid waste pollution will be prevented annually and there will be a £100,000 annual saving in the disposal of special waste.

Case study: Iceland Frozen Foods

Iceland has won a number of awards for its CFC initiatives. Whenever a customer buys a new refrigerator from Iceland, the company collects the old model free of charge and ensures that the harmful gases are removed safely. A portable CFC recovery unit has also been developed by Iceland engineers to ensure that CFC gas does not escape while carrying out domestic repair work.

Most of the new models Iceland sells have only half the volume of CFCs of those they replace. All of its new cold stores, with the exception of one chamber at Deeside which uses ammonia, operate on R22, which it describes as "the most ozone-friendly gas currently available for commercial use".

Case study: J. Sainsbury

All Sainsbury's cold stores in distribution depots use HFC22 and since November 1989 all new and refurbished supermarkets use HFC22 as their only refrigerant. HFC22 is not controlled by the Montreal Protocol, which sets guidelines for CFC use. It has only 5% of the ozone depletion potential of commonly used refrigerants such as CFC12. Even so, the company is working with chemical manufacturers to develop alternative refrigerants, which will be totally ozone friendly.

In the meantime, Sainsbury uses electronic leak detection as part of its store maintenance regime. The new Streatham Common supermarket has a unique coolant gas detection system, which automatically alerts both staff and the maintenance contractor if a leak should occur.

Sainsbury is also encouraging suppliers to conduct tests on CFC-free, blown-foam insulation materials for display cabinets and cold stores. When freezer equipment is disposed of, all existing refrigerants are decanted and returned to storage depots for reuse. This nationwide recycling service, established by Sainsbury with seven major refrigeration contractors, is believed to be the first of its kind.

Case study: IBM UK

IBM UK uses CFCs at its manufacturing sites as a cleaning solvent. According to an article in *Personnel Management* in April 1990, it has now set out to reduce its use of CFCs to 20% of its 1986 level by the end of 1992 – well in advance of the Montreal Protocol. IBM has also stopped using polystyrene cups and packaging, which use CFCs in their manufacture. It no longer uses any CFC-based aerosols.

9.1.2.1 Towards pollution-free travel

Every company can make a significant contribution to reducing air pollution by establishing environmentally aware travel policies. For example, car fleets, even of just two or three vehicles, can be converted to lead-free petrol either immediately, if new, or when replaced. Enforcing this policy has cost benefits to the company, because lead-free petrol is cheaper.

Many company cars are also fitted with catalytic converters, which are designed to cut down on harmful emissions to an even greater extent. However, this will normally involve an investment, from which there is no direct payback, other than a recognition, from employees and customers, that the company is serious in its commitment to environmental issues.

Companies can also help reduce the volume of vehicles on the road by introducing car-sharing schemes or by subsidising employees' use of public transport. In many cases, this provides a useful additional recruitment incentive.

Oxford City Council has introduced bicycles for staff to use within the city, which has good cycle lanes and cycle filters at traffic lights. It only issues cars to staff, such as engineers, who need them to transport heavy equipment.

The London Borough of Sutton pays its staff the same mileage for bike and car use.

9.1.3 Solid waste management

The disposal of industrial waste threatens to become the major environmental issue of the 1990s in Britain. As landfill capacity shrinks, less suitable sites are being proposed and opposed; housing pressures, particularly in the South-East, are forcing the examination of old landfill sites, many of which are being rejected for building, either because of dangerous build-up of methane, or because they contain toxic residues. Control over what companies can dump is likely to increase significantly during the next decade, forcing them to re-evaluate what waste products they produce and whether they could better invest resources in prevention, or recycling.

How can a company improve its waste management record? It can:

- encourage employees' suggestions for improvements
- look for opportunities to turn 'waste' into profitable by-products or recycle these materials
- monitor performance and make sure it is abreast of current technology
- employ an environment specialist to advise on waste disposal, possible future legislation and to maintain contact with appropriate trade associations – or seek help from its trade association, the CBI or qualified consultants
- publicise its environmental-improvement activities in the local media and among its staff.

Other ideas include:

- pre-treating waste, to make it easier, safer, cheaper to get rid of or useful to another business
- thinking carefully about waste mixing – are you putting recyclable materials in with waste destined for landfill?
- refining your production process so that there is less waste to dispose of.

Every aspect of company operations should be reviewed systematically. The CBI suggests organisations should look closely at:

- research and development
- planning of product or output
- design of manufacturing
- design of residuals
- design of waste handling facility to produce new resources from old residues
- design of the system as a whole to avoid waste.

In addition, manufacturing companies should also bear in mind that sooner or later plant will be shut down or they may want to move on. Now is the time to identify likely future problems from, for example, seepage of poisonous residues into the ground. The asset value of the site will be greatly reduced if it is contaminated.

A gradual clean-up over a period of several years of rebuilding will often be more cost-effective than tackling the whole site at a later date. As the principle "Polluter pays" becomes increasingly applied, companies with this problem are likely to have no option but to clean up any sites which they intend to dispose of or rebuild on.

Even office-based organisations can have a socially responsible waste management scheme. Employees can put all recyclable material such as paper and plastic into separate bins. To ensure that the collected rubbish does go to a recycling scheme, you can either allocate somebody within the company to be in charge of organising collection, or you can let your cleaning contractors take the materials to recycling points. Paper companies often pay for used paper in bulk, so the company need not incur additional cost.

Case study: Recycling City

The Recycling City initiative demonstrated how reclamation industries, central and local government, the voluntary sector and other companies can form a successful recycling scheme.

A Friends of the Earth initiative, Recycling City was set up in Sheffield in the late 1980s. The paper industry provided some of the paper banks, which are located around the city and agreed to operate on a fixed price and guaranteed market.

Previously, price fluctuations arising from instability in the paper market had meant local authorities often could not predict whether the income from collection would cover the costs.

The glass industry already had over 50 bottle banks in Sheffield, but it agreed to supply as many more as were required. It also agreed to buy all glass collected at a fixed price for the three years of the scheme.

Save a Can sited five containers on the edge of the city, while cans collected within the city were extracted from general rubbish by magnets at the city incinerator. The Aluminium Can Recycling Association provided promotional materials and assistance for schools and for voluntary sector collections. It offered target incentives such as bar magnets and hand-operated crushers in addition to prizes for the highest per capita collection ratio. Both organisations have guaranteed a market price for materials reclaimed.

For the first time in the UK, the plastics industry committed itself to reclaiming from domestic refuse. The British Soft Drinks Association has provided 20 containers for the collection of transparent soft drinks bottles.

The British Plastics Federation installed five containers at civic amenity sites for heavy duty, opaque or coloured bottles. Support from the plastics industry was of major importance in the development of a comprehensive recycling strategy.

The oil industry worked with the council on a scheme which included siting oil recovery points in garages and local authority rubbish dumps.

Many voluntary groups were already running recycling schemes to raise money. These banded together to form the administrative unit SCRAP (Sheffield Community Recycling Action Programme).

A grant from UK 2000 provided funds for a development worker to work for SCRAP for a year. After this the voluntary sector hoped to fund the post. The council also created the post of recycling officer to help co-ordinate the project.

A community enterprise set up weekly door-to-door collections to pick up recyclable waste from 10,000 households. The business then sold the collected glass, plastic, rags and paper. This operation, based on schemes in Germany and Canada, was the first of its kind in the UK. It aimed to recycle as much as possible by going to people such as the housebound elderly, who found it difficult to get to the fixed point containers.

Recycling City admits that, "Looked at in the narrowest terms, these rounds are barely economically viable. The amount of income received from collected materials hardly covers running costs and insufficient income is generated to invest in better vehicles, good publicity, and so on". But, explains Pippa Hyam of Friends of the Earth: "The collection rounds should be viewed in a much wider context than this narrow profit and loss definition. It costs disposal authorities a great deal of money to dump their waste. With the ever-increasing pressure on landfill sites these costs will only increase. Each tonne of waste recycled means that the authorities will have less to deal with and this will reduce their costs."

Dr Geoffrey Levy of Anglo-French packaging firm CMB is a representative at the newly formed European Recovery and Recycling Association (ERRA). He points out the importance of the pressure group's efforts: "We have nothing but praise for Friends of the Earth and the Recycling City initiative. They set up the project on a minimum amount of money and although it encountered a lot of problems, other projects can learn from their mistakes. ERRA is already sponsoring kerbside collection schemes in Sheffield and will be setting up its own pilot projects. It is the only way forward for the packaging industry."

Case study: Tesco plc

Supermarket chain Tesco's is well known for its concern about the environment. Its commitment to recycling waste includes a published packaging policy which states that the company aims:

- to use as little packaging as possible consistent with the provision of safe undamaged products
- to use packaging which helps extend shelf life, offering added customer convenience
- to give preference to the use of materials which include recycled materials in their manufacture wherever possible
- to give preference to the use of materials which are recyclable
- to promote recycling through the provision of recycling centres, clear product labelling and in-store information.

Case study: LINPAC Plastics

Packaging manufacturers are not unnaturally sensitive to environmental criticism. LINPAC adopted a relatively stringent global environmental policy in mid-1991, to include environmental and energy auditing, encouragement to suppliers to be environmentally responsible and elimination of CFCs from production processes. An environmental manager reports directly to the board.

The most obvious practical demonstration of LINPAC's commitment, however, has been a major investment in a 2500 tonne/year polystyrene plant. Recycled plastic waste from homes and restaurants will be used to make egg cartons and other food containers.

Case study: Allied Colloids

Allied Colloids found it could minimise waste and save money at the same time.

The company supplies speciality chemicals to a wide range of industries. It produces liquid dispersion polymers, but the waste from this process when mixed with water forms a viscous sludge that is difficult to treat and dispose of.

In 1984, the company installed a settlement tank to extract the waste liquid, polymers and white spirit solvent before they became exposed to large amounts of waste water. The waste polymer and solvents are skimmed off and distilled. The five tonnes of white spirit annually recovered is reused. And the remaining polymer waste can be landfilled for £100 per tonne, as against the £500 per tonne it previously cost to dispose of both together. Moreover, as the waste polymer has been recovered before it absorbs too much water, the volume for disposal has been reduced from 20 tonnes to 10 tonnes per week.

The scheme has some major advantages. As well as reducing the amount of chemical that is sent to landfill, weekly disposal costs have been reduced from £10,000 to £1000 and an additional saving of £1000 a week is made on buying white spirit. The recovery plant, which cost about £25,000, is operated and maintained by one employee. And the payback period on the investment was less than three weeks.

Case study: Dow Chemicals

Dow Chemicals produces latex, agricultural chemicals and insulation materials at its 300-employee King's Lynn plant.

The corporate waste minimisation policy, "Waste reduction always pays" (WRAP), has as its objectives to reduce waste, provide recognition for excellent performance in waste reduction, re-emphasise the need for continuous improvement and reduce long-term waste management costs.

As part of the programme, Dow has made process modifications on its latex plants. Water hoses have been fitted with restriction nozzles to reduce the amount of water used. Water contaminated with latex is recycled. Water-cooled vacuum pumps have been replaced with double-sealed pumps, which eliminate the need for cooling water. A belt press dewatering unit has also been installed.

These modifications have led to a reduction in aqueous effluents and a 90% reduction in sludge sent to landfill. Disposal costs have been cut by approximately 70%.

Case study: 3M

A closer look at the production process can highlight opportunities to reduce or prevent pollution with little or no change in the way products are made.

One example is in the production of the chemical FTHQ (fluorotetrahydro quinaline) which is used to produce an antibacterial pharmaceutical product marketed by 3M Health Care, based in Loughborough.

FTHQ is manufactured in two stages, the first involving the production of a wet powder, and the second resulting in the finished chemical. This chemical is then dispatched to 3M's plant in Pithiviers, France, for conversion into the finished pharmaceutical product.

The product method used in the first stage generated volatile impurities, which were then removed by drying the wet powder. It was during this process that residual solvents were emitted, requiring disposal by incineration, and resulting in emissions to the atmosphere.

After a close examination of the production process, it was slightly modified. As a result, fewer impurities are now generated in the first stage product, allowing wet powder to be used in the second production stage. Residual solvents are now recovered by the preferred method of distillation. As a result of the introduction of this modified manufacturing process, 17.6 tonnes of pollution are now prevented every year, with an annual saving of £32,000 in disposal costs.

Regular reviews are carried out of the packaging requirements for all 3M products manufactured in the UK. At the same time, the environmental impact of packaging materials is assessed. Scotch video sleeves were made of an aluminium foil laminate on cardboard, and contained a set of adhesive labels that could be used by the customer to identify the video. A review of video packaging in 1987 suggested that improvements could be made that would reduce costs and, ultimately, waste.

As a result of the review, a pollution prevention team was set up headed by Peter Copsey – purchasing manager – who worked with marketing staff and engineering and production staff to create a solution.

After a period of close consultation with customers and 3M marketing specialists, the cardboard used to make the sleeve was reduced in thickness from 750 to 610 micron. The foil laminate was removed altogether. During 1987-90, the labels included in video packaging were reduced to one-third of their original size.

These changes reduced the amount of material used, and allowed a less-expensive material to be selected for video packaging. Smaller labels do not need to be folded, reducing costs further.

The benefits of the initiative include:

- 120 tonnes of solid waste pollution prevented annually
- £165,000 annual saving in packaging costs
- Quality of packaging has been maintained.

Case study: The Body Shop

The Body Shop operates a major recycling programme, Project Paperchase. All white and lightly coloured paper is segregated for collection by paper merchants for recycling. According to the company, this is not only environmentally responsible but raises awareness among staff and shows them the importance of individual effort. The company hopes they will become aware of implementing recycling at home.

The Body Shop is extending its direct link distribution from the warehouse to the shops for recovering certain plastic containers and cardboard boxes for reuse and recycling.

In the meantime, a number of shops in the chain have made arrangements with local charities, schools and playgroups, who will collect cardboard boxes. Metal drums, used for transporting toiletries and cosmetics, are crushed and sent for recycling; large plastic drums are sluiced out and re-used. Smaller drums are often sold to fishermen for floats.

A recycling port for newspapers and aluminium is being set up at the organisation's warehouse, for use by the local community and staff. Body Shop only uses recycled paper for note pads, reusable sticky labels, photocopying paper, fax and even lavatory paper. The company is currently trying to source recycled computer paper.

Although only 2% of customers bring in their empty bottles for refilling, the Body Shop still operates its long-standing refill policy.

The Body Shop has worked closely with Friends of the Earth since 1987 to raise public awareness on issues such as recycling waste as well as acid rain and ozone depletion. Jonathan Porritt, former director of the environmental pressure group, said: "Our link with the Body Shop has given us a shop window on the High Street."

Checklist

1. Does your company know all the waste products it produces, in what amounts?
2. Does it have a formal system for identifying both potential and actual environmental impact?
3. Does it have a green purchasing policy – and does it implement it strictly?
4. Does it actively seek ways to reduce both toxicity and volume of waste products? Does it perceive this activity as a source of cost saving rather than a drain on resources?
5. Does it actively involve employees in monitoring environmental issues and suggesting improvements?

6. Does it have effective plans to minimise the damage from accidents?
7. Is it using the latest pollution-prevention technology wherever possible? Does it have a programme to develop its own technology?

9.2 Energy conservation

"Global warming is a real threat. Therefore the time to do something is now." The speaker is not a politician, nor a member of an environmental pressure group but Chris Hampson, executive director of Imperial Chemical Industries (ICI). Speaking in October 1989 at the Watt Committee on Energy, Hampson pointed out that analysis has shown that carbon dioxide in the atmosphere accounts for 50-60% of the greenhouse effect. Within this total, burning of fossil fuels such as coal, oil and gas, accounts for 40-45%.

So, explains Hampson, energy conservation is seven times more effective at reducing the major problem of CO_2 emissions than other supply options. Moreover, it is known to work.

He cites the figures:

"In 21 countries belonging to the International Energy Agency, economic output grew on average by 32% between 1973 and 1986, and yet energy demand rose by just 5%. In the US, which consumes a quarter of the world's fuels, the annual demand for energy is still below that of 1973 even though the country's GDP is up by 40%. Similar figures are available for Japan."

He suggests three routes to follow:

1. Improved fuel and energy conservation in new or existing power generation facilities
2. More general energy-saving programmes for public electricity consumption
3. Specific energy-conservation projects in the major power–consuming industries.

He rounds off: "Energy conservation is not the only way to resolve the environmental issues around energy generation and use, but it is something that we can practise now and where the effects can be predicted with confidence."

The Association for the Conservation of Energy concurs, listing three important sectors where attention to detail could have an effect:

- commercial lighting
- industrial motors
- domestic refrigerators/freezers.

These three sectors account for more than 42% of total electricity used. In lighting alone, which accounts for 15% of total energy at a cost of £1.6 billion a year, energy consumption could be halved by new technologies such as high frequency lamps and occupancy sensors.

The government also recognises the problem and has been running a campaign since 1983 through its Energy Efficiency Office. Its target is to reduce energy consumption by 20% from current levels.

Energy costs also have a direct bearing on bottom-line profitability. So what can a company do to ensure it is cutting back on fuel consumption (and bills)? Among the options are:

1. Conduct an energy audit
2. Install low-energy lighting on timers
3. Use energy more than once – for example, refrigerators use a lot of energy, but they also give off heat. Can this be used to heat the plant/shop/office?
4. Install occupancy sensors
5. Educate the workforce – publish posters and leaflets explaining why energy conservation is important.

Case study: Wessex Water

Wessex Water's Avonmouth works produces methane gas from sewage sludge in sufficient quantity to heat and power the treatment works. This is a considerable achievement since energy is a substantial part of the company's operating costs. The scheme is so successful that any surplus electricity generated is sold to the local electricity board.

During 1988-89, the works won a South West Electricity Board Gold Award for its economic use of energy in relation to sludge disposal.

Case study: ICI

"ICI generates an eighth of the British private energy supply and our energy bill is about the same as we spend on salaries and wages," confides executive director Chris Hampson.

The UK chemical industry is the third biggest consumer of industrial energy users, yet it represents only 10% of the manufacturing output of the UK. So ICI is under considerable pressure to work towards energy conservation.

In 1983, ICI Fertilisers decided to replace its two oldest plants at Severnside in Bristol. ICI built a new, smaller plant that could match the output and energy efficiency of its best capacity plants. The new plant, which used new technology based on advanced engineering and modern distributed control systems, required only half the amount of steel for its construction. It also achieves a reduction of 60% CO_2 and 75% reduction of ammonia in liquid effluent compared with conventional ammonia plants.

Another example is the production of chlorine, a basic building block in today's chemical industry. In the 1970s, the most widely used process for electrolysis of brine to make chlorine was the mercury cell. This is highly energy intensive and the mercury is recognised as an environmental hazard.

ICI explored alternative technologies and came up with a non-mercury membrane electrolyser, the FM21 cell. This is available from ICI on licence and has now been introduced into more than 20 plants throughout the world. Its power requirement is over 20% lower per tonne than the mercury cell.

The company is also looking at building a combined heat and power plant, based on natural gas at Teesside. The plant would provide energy for ICI's own use and the remainder would be sold to the UK market.

The waste heat would supply the total steam requirements of the complex, replacing the present coal-fired facilities.

Case study: J. Sainsbury

Sainsbury's began its energy-saving programme in earnest in 1974 and has since won a number of awards for energy efficiency. For example, a new store near Guildford won the Electricity Council's 1989 Beta award.

The store uses recycled heat from refrigeration plants. Use of such new technology, combined with radical changes in lighting, environmental control and refrigeration has meant that Sainsbury's supermarkets use only 60% of the energy that they would have ten years ago.

Checklist

1. Does your company monitor energy usage in its buildings and equipment?
2. Does it have an active programme of energy saving?
3. Does it encourage employees to save energy, e.g. through car-pooling?
4. Does it take energy-saving factors into account when building/buying new plants/premises?

9.3 Urban renewal

Environmental improvement is an issue that many companies have tackled. They have set about solving the problem of rundown inner-city areas, urban degeneration and conservation in a variety of ways, but most commonly by forming partnerships to tackle the problem. The first partnership was in Calderdale and had the firm backing of HRH The Prince of Wales, who has been in support of the idea from the outset.

The partnership, backed by Business in the Community, brought together a focus group from the public and private sectors, to pursue practical projects ranging from environmental improvements through to business expansion, educational experiments, and a major industrial development.

This started the trend for a series of business partnership initiatives in areas such as Newcastle, Bristol, Nottingham and Teesside.

Enterprise agencies have also been instrumental in developing urban renewal programmes.

Companies which do not want to join a large partnership arrangement can always set up their own projects for improving their surroundings. Some companies put money into local conservation projects or give regular sums to the National Trust or other conservation organisations.

Other companies try to site their new buildings on derelict or rundown land, landscaping and planting trees in the area at the same time as building. A construction company has encouraged urban renewal by lending its expertise to help people build themselves a new home and a new life in the inner city.

Every organisation can find a way of improving the environment for the community. It is an obvious and highly visual way of enhancing its reputation with the general public.

Case study: J. Sainsbury

Over half of Sainsbury's stores built since 1986 have used derelict or rundown urban sites. Sainsbury's also chooses sites which are unsuited to other types of development, because they are close to motorways or railways.

The company believes in a comprehensive approach to landscape design that recognises the obligation of a new development to its local environment.

To this end it employs some of the country's leading landscape architects and supports each scheme with a long-term aftercare programme or regular maintenance.

Wherever possible, the company uses existing trees, bushes and shrubs to provide scale and shelter. It also mass-plants young trees and shrubs as well as semi-mature trees.

The company supports green belt policy and will not seek planning permission on green belt land. In rural sites, it has given land to nature conservancy and it has also retained local wildlife and habitat where possible.

In some developments, tree surgeons, employed by the company, have moved existing trees using modern technology and successfully kept them alive and healthy.

Case study: British Telecom

After flotation, British Telecom undertook a major internal study on the role of the company within the context of inner cities. As they became aware of the severity of rising unemployment, a decline in manufacturing capacity and depressed housing conditions, the board members decided to create a community action budget to tackle the issues.

During 1989 and 1990 British Telecom provided financial support for more than 90 projects. These fell into three categories:

- Resources for training schemes for the long-term unemployed, women returners, and disabled people. In many cases BT provided the start up costs for training schemes and the government or the Training Agency met the day-to-day expenditure.
- Enterprise training and the provision of small workspaces for new businesses. Working with inner-city task forces or voluntary agencies, BT has provided capital to convert disused buildings into enterprise centres where young people have a base to start commercial activities. An integral part of these centres is enterprise training sessions. Youngsters are trained in marketing, accounting and other related subjects. BT supports inner-city projects to reclaim industrial wasteland and peripheral housing estates. It also works with social workers and youth organisations to set up community improvement schemes in these areas.
- Social welfare programmes. In some areas, BT gives a grant to help community development; in others it funds a community worker. It particularly favours community computer centres, where local people develop community services and acquire basic computer skills. The company has also provided practical support in developing leadership teams in major provincial cities. The teams work with local authorities and government departments to develop economic policies by attracting inward investment and acting as catalysts for development and construction.

The criteria for making grants are under constant review so that they reflect the changing economic position and demands of society. In almost every case, British Telecom acts alongside other organisations, such as Business in the Community, and in some cases with other companies. It recognises that the long-term solution to our inner-city problems cannot be solved by any one agency but only through partnerships.

Checklist

1. Do you support:
   local/national nature conservation groups?
   partnership agreements for urban regeneration?
2. When considering a new site, are environmental/landscaping issues a factor?

3. Do you have a policy against green belt planning applications?
4. Could you band together with several local companies and other agencies to set up an environmental improvement scheme for your area?

9.4 Environmental management

For obvious reasons, companies leading the field in environmental awareness tend to come from the manufacturing or primary industry sectors, although the proportion of service company organisations with active involvement is steadily rising. The key in either sector is to have a coherent environmental policy. Manufacturing companies which wish to improve their environmental performance should ensure that they:

- employ an environmental expert
- set up a department responsible for environmental issues
- join relevant trade organisations
- ensure the firm backing of the board and senior management
- issue a short environmental mission statement – operating companies and subsidiaries will formulate their own based on it
- update equipment with the best available environmental technology. Companies that design their own equipment should introduce environmental criteria to the design process
- issue a newsletter to employees informing them of the company's commitment and raise their awareness of the issue; offer awards for any environmental improvements they may suggest.

Other businesses can:
- formulate a brief environment policy statement to show commitment to staff, shareholders and the general public
- allocate a member of staff to be responsible for general environmental matters
- set up staff award schemes for new environmentally friendly ideas
- only use recycled paper
- use environmentally friendly cleaning agents
- ensure that all new products bought for the business have the best available environmental technology

– publicise the company's efforts in the annual report/company magazine.

A boost to environmental management processes should be provided by the recently launched BS5750. The British Standard for Environmental Management Systems sets out a "systematic and integrated approach to environmental management and ... is strongly linked to existing quality management practice". The new standard is compatible with proposed European legislation on environmental auditing.

Case study: 3M

John Elkington, author of *The Green Consumer Guide*, is unequivocal about 3M's environmental performance: "Without a shadow of doubt, the most impressive environmental success story has starred 3M."

The reason for its outstanding success (and the disproportionate mention in this book) is that the programme has the firm backing of senior management. Chairman of the environment council is Dr Peter Fleming. The council includes three directors. Formed in late 1989 it meets every six weeks and enables senior managers from public relations, research, marketing, distribution, engineering and manufacturing departments as well as the health care division to monitor environmental issues. The council sets quantitative targets, monitors progress, establishes responsibility and identifies areas for action. Line managers then have responsibility for working out detailed action plans and reporting on progress.

The 3M environment council is unique in the UK. It creates a forum for focusing attention on environmental issues and stimulates a climate in which these issues can be positively addressed.

All employees can win a Bond of Excellence award for ideas, effort or outstanding service. Staff are awarded with a "bond" which is equivalent in value to one share.

For example, the secretary who introduced "green bins" into the Bracknell offices early in 1990 has received this recognition. The bins only contain recyclable paper and the "green" bags are picked up separately by the refuse collectors.

As consumer pressure intensified, 3M brought in an extension of the 3P programme in 1988. Says Smith: "This project is called 3P Plus and places more emphasis on environmental benefits than on cost of saving. Originally, environmental projects had to stand alone and pay for themselves. Under the extended initiative, the projects have to make some saving, but cost saving is not the prime purpose."

Case study: B&Q

B&Q's board has appointed an environmental co-ordinator to supervise the development of environmental policy and the implementation of environmental action plans. The co-ordinator is supported by specialist environmental consultants and by an Environmental Action Unit, made up of senior managers from a variety of departments across the company.

The environmental co-ordinator makes a monthly, hour-long presentation to the board, concentrating on three key areas:

- the day-to-day running of the business
- the product range in general
- key issues, such as peat or timber.

To enforce its policy, B&Q carries out environmental audits of its own operations and requires its suppliers to do the same.

The company involves its employees in the programme through articles in the company newspaper, through a Green Bright Ideas suggestion scheme and an Environment Week in June. The Environment Week is supported by a manual and video distributed to employees.

Supplier environmental audits
B&Q introduced its policy to suppliers at a conference attended by 200 of them in December 1991. All suppliers now have to create and implement an environmental policy supported by a thorough environmental audit.

Suppliers' performance is assessed through:
- a comprehensive 40-page questionnaire
- telephone interviews and site visits
- independent audits where necessary.

To help suppliers comply, B&Q has produced a detailed manual and made available assistance from a team of environmental experts

Case study: British Telecom

Like other big companies, BT uses vast amounts of materials, from paper to batteries, all of which have an implication for the environment.

BT has produced a statement of its commitment to ensure that its operations are environmentally friendly. Those commitments include active support for waste recycling and energy saving initiatives, and for using materials which are less damaging to the environment.

BT is making sure that the products and services it buys are manufactured, used and disposed of in an environmentally friendly way.

It is phasing out the use of CFCs and has cut harmful vehicle emissions by switching to unleaded petrol with plans to change to a mostly diesel fleet. It is also actively supporting a number of ''green projects'' and organisations to support the improvement of the overall national environment.

It is unique in having an Environment Liaison Panel which the company consults on all environmental issues. The advisory panel is chaired by consultant Pat Delbridge.

One particular BT success is a pioneering scheme to recycle the batteries used by BT in payphones, testers, engineers' hand-drills and other operational equipment. It is expected to save 160,000 of them a year from being dumped. BT has drawn up an arrangement with the manufacturer,

Varta, under which the nickel-cadmium batteries are shipped back to Germany for recycling.

Lead acid batteries used in telephone exchanges are also being recycled by a specialist company and BT has for a long time been sending old vehicle batteries back to their makers.

In only one area is BT engaged in any major controversy – that is over telephone directories. The cause is the glue. Waste-paper mills don't want the directories because the glue contaminates the pulped paper, although there are other outlets for old directories, such as bedding for animals. But BT is working on the problem so that directories can be disposed of easily along with other paper waste.

And BT will produce three million directories over the next year on recycled paper in an ongoing trial.

The BT environmental commitment:

BT will
- Meet and, where appropriate, exceed the requirements of all relevant legislation – where no regulations exist, we shall set our own exacting standards
- Promote recycling and the use of recycled materials, while reducing consumption of materials wherever possible
- Design energy efficiency into new services, buildings and products and manage energy wisely in all directions
- Reduce wherever practicable the level of harmful emissions
- Minimise waste in all our operations and product development
- Work with our suppliers to minimise the impact of their operations on the environment through a quality purchasing policy
- Protect visual amenity by the careful siting of building structures and deployment of operational plant in the local environment and respect wildlife habitats
- Support through our community programme the promotion of environmental protection by relevant external groups and organisations
- Include environmental issues in BT training programmes and encourage the implementation by all BT people of sound environmental practices
- Monitor progress and publish an environmental performance report on an annual basis.

Case study: CarnaudMetalbox

CarnaudMetalbox (formerly CMB Packaging) has an environmental policy that recognises its environmental duties to its employees, customers and the communities in which it operates.

In addition, the CarnaudMetalbox businesses are responsible for preparing and declaring their own local environment policy statement in line with group policy.

CarnaudMetalbox accepts the need for clearly defined and assigned environmental management responsibilities and for the establishment of appropriate environmental management structures within the organisation.

Each CarnaudMetalbox business assigns a senior manager to establish that its environmental management organisation is committed to identifying, measuring, controlling and minimising the environmental impacts arising from its operations and from the use of its products.

Business environmental management teams are responsible for preparing detailed action plans to identify and measure the environmental impacts arising from their operations.

All CarnaudMetalbox businesses ensure that they are conversant with all environmental regulations and legislation applicable to their operations and products. A key feature of action plans is to assess performance against relevant environmental regulations and company environmental standards.

Compliance is part of wide-ranging Environmental Care Action Programmes enacted by CarnaudMetalbox businesses to address the environmental impacts associated with their operations.

The businesses report progress to the executive committee on:

- environmental impacts associated with their operations
- environmental regulations/legislation relevant to their operations and products
- action being taken to comply with the legislation
- action plans to limit and control other impacts
- communication and training programmes planned for employees.

Considerable technical resources are applied to resolve environmental problems and develop clean technologies, and action is taken to remedy any non-compliance.

Environmental initiatives include:

- solvent emission abatement
- solvent reduction and substitution
- vinyl compound substitution
- elimination of CFCs in expanded polystyrene.

An integral part of CarnaudMetalbox's corporate environmental commitment is to develop a company-wide environmental culture through communication programmes which increase the awareness and understanding of environmental issues by all employees.

The company's environment communication programmes inform employees on environmental issues. The programme includes:

- *Environment Today* – a regular publication raising employee awareness of environmental issues
- key issue briefing documents – informing CarnaudMetalbox managers about the business implications of specific environmental issues
- case studies – examples of environmental responsibility from across CarnaudMetalbox
- News Review – a monthly update on developments for environmental managers and their teams
- Environment databank – an easy-access environmental reference facility
- environment networks – sharing environmental experience in all CarnaudMetalbox businesses

- education and training – developing the skills of the environmental teams

The company is also committed to establishing effective partnerships with its customers, suppliers and other external communities, to address, in particular, problems associated with post-consumer packaging waste.

The Communication Programme provides customers, shareholders and other external communities with information on CarnaudMetalbox environmental activity. CarnaudMetalbox participates extensively in the environmental initiatives of trade and industry associations.

Case study: The Body Shop

The Body Shop has an environmental department that advises on environmental policy and activities. Each department also has an environmental advisor, who is responsible for looking into the environmental implications of its activities and for resolving with the department's staff any environmental problems they identify. From 1992, there will also be networks of environmental advisors for the retail shops, both in the UK and overseas. The company publishes an environmental charter, to ensure that employees understand the environmental objectives and their entitlement to relevant training.

The Body Shop carries out an annual environmental audit, at both headquarters and in the field. Part of this is an energy audit. Staff training incorporates a strong element of environmental issues and is reinforced in the retail branches through a travelling roadshow.

Case study: Safeway

Setting clear targets and disseminating them throughout the organisation is an important part of making change happen. As part of its environmental policy statement, Safeway published the following:

"Our overall objective is that environmental protection continues to play a central part in Safeway's business development, and that consideration for it is increasingly evident in all the company's activities."

Environmental targets for specific areas are as follows:

Waste
- A reduction in the volume of input waste by 5% within three years (at store back door) measured by the number of pick-ups as calculated from total disposal costs and cost per pick up.
- A 20% increase in the recycling of the remaining bulk of current waste (excluding materials already recycled) measured by relating volume removed against total volume.

Recycling by customers
- That every store capable of installing and operating facilities in line with the company's code of practice should do so within two years.

Noise and environmental complaint
- A 25% reduction in complaints in three years.

Environmental audit
- That an internal environmental audit on one aspect of each division be undertaken within the next 12 months.

Paper use
- A 25% reduction in paper within 12 months.

Petrol consumption
- A 5% reduction in petrol consumption within 12 months.

Car policy
- That all new cars (both purchased and leased) should have the option of a catalytic converter or a diesel version as a choice against current models within three months.

9.4.1 Environmental advisory panels

One way for companies to keep up to speed is to set up an environmental advisory panel, board or council. Designed to be independent and composed of company outsiders such as academics and luminaries, the environmental advisory panel allows the company and its directors to tap into environmental expertise to track new legislation and keep up with trends.

Case study: Dow Chemicals

Dow Chemicals, the US-based multinational, set up a Corporate Environmental Advisory Council in 1991. The council will eventually consist of up to 14 members from around the world and will meet three or four times a year.

Frank Popoff, Dow's president and CEO, speaking at the council's launch in 1991, said: "We recognise that the public has a right to know what we are doing and a right to contribute to our decision-making process. Over the years we have learned the importance of opening our doors, seeking new ideas and gaining the support of our neighbours."

Committee members include environmental academics from America and the UK, the former premier of Quebec, an ex-member of the Pollution Prevention Directorate of the French government and a former environmental correspondent for the *New York Times*.

According to Dow, the geographical diversity of the council reflects the fact that over half of the company's sales are outside the US. Committee members are regarded as serving not as official representatives of any organisation, but as individuals and are asked to serve for a 24- to 36-month period.

Popoff added that the advisory council is consistent with Dow's commitment to "Responsible Care" – an industry-wide initiative in the US which requires members of the Chemical Manufacturers Association to seek public input on environmental performance. Dow also has community advisory panels at several plant locations which meet regularly with company representatives to discuss issues of local concern.

Shanks & McEwan, the UK-based waste-management and incinerator operator has been advised by an environmental board since 1989. The advisory board is an integral part of the group's environmental policy and acts, together with a formal quality assurance scheme, as a check on the company's environmental performance.

"An environmental policy is just a page of nonsense unless you have a management structure that makes it work," says Roger Hewitt, Shanks' chief executive.

Financial institutions which offer environmentally screened investments also use advisory panels – usually called screening committees – to examine their investment decisions and lend credibility to the scheme. The TSB, for example, has a committee chaired by David Bellamy, the botanist and broadcaster.

These companies and others have found that an advisory panel can make a valuable contribution to environmental management decisions. The benefits include:

- enhancing public image – the company is seen to be taking its environmental responsibilities seriously
- cost-effective access to expert advice
- timely incorporation of new legislation and trends into company strategy
- a safety net to catch environmentally damaging company policy before it is implemented.

Establishing an advisory panel
To be truly effective an advisory panel on environmental issues will have a protected independence from the company and the freedom to investigate the company's affairs. There are therefore two important issues to be considered by a company prior to setting up a panel:

1. Is the company willing to listen to and act on unpalatable advice from outsiders who may not be concerned with the financial performance of the business?
2. Can the advisory panel's need for independence be reconciled with its need for access to sensitive information about the company?

Unless a company is fully committed to the principles of an environmental panel then its operation assumes the role of a superficial PR exercise with a number of potential dangers. Not least of these is the risk that members of the panel, frustrated at having their advice constantly ignored, reveal the company's environmental transgressions to the press or attract unwanted attention by resigning.

It is important, too, for senior management to align the interests of the panel with those of the company, to prevent the organisation obstructing its work. For example, by being slow to produce information so that meetings – which are usually held quarterly – are ineffective. Or by failing to incorporate its views into the management decision-making process.

In establishing the panel, it is essential to be clear about its role and to ensure that role is facilitated by the terms of reference. Most companies see the advisory panel as neither watchdog nor ombudsman, but as a means to keep abreast of environmental issues so that they can plan for shifts in the market and new legislation. Some companies, such as Shanks, want the advisory panel merely to comment on main board decisions.

Although some companies with established advisory panels say they use them to help formulate strategy, it is usually only in the most abstract sense. Hewitt, for example, sees no role for the panel in deciding company strategy and when Shanks recently bought Rechem, the high-temperature incinerator operator, the environmental panel was only told after the event.

"We cannot make an external body party to price-sensitive information," he says. "We cannot discuss general or specific strategy with them because it would turn outsiders into insiders."

To protect their independence, panel members are often paid only a small fee, or just their expenses. A by-product of this is that they can be viewed as a relatively low-cost way to buy in the advice of specialist environmental consultants. Indeed, to protect their own position, some experts like Tim O'Riordan, professor of environmental affairs at the University of East Anglia and a member of Dow's council, refuse any form of payment. Under these circumstances, the cost of setting up an advisory panel and servicing it is composed mainly of the time and effort invested by management, making the environmental panel an economical as well as extremely powerful management tool.

Hewitt puts the total cost of his company's advisory board, including administration and company time, at about £100,000 a year, which he considers to be good value compared to the cost of non-executive directors.

The effectiveness of an advisory board depends on three factors:

- the quality and independence of the board members
- establishing meaningful terms of reference and an agenda that addresses the company's activities through frank and timely discussion
- the company's commitment to the advisory board – both in terms of providing it with information and listening to and acting on its advice

Consumer panels are another variation on advisory boards. These are discussed in more detail in Chapter 2, but usually represent a cross-section of the company's customers. BT, for example, runs three specialist panels, including one on environmental issues.

Emergency response and crisis management
The impact of large-scale industrial disasters, both on the environment itself and on the reputation of the company responsible, are incalculable. For example, the grounding of the Exxon Corporation's *Exxon Valdez* in April 1989 resulted in the spillage of 11.2 million gallons of crude oil off the coast of Alaska. By mid-September 1989, when the clean-up operation was winding down, the estimated environmental cost included the deaths of 34,434 sea birds, 9994 sea otters and 147 bald eagles. By mid-1990 Exxon had spent £1.1 billion on cleaning up after the incident.

As a result of this and a spate of other environmental disasters and scares, enlightened companies have increasingly moved away from complacent denial of risk towards emergency response and crisis management. For instance, in its 1991 corporate brochure on Health, Safety and Environmental Policy, BP realises that: "however hard the oil industry works to prevent accidents, it must always recognise that they do happen".

Case study: BP

In February 1990 BP's emergency response procedures were put to the test when 1000 tonnes of Alaskan crude oil leaked from the chartered tanker *American Trader* into the sea off the Californian coast. The spill was just two miles from popular leisure areas and close to a number of sensitive wildlife habitats. However, the speed with which BP put its Crisis Response Plan into action drew widespread praise, not least from the often critical press. By the time the first oil came ashore, five days after the incident, booms had been used to cordon off sensitive areas and harbours. More than 2000 beach cleaners dealt with contaminated sand and a bird centre handled wildlife affected by the oil. A US coast guard official quoted in *Time* magazine said BP America's response had been "without equal".

The company's emergency services again swung into action in April 1990 when a tanker "collided" with a North Sea oil platform. This time, however, the "collision" was not a real incident but part of a simulated exercise that assumed a full-scale catastrophe with fire, explosions, loss of life and a massive oil spill had occurred.

Called "Exercise Highland Capital" it was the largest ever civil exercise in the North Sea and involved nearly 1000 people and 20 outside agencies. The exercise was one of the first opportunities to test the effectiveness of BP's newly created Crisis Management Team. The London-based team, which is led by a managing director and includes the chief executives of all the BP businesses, was set up to spearhead BP's response to any major crisis.

Exercise Highland Capital was followed in November 1990 by Exercise Belgrave Alpha, which simulated a massive explosion and fire at a BP Chemicals plant. Two more exercises took place during 1991.

Simulations like these also test the back-up teams such as the BP Group Crisis Management Centre which provides and manages support for the BP Group during a crisis. In addition, the Oil Spill Service Centre at Southampton, set up by BP in 1981, is now the largest privately owned facility in the world. It has a £10 million stockpile of equipment and a nucleus of skilled staff. Since 1985, when the centre was made available to other oil companies, 13 have joined as partners.

9.5 Environmental auditing

The recent environment protection legislation will make it more imperative than ever that businesses look closely at how they relate to the environment, and put in management systems and technologies to reduce their impact on it, said the CBI at a conference on environmental auditing in June 1990. It estimated: "All businesses are affected by the environment debate, but to date only relatively few are using the systematic approach which an environmental audit offers."

Martin Charter, managing director of KPH Marketing, a company that specialises in environmental audits, endorses this view. "Within the UK, environmental auditing is a relatively new discipline outside the oil, chemical and pharmaceutical industries. There have been an estimated 200 completed projects to date. However, decision-makers across industry are now coming under a variety of pressures to establish an environmental policy. An environmental audit is a necessary precursor for this.

"By taking a broad view of environmental auditing and by understanding its interconnections both in and outside the organisation, companies will be able to generate creative, cost reducing and revenue-generating ideas, that will have a direct impact on the bottom line.

"Senior management must face this responsibility and champion the change and empower management and staff to implement the new policies. The results are likely to improve morale, produce a better corporate image and ultimately improve market share and profitability."

An environmental audit explores all aspects of a company's manufacturing, office and field safety procedures and attempts to:

- analyse its effect on the environment
- suggest ways of minimising its effect.

Although, like a financial audit, it provides a snap-shot of the organisation at one time, the environmental audit is different in that it is intended to force positive change. Attention is directed not simply to the environmental bottom line, but to every point where the organisation may have a negative impact on the environment.

For most companies, an audit will reveal areas where action is needed, either in terms of policy formulation, or preventive implementation. Top management must become involved at this point to set priorities and establish broad budgets.

European Community legislation may well make environmental audits obligatory for public companies over the new few years. Those companies which invest in auditing systems while it is still voluntary stand to gain significant benefits in terms of market positioning.

Case study: Allied Signal

Based in the USA, Allied Signal is a major manufacturing corporation with over 240 plants worldwide and over 11,000 employees working in the automotive, aerospace and engineered materials sector. In 1978, upon the recommendation of an outside consultant, it embarked on a Health, Safety and Environmental Surveillance Programme.

The programme's purpose was to ensure compliance with existing legislation and check that operating companies were able to comply with future standards.

The audit function is carried out by the Corporate Health, Safety and Environmental Sciences Department. Within this 14-person team are three full-time environmental auditors, one each for health, safety and the environment. The department is headed by a vice president reporting to the senior vice president of operating services.

The audit covers seven areas:

- air pollution control
- water pollution and spill prevention
- solid waste disposal
- occupational health
- medical programmes
- safety and loss prevention
- product safety.

From an annual budget of US$750,000, the company conducts 50 audits annually, a sample of about 3%. Each audit covers one of the three areas.

Audited sites are chosen from each of the corporation's main business areas and operating companies. Facility managers are notified of a review one month in advance.

Each audit team uses techniques such as formal audit protocols, written questionnaires, informal interviews with key members of staff, physical measurement and documentation checks. An audit takes around four days. The team then issues a written report in draft for the facility manager and line and corporate staff, followed by a final report which takes into account any comments.

The facility manager has to prepare a written response to this report within one month and draw up and execute an action plan to remedy any deficiencies noted. About 20% of these action plans are followed up again by the audit team.

The company places environmental responsibility with sector presidents. Each year they must write an environmental assurance letter, guaranteeing that appropriate health, safety and environmental systems are in place and working. They must also state that any deficiencies are being dealt with – and how.

Allied Signal is making a substantial effort to keep its business practices both within and in advance of legislation. Because legislative requirements vary from country to country, it aims to use the strictest requirements as the corporate standard. Nonetheless, the sheer size of the auditing task means that the process is mainly reactive rather than proactive.

This case study was provided by Matthew Nicol of Bioscan (UK) Ltd and Martin Charter of KPH Marketing Ltd who have formed a working partnership to examine corporate environmental stances from audit through to implementation.

Case study: Texaco

Texaco operates an environmental auditing programme at all its UK operational sites. The programme involves regular checks for air and water pollution, and inspection of waste handling and emergency response procedures.

As a minimum the facilities must comply with legislation, but Texaco has also produced worldwide Environmental Operating Practices (EOPs) which are generally considerably more rigorous than local legislation. The EOPs are set at a level agreed by the company's senior management and are supplemented by guidelines generated within the UK which match the local operating environment.

Through the EOPs and the guidelines all Texaco facilities are kept informed about the environmental standards to which they are expected to operate. Environmental audits act as a check to ensure compliance with standards and to measure environmental performance. Auditors draw up a plan of action for any deficiencies detected.

Auditors' findings are discussed and agreed with site managers before they leave the site and are followed up with regular reports. Environmental audits are also carried out before the company buys or sells land. Environmental complaints are thoroughly investigated and clean-up procedures put in train in cases of contamination.

When its Safety and Environmental Affairs Department was created in 1989, Texaco became one of the first major oil companies to appoint a director with sole responsibility for this area.

Case study: McDonald's' cups

An instructive example of the difficulties surrounding cradle-to-grave environmental audits concerns McDonald's and the disposable cups in which it sells soft drinks. In the late 1980s, an environmentalist campaign convinced the fast-food company that it should phase out polystyrene cups, because they were made from a finite resource, petroleum, and because they led to the production of chlorofluorocarbons. Foam cups were also held to be environmentally unsound because they were neither recyclable nor biodegradable.

As McDonald's switched to paper cups, however, it came under attack from the scientific community. In a controversy-raising article in *Science* magazine, Martin Hocking, professor of chemistry at the University of Victoria in British Columbia, came to the conclusion that paper cups were more environmentally damaging than foam ones.

Hocking's analysis suggested that paper production used more energy and burnt more petroleum in transportation costs. It also generated more liquid wastes. Other scientists came up with different equations and the dispute shows no signs of being settled.

The US Society of Environmental Toxicology and Chemistry has set up a committee to recommend how to conduct a cradle-to-grave environmental audit. One of the issues it will consider will be how far back to take the comparisons – Hocking's analysis did not consider the energy use of the chain saws used to cut down the trees, points out MIT's *Technology Review*, nor did it look at the environmental impact of manufacturing the lumbering equipment.

The primary lesson from the McDonald's case is that environmental audits, if they are to be credible, must be done with a great deal of scientific rigour and should ensure that the assumptions made are acceptable to as wide a body of expert opinion as possible.

Checklist

1. Does your company hold regular environmental audits? If so, is there any procedure in place to follow an audit up?
2. Do you publicise positive developments to employees/the general public?

10. Maintaining an ethical climate

How often are people in your company asked to do things which they regard as unethical, immoral or illegal? In many companies, far more than top management would like to think, if a recent study by two associate professors at the University of Columbia, New York, is to be believed. John Delaney and Donna Sockell surveyed over 1000 recent business school graduates and found that, on average, each faced more than four ethical dilemmas a year. Nearly two in every five of these dilemmas were perceived by the graduates to involve illegal actions.

In most of these cases, the graduates stood to gain very little from doing as they were asked. It was most often the company that benefited (although in over 40% of cases, a more senior manager was the partial or sole beneficiary).

Fully half of these young employees took a stand and refused to do as they were told. One in three of them was punished by the company – for example, by being passed over for promotion, reprimanded or eased out of the door. Just over a quarter obeyed the instruction, although they believed it to be wrong; the rest either quit or did as they were told while covering their backs by reporting their concern to someone else, either inside the company or a regulatory authority.

Most interestingly, about 40% of those who did act illegally or unethically and kept their mouths shut were rewarded in some way. The rewards do not have to be obvious, such as financial or promotion; in many cases, they consist of allowing people into the "inner circle" of shakers and movers within the organisation. People who aren't prepared to compromise their principles simply don't get asked.

The only time that shareholders (and frequently top management) learn about such goings-on within their organisations is when something goes wrong. Either customers complain and force an external enquiry; or a concerned employee takes his or her case public. The recent Serious Fraud Squad investigations into boardroom activities at Polly Peck, for example, were a direct result of whistle-blowing by a former executive.

It isn't just the damage to the company's reputation which is at issue here, although that is serious enough. (Customers think twice about doing business with a company they cannot trust; and would-be employees also tend to be cautious about joining a company with a reputation for dishonest or unethical behaviour.) Equally at stake is the motivation of people already within the organisation. Even if the illegal behaviour is not brought out into the open, it results in the company's effective isolation from the influence of people who have much to contribute. It also helps to focus managers' attention on short-term, pragmatic goals, to the virtual exclusion of the long-term objectives so essential for establishing corporate direction.

Worse still, the company that does not encourage high ethical standards in its dealings with customers, suppliers and employees encourages unethical behaviour towards *itself*. If the company permits overcharging of customers, it is not surprising that employees come to similar conclusions about the permissibility of fiddling expenses, overstating overtime, minor "shrinkage" and so on.

The dilemma for top management is that it is expected to maintain an ethical climate, yet has only limited control over the hearts and minds of the people who work in the organisation. Yet applying effective management principles can reduce the problems.

There are at least two major issues here:

- how do executives keep themselves out of trouble?
- how do they control the activities of perhaps thousands of individual employees, any one of whom may be misguided or mis-motivated into behaving in ways that may damage the corporate reputation?

Some years ago, a research project in the United States investigated what it called "corporate deviance". The research showed that these executives are frequently otherwise remarkably law-abiding citizens and often pillars of the local community. However, they have built up a wall between the morality that applies in their personal life and that which applies in business.

What appears to happen is that the company becomes such a dominant part of the executive's life that his or her sense of moral values becomes distorted. If it is right for the company, it must be right for the community. Few of these executives act in isolation. They usually gather round them a coterie of equally committed managers who reinforce each others' values. People who would not approve, or who might blow the whistle, are excluded from the club – where the action is – making those within it feel even more close-knit. The club then develops a momentum of its own, becoming difficult or even impossible to control.

The need to take urgent action on ethical controls has come into sharper focus in the United States recently as a result of a major review of responsibilities and penalties by the Sentencing Commission. New guidelines, introduced in December 1991, allow for substantial reductions in fines for organisations that can prove they have an effective system or programme to ensure that employees at all levels behave honestly. They also place a responsibility on executives to be proactive in seeking out potential violations. According to the Commission: "An individual was 'wilfully ignorant of the offence' if the individual did not investigate the possible occurrence of unlawful conduct despite knowledge of circumstances that would lead a reasonable person to investigate whether unlawful conduct had occurred." In other words, if top managers don't actively discourage illegal behaviour by installing and using proper management systems, they can be held personally liable.

So what can a board of directors do to ensure that a company does behave ethically? There is no simple answer, nor is it likely that any company can totally eradicate the possibility of wrong-doing. But the board does have a duty to take what practical steps it can, and these should normally include the following:

Set a clear example

Much of the work we and others have undertaken in communications indicates that messages from on high are rarely taken sufficiently seriously by those at the ground floor. The perception by top management that simply saying something should be done will automatically lead to its accomplishment is very common – and very misconceived. For a start, there is the whole massed rank of middle management to subvert priorities and substitute its own. Then there is the cynicism of people at the coal face who assume that fine words are just that – if they get the message in the first place.

The key to setting an example is visibility and practice. Among actions top management can take are:

- include ethical considerations on the board agenda, every time
- make a big fuss of ethical issues in the annual report and elsewhere
- create opportunities to demonstrate ethical commitments – even manufacture drama if necessary. For example, Clark's the shoe makers used the requests by environmentalists to help stop the use of whale oils in leather curing as a major opportunity to make an ethical statement
- deliver the same message internally and externally
- be seen to be active in charities. (This does not simply mean appearing on the governing bodies; far better to take part – as for example, Kingfisher executives sleeping out to raise cash for the homeless.)

Publish a code of ethics

Some kind of touchstone or guidance is essential to help managers decide when – in the view of the company – an action is right or wrong. Only the board can make that decision, although it may delegate some of the groundwork to a sub-committee.

About 70% of Britain's top companies have some form of company statement that they use for setting broad standards of behaviour. However, establishing a statement of values – what the company stands for and how it will treat each of its stakeholders – appears in many cases to be easier than creating a code of ethics. Many companies avoid issuing codes of ethics for fear of suggesting to the outside world that they have a problem in this area. But the reality is that every company has this problem, even though it is not readily apparent.

A study by the Institute of Business Ethics, published in May 1992, found that 29% of 164 leading UK companies had a written ethical code – against 18% in 1991. Some companies have had codes for a good many years – IBM for 30 years, Esso, which sponsored the study, since 1977. According to the *Financial Times*, 84% of all US companies have written codes.

Among firms with a strong belief in promoting a formal code of ethics is Cadbury Schweppes. Sir Adrian Cadbury explains that company policy towards gifts obliges employees to consider two rules of thumb: "Is the payment on the face of the invoice? Would it embarrass the recipient to have the gift mentioned in the company newspaper?" The first ensures that all payments, however unusual, are recorded and go through the books. The second is aimed at distinguishing bribes from gifts, a definition which depends on the size of the gift and the influence it is likely to have on the recipient.

Some companies, such as Forte, Body Shop and Shell, encompass ethical principles in general statements of business philosophy. Others, such as Coca-Cola and British Gas, issue separate codes of business conduct. Several of these are reproduced in Appendix 2.

A draft code of conduct

The need for guidelines and how to use them

Your role in maintaining the corporate reputation
- behaviour towards people outside the company
  - customers
  - suppliers
  - the general public
  - etc
- behaviour towards your colleagues at work
- behaviour towards the company and its property
  - time
  - assets
  - intellectual property
- confidentiality
- activities outside working hours
- conflicts of interest

What to do when you are concerned about other people's behaviour or about company policy

What the company owes you.

Ronald Berenbeim of the Conference Board is reported as identifying three key steps in developing and using an effective code of ethics. These were quoted in the *Financial Times* as:

- The drafting of the code should be participatory, including all levels of employees in discussions to gain an understanding of the corporate culture and values.
- Everyone should receive a copy of the code and be involved in discussions on its meaning and implementation.
- Any breaches in the code should be reported and discussed internally, so that staff are aware that it is, as he says, "a living document".

Part of the value of an ethics code is that it formalises the process of assessing actions against what is right. The very existence of the code is a partial protection for the employee who observes unethical behaviour, because he or she can demonstrate conformance to company policy. It also legitimises taking the issue outside the immediate work team, if the individual cannot resolve his doubts with his immediate boss. The Coca-Cola Company tells its employees in its code of business conduct: "The guidelines contained in the code are of necessity broad principles. As a result, employees may from time to time need assistance in determining how the code applies to situations which confront them. Questions about the code's application to specific circumstances should be directed to an employee's supervisor or to the company's general counsel." In other words, if you can't resolve the problem, there is an outside source to talk it over with and you have an obligation to do so.

Valuable as it may be, a code of ethics is only part of the answer, however. Unless it is supported by an infrastructure that reinforces the values expressed, it is no more than another memo from headquarters.

Monitor performance

Monitoring the performance of executives and managers against the ethics code is essential. An ethics code is only of value to the extent that people take notice of it. The company has to take active steps to police the policy.

Companies on both sides of the Atlantic use a variety of means to achieve this. Some, such as Perkin Elmer, require all managers to confirm that they have not deviated from the ethical guidelines; the company conducts sample audits to check that these statements are true. Others – about one in four of Britain's top companies – make ethical monitoring a specific responsibility of non-executive directors; in some cases, this means setting up an ethical sub-committee of the board. Among the danger signs to look for are the establishment of secretive cabals where a small group of key individuals withhold information that would normally be more widely available. (This appears to have been the case at Guinness, for example.)

Ethical committees, relatively common in the United States, are few and far between in Europe, although we can expect to see them gradually become an accepted part of corporate governance. In the UK, the Royal Bank of Scotland refers ethical issues to a board-level committee, where external directors dominate. Similarly, Esso SAF in France has an ethics committee consisting of the finance director, the financial controller, the general counsel and the internal audit manager. Appointed by the chief executive, its remit is to examine ethical issues and recommend actions and policy. The committee has the authority to insist that managers behave in accordance with company policy and/or the law.

MacDonald and Zepp point to Motorola as a company which has experimented successfully with the concept. They suggest: "Committee membership should be rotated among employees thereby exposing them to the ethical problems submitted by either employees or managers." These committees normally deal with policy-making rather than specific complaints or unethical actions. Committee decisions can then be used as firm clear guidelines for future action. According to MacDonald and Zepp, these committees are more popular in US businesses than ethical ombudspersons.

A few companies have also given individual directors the responsibility to intervene to maintain ethical standards. For example, in the late 1970s Gillette appointed a vice president, product integrity. When managers in one division proposed to launch a new shaving cream aerosol, knowing that it would only deliver three-quarters of its contents, he blocked the product. The managers argued that the customers would never know but the VP, supported by the board, insisted that the launch was delayed for many expensive months while a new propellant was developed.

MacDonald and Zepp suggest creating the post of ethical ombudsperson to guide employees on ethical questions. They state:

- an ombudsperson should have an investigative counselling and advisory role. He or she investigates ethical matters and advises on potential problem areas.
- no one is obliged to discuss matters with the ombudsperson – employees can request help or advice on their own initiative if they feel they need it
- an ombudsperson must be independent, trusted by both management and employees. Confidentiality is also essential for the position to be effective
- an ombudsperson needs experience within the company – the position is suitable for an older respected employee who has assimilated the corporate value system. The position is appropriate for someone approaching retirement or a 'plateaued employee'.

Use the reward and punishment mechanisms to reinforce correct behaviour

- Write ethical responsibilities into every manager's job description – and use them in appraisal
- Reward exemplary behaviour: with cash maybe, but recognition always
- Punish breaches of the ethical code – publicly. If you simply warn someone in private, it will be perceived by others as a tacit condoning of the unethical behaviour
- Use the key motivators of *influence, promotion and access to resources.*

One of the features of the financial scandals within the City of London has been the reluctance of some employers to punish people who were guilty of unethical behaviour. The message to other employees was that it is all right as long as you can get away with it. The swift action by the Guinness board provides a contrary example. The fact that the CEO was obliged to leave carried an equally strong message about acceptable and unacceptable behaviour.

Recruit ethical people

Discuss ethics at recruitment interviews and employ people for their ethical attitude as well as their experience and formal qualifications. Make it clear to interviewees that this is an ethical organisation.

One possible (though difficult to prove) beneficial spin-off of an emphasis on recruiting ethical people is that job candidates may be less likely to lie at interviews. A recent study of the ethics of job candidates and interviewers by Clive Fletcher of Goldsmiths' College, University of London, found that, while 97% of interviewers felt that complete honesty on the part of candidates was essential, 20% of candidates admitted they were seldom or never completely honest during interviews.

Case study: The Body Shop

The Body Shop has two training schools, one in London and one at head office in Littlehampton to induct new recruits into the company culture. Much of the programme focuses on raising the new staff's awareness of environmental and social issues and of the company's codes of practice. People who do not share the basic values The Body Shop espouses are counselled out of the job at this point. The induction training, says the company, covers a wide range of issues not necessarily related to the products or the company directly. It is done to raise the consciousness of staff on a wide variety of issues.

Once at work, employees are swiftly exposed to volunteering. Participation in local voluntary work helps to reinforce the corporate values.

Train

An increasing number of business schools now have ethics on the curriculum. Harvard, for example, was influenced by a large gift that specified all students must attend business ethics classes. But the primary responsibility for ethics education has to lie with companies themselves.

Even small companies can institute ethics training. For example, Coils and Cables, a 44-employee company, backs up its ethical code with lunch-time role-playing sessions. The managing director leads these sessions every two months, inviting employees to discuss issues such as "Should a manager accept an all-expenses paid weekend at the World Cup from a supplier?"

Ethics training should also be reinforced by the example set by top management. If the executive team is clearly seen to be taking ethical issues seriously, so will other managers.

Ethical training should:

1. Enable people to identify when an ethical dilemma is present
They need to be able to:

- Determine where and how conflicts of interest might arise
- Establish whether the dilemma is real or potential
- Understand and examine their own attitudes and motivations
- Become sensitised to the nuances of ethical issues.

It also helps to be able to rank behaviour on a particular issue. For example:

What constitutes a bribe?
  - use my mobile phone
  - desk diary
  - lunch
  - bottle of whisky/crate of wine
  - guests at sponsored theatre event
  - guests at unsponsored theatre event
  - day at Ascot in Royal Enclosure
  - holiday for two in the Bahamas
  - packet of used fivers.

2. Provide a decision-making framework
This would typically involve six stages:

- articulate the problem
- consider the implications
- consider the context
- invite other opinions
- balance the arguments
- the final check – have we made the right decision?

Case study: Ethics training at Allied Signal

Allied Signal, a US electronics company sends all senior managers on a three-day course, which has three primary objectives:

- to help executives recognise the ethical components of decisions they make
- to help them put the ethical issues in context
- to teach them how to predict and avoid ethical dilemmas.

The programme is highly structured with day one dealing with business ethics in general; day two focusing on Allied Signal's responsibilities to its employees; and day three exploring responsibilities towards other stakeholders. Case studies, role playing and the participants' own experience are all used to force discussion of sometimes difficult issues.

Case study: IBM

IBM reinforces its code of conduct by making ethical issues part of the normal day-to-day decision-making procedures. All managers are issued with a reference card, entitled "Thinking it through", which rehearses the key questions they should ask whenever a less-than-straightforward, routine issue arises. The card takes them through the following fundamental questions:

- What do I want to do?
- Does it deviate from any IBM guidelines?
- Does it break a fundamental rule?
- Why should we do it? What are the benefits or gains?
- What are the impacts? Who are the stakeholders? What are their issues?
- What could go wrong? How likely is it and how severe would the impact be?
- Can I minimise the risk?
- Does it break a fundamental rule? (again)
- Decide/ document.

Alongside this routine sits a list of 17 different stakeholders, to remind the manager that any of these might have a legitimate interest in the decision he makes.

Create a framework for registering concern

Auditing and training will still not necessarily bring all wrong-doing to light, particularly if senior managers are involved. So companies need mechanisms which encourage people who feel disquiet about activities to register their concern.

In some companies, a non-executive director acts as an informal ombudsperson on such issues; in others, such as the John Lewis Partnership, there are frequent discussion groups where employees are asked to speak up on ethical issues. John Lewis also has an anonymous letters page in its staff magazine to which people can write if they feel something is immoral, illegal or unfair.

Case study: Scott Bader

At Scott Bader, a Northamptonshire chemicals company wholly owned by its employees, elected committees deal with all aspects of company policy. If an employee feels that a certain policy is against the ethical code of the business, he or she can ask for policies to be reviewed without fear of repercussions. The company's strong ethical culture has much to do with its 4% annual staff turnover.

Case study: Perkin-Elmer

Perkin-Elmer, a US-owned firm making analytical instruments, not only requires all employees to sign a code of ethics, but insists they report all instances of improper business conduct to their supervisor or to a responsible person such as a division manager or legal department. And it says it is the firm intention of management to enforce the policy. In addition, each site has a supervisor's manual which identifies the ethics of each department. This document makes sure what the department does fits into the company's ethical code.

Perhaps the extreme example of this kind of openness is the US equivalent of the Atomic Energy Authority which has an annual staff competition for the best dissenting essay. The programme, which is highly regarded internally, is a recognition of the fact that it is better to have potential whistleblowers bring issues directly to the board, than to have them air their feelings in the press first.

Experience shows that, in almost every case where an employee feels compelled to blow the whistle publicly, both the organisation and the individual suffer. (Often the individual suffers most, because once his or her identity is made public, they become almost unemployable.)

It also helps to bring in other outsiders. A US insurance company invites a small group of customers to visit the headquarters with a remit to audit anything they wish. The customers say what they like and don't like about the company's behaviour and these comments are used by top management in planning.

Key questions to ask at board level include:
- are we creating a climate of trust with our employees, our customers, our suppliers and the communities in which we operate?
- are we encouraging these groups to tell us what they think, and are we listening to them?
- when we have an ethical issue to consider, do we involve these groups, or do we simply make decisions at the senior management level?

One of the obvious, but little-used mechanisms for creating this kind of open flow of information is the interest group panel. British Telecom, for example, has made major steps forward in its relationships with disabled customers by setting up a customer panel where they can advise on services and the management processes that support them.

Build openness into the workplace

Many companies are now examining their predominant management style, to assess whether it supports their business objectives. In most cases, they are finding that an open style of leadership is essential if they are to remain competitive. As a result, a great deal of time and management effort is being ploughed into developing appropriate behaviour among managers, helping them to delegate, to listen, to empower, coach and counsel. The more adventurous companies also encourage their managers to develop self-critical skills and to encourage constructive criticism from their direct reports and colleagues. These abilities are more difficult to acquire – they require a degree of personal maturity many people never attain.

The benefit of an open style is that contentious issues are aired within the work team – the unit where most unethical decisions are made. If people feel that criticism will be accepted and recognised as a positive contribution to the business, they are far more likely to register concern and to argue the moral case as they see it.

A handful of companies have encouraged this kind of openness by providing managers with feedback from direct reports, among them W.H. Smith and The Woolwich Equitable Building Society. These upward critiques of a manager's behaviour provide valuable information for improving performance and most managers at the receiving end tend to welcome continued feedback from below (once they have got over the first shock!).

Case study: NHS Whistle-blowers

In June 1992, the government announced its commitment to new measures to protect whistle-blowers inside the National Health Service. Health Secretary Virginia Bottomley promised new guidelines aimed at preventing the gagging of whistle-blowing staff who publicly voice fears about health service standards.

Speaking at the Institute of Health Services Management conference, Mrs Bottomley said that she recognised the fears of healthcare professionals and other staff that management reforms in the NHS could compromise their ability to express genuine concerns.

"A proper balance must be struck between the duty of staff to raise matters of professional concern," she said, "and the need to safeguard confidentiality."

Under the new guidelines, managers will be expected to provide channels to allow complaints, if necessary, to reach the highest levels.

Making it happen

The idea of *managing* ethical behaviour may seem alien to many executives. Yet, in reality, it is already part of the management job, in the sense that line managers have specific legal responsibilities for employee safety, preventing discriminatory behaviour or sexual harassment in the workplace, and so on. From a standpoint of avoiding hassle alone, it pays for managers to be aware of the potential problems and to have the competence and support they need to direct the behaviour of individuals so those problems do not arise.

The requirement within the 1990s and beyond will be to systematise our approaches to issues with ethical dimensions in such a way that they become readily manageable. Ad hoc decision-making must give way to decision-making within the context of clearly understood and shared values – shared not just within the workgroup but within the broader communities, of which the workgroup is a part. It won't be easy, but the process may be helped by the necessary introspection most large companies are putting themselves through, as part of their attempts to build organisations capable of thriving in a world of rapid change. The wholesale reconstruction of the modern enterprise frequently involves incorporating new values that will shape people's behaviour for the coming decades. The opportunity for top management to make strong ethical values part of "the normal way we do things here" has never been greater.

11. Getting the message across

The issue of communication has come up frequently within the course of this book. The reason, quite simply, is that while all of the activities discussed are no doubt worthwhile doing for their own sake, the benefit to the organisation is greatly enhanced if they are widely publicised.

If a company is truly making a community investment then it behoves the company to maximise the benefits to its reputation. The limits to this exposure will usually lie in:

- not wanting the corporate message to overshadow that of the community partner. (If it does, people are likely to see it as advertising and adjust their credulity accordingly.)
- the nature of the involvement. (Employee involvement is more news-worthy than straight cash donations, for example.)
- the degree of resources and creativity which the company puts in.

Effective communications are *planned* and *co-ordinated*. We frequently see companies with a different and contradictory message in, say, their recruitment advertising and the advertising they put into consumer magazines. An effective approach to communicating social responsibility action brings together the key managers – human resources, public relations, social responsibility/community investment/public affairs, marketing and environment, at the minimum – on a regular basis to discuss initiatives and agree how, when and by whom they will be communicated to both internal and external audiences.

A communication budget should be an early and integral element of budget planning. The amount of the budget will vary according to circumstances, but in general communicating to an internal audience will require a relatively small budget, as long as existing media can be used, while communicating a major national initiative to the public in general will require (as we saw in the chapter on sponsorship) a budget at least equal to the operational costs of the project.

Some practical questions to help make such budget decisions include:

- how important/relevant is the issue to the corporate brand? to divisional brands? to local reputation?
- how direct is the pay-off to our reputation at each level?
- how important/relevant is the issue to each audience (employees, customers, suppliers, influencers, local community etc)?
- how important is each of the audiences to the business objectives?
- what choice of media is currently available to reach each audience?
- how cost-effective is each medium (on its own or in conjunction with others)?

The answers to these questions can be built into simple matrices, which compare community importance against business importance (much along the lines of the Giving Matrix – see page 172) and the various audiences against the cost and practicality of reaching them. The two matrices can then be combined to compare the priority issues against the priority audiences. The results may subsequently need to be modified to take into account special circumstances. At the very least, decisions to invest communication time and money into high-cost, low-impact media (for which a good case can often be made if the audience is small enough and influential enough) then at least they will have been made from a position of understanding rather than ignorance.

The impact of communication will depend on:
- the likely public interest in the issue
- the creativity with which it is addressed
- the variety and scope of the media. (The more often people receive a message, and the more numerous the ways they receive it, the greater their recognition and acceptance is likely to be.)

For an external audience, the media available include:
- press relations (newspapers, television, radio – national and local)
- videos for distribution to schools and interest groups. Retailers have a special advantage in that they can play videos in their public premises, for example, while customers queue.

- the annual report, or a separate social report
- schools information packs
- speaking at conferences (the same names occur so frequently at conferences on social responsibility issues, because so few other companies seek the opportunity to talk about what they do!)
- talks to schools, local societies and so on. (For example, Volvo in Sweden uses retired employees to carry out this ambassadorial role.)
- displays at conferences and exhibitions
- posters and other display materials at company premises. (For example, for Red Nose Day many companies signalled their involvement by attaching large red noses to their buildings.)
- placing the company logo on sponsored publications, or on the programmes for events, which the company or its employees support
- open days
- 0800 information lines – GE in the United States has increased market share by having staff available on a helpline 24 hours a day, 365 days a year
- advertising, through commercial media or on product packaging.

External communications are often most effective when they associate the company with a specific initiative. If the initiative is innovative and likely to catch public imagination, so much the better.

It also helps to be very clear where the communications should come from. Is the objective to enhance the reputation of the corporate brand, divisional brands or local presence? Or all of these? It is very easy to lose the impact of a major investment because the promotional opportunities are only seized at one level. If the company has a regional network, it should invest effort as heavily in marketing corporate initiatives to the operating units and local offices, as it does to the public in general.

For an internal audience, many of the same media apply, but the approach may be different. For example, CarnaudMetalbox produces a newsletter to keep employees informed of environmental activities, but expects the circulation to include quite a wide external audience as well. Similarly, the employee annual report is likely to have more space to focus on community activities than the shareholder version.

Some companies we have encountered make over up to a third of the pages of their company newspaper to community activities, either initiated by the company, or the result of employees' own initiative. Other communication channels available include electronic mail, teletext systems, in-company television (Ford has its own employee news programme, which carries some items on relevant issues) and team-briefing systems.

A development we would like to see is more information to employees about opportunities to volunteer, either in the company newspaper or through information packs, which could be distributed to employees and their families. It is also remarkable how few companies think to circulate to employees the press releases they send out to the media.

Effective in-company communications tend to be multi-dimensional – top down, bottom up and horizontal. Most communications in this area tend to be downwards. But it is equally important to gather information on what employees think about these issues, if the company is to tap into their commitment and enthusiasm. Moreover, it also pays to encourage employees to share experiences and ideas across locations and divisions. A useful suggestion is to hold an annual social responsibility fair, at which employees can exhibit their accomplishments, both to colleagues from elsewhere in the company and to invited external guests.

Although we have so far spoken mainly of communications, in reality much of the requirement is for internal marketing. That implies not merely education and information, but motivation. All the above media can be used to recognise people's contributions to community action, but it may help to add more focused methods of recognition. For example, many companies operate schemes designed to recognise those people who choose to spend their own time, as a team, a store or as individuals, in putting something back into the communities, in which they work.

Analysing the communications opportunities

It is useful to examine critical social responsibility issues on a regular basis, both in terms of what communication is being made and what should/could be made.

The way in which this information is presented will vary according to the scale of the initiatives and the structure of the company. However, the following template may provide a useful guideline.

A. What are we doing now?

ISSUE: Equal opportunities

| | Level | | | |
| | Group | Division 1 | Division 2 | Branch |

Sub-issues:

Opportunity   (Descriptions of activities and
2000   communications media)

Ethnic
monitoring

etc

B. How could we extend existing initiatives?

ISSUE: Equal opportunities

| | Level | | | |
| | Group | Division 1 | Division 2 | Branch |

Sub-issues:

Opportunity (Description of how initiatives could be
2000   extended and the communications that could
             assist them)

Ethnic
monitoring

etc

C. What new initiatives should we launch?

ISSUE: Equal opportunities

	Level			
	Group	Division 1	Division 2	Branch

Sub-issues:

Minority mentoring	(Description of initiatives and communications options for supporting them)
Access for disabled	
etc	

Winning individuals or teams (one from each operating division) attend a celebrity prize-giving ceremony where they are presented with a £500 cheque for their charity or community organisation and a commemorative certificate.

Although communication audits are becoming relatively common, not many companies use them to cast light on social responsibility issues. Yet asking employees for their opinion on what should be the company's priorities, as Whitbread has done for example, is a valuable way of gaining feedback. A well-constructed audit should also provide useful data on how employees regard the company's performance in areas such as equal opportunities, customer care or ethical climate.

However information is gathered, it is useless unless it can be analysed and put to work. Part of the role of the social responsibility steering committee should be to commission studies, to interpret feedback from stakeholders and to ensure that valuable comments and ideas are not lost. In doing so, they should incorporate their efforts for continuous improvement into the central nervous system of internal communication, the business plan. Although few companies yet disseminate the business plan to all employees, simply building social responsibility objectives into the plan speaks louder than any other medium. It says, in particular, that the company is serious and committed to action.

12. The role of the social responsibility audit

Our research uncovered a number of companies, which had – usually fairly recently – instituted environmental audits, customer service audits and audits of specialist issues, such as equal opportunities in hiring and promotion. We did not find any company, however, which undertook a comprehensive audit of all activities which could be grouped under the heading of social responsibility.

The problem for the concerned company is that, while it is busy tackling perceived priority issues, matters may be going seriously awry in areas which are not subjected to senior management analysis and scrutiny.

We believe strongly that the social auditing process should be as broad as possible, to protect the organisation from as wide a variety of potential problems as possible.

So what is a social responsibility audit and how does it work?

In principle an SR audit is like any other business audit. It attempts to answer the management need for information on where the organisation's performance is now, and where it ought to be.

Normally, an audit will operate at three levels:
1. Policy:
   - are there written policies for each area of social responsibility?
   - do they reflect current thinking/knowledge?
   - do people within the relevant parts of the organisation know that the policies exist and roughly what they say?

2. Systems and standards for measuring performance in each area:
   - do the systems exist?
   - do they measure the right things?
   - do they work?/are they used?
   - are the standards high enough? (i.e. will they be overtaken

by legislation?) Can we seize competitive advantage by achieving higher standards? How do our standards compare with best practice elsewhere?
- are the standards clearly understandable and precise enough to be measured accurately, year on year?

3. Recording and analysing performance:
   - current
   - versus previous years
   - versus targets set.

In practice, initial audits are likely to discover that the necessary measurement systems do not exist. In many ways, the SR auditor is then in a similar situation to the financial auditor, who finds that there is no system to record invoices.

In those circumstances, he or she can:

- record the existence of active programmes and specific achievements within them
- recommend where the company should develop systems and standards and what these should contain.

Every area of social responsibility can be measured in this way. To give some examples:

- equal opportunities
  - percentage of workforce as total and percentage at different levels from each minority group
- pollution control
  - parts per million of emissions
- raw materials purchase (e.g. tropical hardwoods)
  - what steps could the company reasonably take? How many of these (%) has it taken?
- customer service
  - measurement of service quality by questionnaire or focus groups
  - complaints
  - repeat business
- supplier issues
  - attitude surveys
  - level of contact/sharing
    and so on.

Finally, an SR audit will seek to examine the degree of involvement and commitment to social responsibility at various levels in the organisation. For example:

- top management only
- the management group as a whole
- all employees
- all employees plus some suppliers and customers.

This information, once analysed, has two main uses. Firstly, it helps the company establish a coherent social responsibility plan – a framework of activities that meet the needs of various SR policies.

Secondly, it provides an excellent public relations platform, particularly if the company can point to continuing improvements both in standards aimed at and in actual performance. These issues are of interest to all stakeholders, but particularly to the employees, for whom pride in their employing organisation is an important part of motivation.

We recommend that, at the minimum, companies publish the results of an SR audit in their company newspaper. More ambitiously, they should consider publishing a separate social audit report to accompany the annual financial report and accounts.

Appendix 1: The survey of social responsibility in business

One of the most useful elements in the first edition of this book was the survey we conducted in 1990 among companies known to have an interest in social responsibility. We have subsequently repeated the survey, but extended it to cover more management issues.

The initial sample size in both cases was 42 questionnaire responses from UK companies, operating in a wide variety of industry sectors, both private and public, manufacturing and service. In both cases, the vast majority of companies were large or medium-sized. Other companies simply sent materials which described their programmes and approaches or returned questionnaires after the statistical analysis had been completed. We have not used these on a statistical basis, but wherever possible we have drawn on them for supporting evidence.

For the most recent survey we also obtained a small number of responses from continental Europe, which have not been included in the totals. While there were not sufficient of these responses to create a valid sample for comparison, they generally agree closely with the UK results. (The one exception is on whether the recession has resulted in cut-backs in corporate giving, where a much higher proportion said it had, compared with the UK respondents.)

The most striking observation from a comparison of the two surveys is the general consistency of the results (although there are one or two marked differences) in spite of the very different economic climates when each survey was carried out.

We first explored the *general environment for social responsibility*.

All respondents (compared with only 83% in 1990) considered that companies in general are becoming more conscious of their social responsibilities and most (92%) believed that companies are responding to those needs. All but one respondent believed that his or her company was becoming more conscious of its social responsibilities. The most frequent reasons for doing so (in the same order as for 1990) were:

- to enhance the corporate image (88%; 71% in 1990)
- as part of a corporate philosophy (81%; 57% in 1990)
- to support marketing activities (60%; 50% in 1990)
- as a result of competitive pressure (26%).

Only small percentages (14% and 15% respectively) were responding to public or legislative pressure. One company only was influenced by a major PR disaster.

On the other side of the social responsibility fence sit the various charities. Asked for their opinions on whether charities and community groups position themselves well to receive aid, our respondents were equally divided in their answers – again, exactly as in the previous survey.

As part of this section, we also looked at the degree to which companies had created the infrastructure to manage a broad range of social responsibility issues. We asked first if they had policies, guidelines, implementation procedures and methods of management for each of the following:

Business ethics
About half of the respondents had policies on ethics and slightly more (55%) had guidelines or codes of conduct. The figure rises to 64% at corporate level (26% at divisional level) for companies that have one or the other, but is still much lower than in the 1990 survey, where 83% had a general statement of business ethics. Our suspicion (supported by the materials sent to us by respondents and a similar number of companies, which did not complete the questionnaire) is that the true figure is the more recent – not least because other surveys of large companies only have suggested that 70% have codes of conduct. However, the confusion in terminology in this area (between visions, missions, statements of values, codes of conduct, ethics statements, statements of business philosophy and so on) does not help.

Only 40% had procedures to implement their ethical policies and less than half that number had any method of measuring whether the policies and procedures were working.

The environment
Just over three-quarters of respondents had environmental policies, with 52% producing guidelines (78% in 1990), 45% having implementation procedures (52% in 1990) and 26% having some form of measurement or auditing. The most common areas of environmental policy concerned pollution and

energy usage, followed by use of non-renewable resources and urban renewal, and the pattern of activities followed closely in suit.

The arts
Just over half had policies and 31% produced guidelines. Only 14% measured the effectiveness of their activities in this area.

The local community
Some 83% had policies, 55% guidelines, 24% had implementation procedures and 29% a system of measurement.

Schools
Three-quarters had policies, 43% (88% in 1990) guidelines, 38% (60% in 1990) had procedures to implement them and 24% had a system of measurement.

Employees
83% had general policies, 69% had guidelines and procedures, and just over half had some form of measuring progress. The vast majority (88% and 90% respectively versus 95% and 98% in 1990) had specific policies towards equal opportunities and health and safety. Not far behind, at 83%, came developing talent. Less than half had policies on employment security (compared with 71% in 1990) and only 14% (versus 21% in 1990) had policies on whistleblowing.

When it comes to specific activities in support of policies, a similar pattern emerges.

Customers
Three-quarters had policies on responsibilities towards their customers and 64% produced guidelines. Just under 70% had clear procedures to put the guidelines into practice and slightly less (60%) had some form of measurement – reflecting the growth of market research and customer satisfaction techniques. Not surprisingly, the policies tended to be focused around customer service (64%; 78% in 1990), with fair trading, product safety and fair marketing policies in 50%, 50% and 43% of companies respectively (very similar to 1990).

Suppliers
Half of the companies had policies concerning relationships with suppliers and 38% had guidelines and procedures to implement them; 26% measured adherence to the policy and guidelines. Two-thirds of companies had an active programme of purchasing ethics.

Shareholders
Again, half of the companies had relevant policies and 38% had guidelines. Only 24% had procedures to fulfil their responsibilities towards shareholders and only 17% carried out any form of measurement relating to how well they did so.

By and large, formal procedures for managing activities in each of the social responsibility areas tend to be underdeveloped. The only areas where half or more of companies have procedures are product safety, customer service, equal opportunities, health and safety at work, developing employees' talent, education and schools liaison, pollution control and energy usage. Not surprisingly, most of these are areas where there is either strong, direct commercial pressure or legislative requirements.

Even less developed are systems to monitor and measure the success of social responsibility activities, with less than one in three companies measuring performance even in critical areas such as equal opportunities or health and safety. Clearly, if these companies are not measuring performance, they can only use guesswork to identify whether or not they are improving.

We looked next at *how companies fund their social responsibility activities.*
The vast majority (85% versus 67% in 1990) had an annual budget and expenditure plan set at a corporate level, but 43% (45% in 1990) set budgets at divisional level. Some had budgets at both levels.

Actual allocation of funds for community activities was handled by the board or a board-level committee in just over half of companies (59% in 1990); by a public affairs department or specialist community affairs department in 62% (55% in 1990); and through a staff committee in just 21% (12% in 1990).

All but 15% were spending more in real terms than five years ago. However, 43% said that the recession had had a negative impact on the level of their corporate giving (80% of respondents from continental Europe!) and 19% felt it had decreased the importance of social responsibility on their company's business agenda.

There seemed to be a fair level of agreement as to where additional spending should go. Asked which areas would become more important to their company, the respondents replied, in order of importance, that customer service, equal opportunities, energy usage, health and safety, developing talent, education and schools liaison, pollution and the use of non-renewable resources were all assuming greater significance. Seeding community initiatives, such as crime prevention, homelessness or small business development, was expected to grow in importance for 60% of companies. At the other extreme, while one-third of companies expected job security to come higher on the agenda, half as many thought it would fall in importance. Moreover, in line with our previous findings in 1990, the arts are only expected to become more important in 21% of companies, while 14% of respondents actually expect them to decrease in importance to their companies.

Next, we examined the method of *structuring social responsibilities*.

Some 55% of companies had an individual or department with specific responsibility for social responsibility issues and these reported to a plethora of different titles, including: chairman, deputy chairman, managing director, company secretary, finance director, president, HR director, director of corporate affairs, group communications manager, trustees and charities + sponsorship committee. This seems to support the view that companies are unsure where to place what is essentially a new discipline. The situation is analogous to data processing or IT, which is not viewed as important enough in most companies to justify its own boardroom seat, but may be found under finance, operations, manufacturing or any of a dozen other executive umbrellas.

Responsibility for social issues tends to be concentrated at board level (in 83% of companies), but with 45% of companies also distributing responsibility to the divisions.

More than half (55%) of respondents said they had a champion for social responsibility at board level. However, only 29% thought social responsibility issues were very high on top management's agenda (55% thought they were quite important and 10% unimportant). The figures may be optimistic, suggested one manager, who wondered how honest responses would be!

Under the theme of *managing social responsibility*, we first investigated how often companies reviewed and assessed their policies and programmes. Most (55%) carried out annual reviews, with 14% reviewing quarterly. A small minority (5%) review policies and programmes every month, while 12% do so at other, sometimes irregular intervals. One in seven does not review its programmes at all.

In 62% of cases, the company has a formal strategy for enhancing social responsibility performance.

We also asked respondents to indicate what they perceived to be the most important factors in successful social responsibility management. The spread of opinion was remarkably wide, with no discernible pattern other than a general agreement that top management commitment was one of the two most critical factors. In order of importance, the key factors were felt to be:

- top management commitment (88%)
- employee involvement and commitment (79%)
- clear policy guidelines and procedures to follow (69%)
- defined goals and priorities (64%)
- systems for measuring and reporting results (52%)
- consistency (45%)
- training and skills development for managers responsible (45%)
- transparent decision-making processes (30%).

When we related this to a specific project, which they considered to be their most successful community/social responsibility project, the most significant factors were:

- appropriateness to the company's role in the community (76%)
- how well the project was managed (64%)
- being well publicised, with a high PR profile (50%)
- high level of employee participation (40%).

Our tentative conclusion is that there is a need both for management processes to support the broad social responsibility programme, and for individual projects; and that these may differ considerably in their objectives and emphasis.

The most significant challenge facing people responsible for managing social responsibility issues appears to be lack of cash for just over half of the respondents (36% in 1990). Lack of top management commitment is a problem in 36% of companies. By contrast, the 1990 survey found getting the organisation's view across to pressure groups to be the second most significant problem (31% versus 7% in 1992) – perhaps a reflection of companies' loss of interest in external views when survival is at stake – and lack of top management commitment to be a problem in only 19% of companies. As in 1990, poor quality of community projects on offer was only an issue for a very small minority.

Lastly, we attempted to explore how companies *maintain an ethical climate*. Not surprisingly very few companies (10%) had any form of ethical committee at board level and in most cases these turned out to be just the board members discussing ethical issues during their normal meetings. None of the respondents had received any specific training in ethical issues that might affect their companies.

When it came to informing the various stakeholder interests of the company's policies and activities in social responsibility (particularly important in setting an example) the responding companies were relatively efficient at communicating with employees and shareholders (57% and 54% respectively). Only one-third published any statement of their social responsibility policies and activities to customers or the general public, however; and even less (17% and 19% respectively) to suppliers and pressure groups.

There may well be an inadequate flow of information on social responsibility issues *into* the organisation, too. While 38% of companies gather external views on social issues via market research, only 29% have appointed non-executive directors from outside the business world to provide an alternative view. Less than a quarter of companies employ external consultants to advise them in social responsibility areas.

Most companies do not even expend much effort in sharing information for mutual advantage with other organisations interested in social responsibility issues. Only 21% did so frequently, 38% occasionally, and 26% rarely or never. However, this represents an improvement on 1990, when 55% said they did not exchange information on social responsibility issues.

On a more positive note, the proportion of companies which say they have made decisions on socially responsible grounds against their direct commercial interests has increased in this survey from 24% in 1990 to 33% in 1992.

Summary

Applying management processes to social responsibility still has a long way to go. The picture that emerges, both from this survey on its own and by comparison with the survey undertaken in 1990, is, however, generally positive. Companies are more aware of social issues, they are developing structures to manage them effectively (even if in a piecemeal and often unco-ordinated manner) and they are sharing information about good practice more freely.

It takes time for management practices to move out of the scope of theory and a few isolated exemplars and become part of the workaday furniture of the organisational structure. The names of the companies participating in our survey are not all the well-recognised pioneers; they include small businesses and partnerships, and large companies, which have only recently begun to formalise these areas of activity. We hope that this is an indication of a gradual maturing and wider dissemination of social responsibility management.

Appendix 2: Codes and policies

The issue of codes of practice or guidelines, statements of values or business principles – call them what you will – has recurred frequently in this book. The reason, quite simply, is that someone has to set the framework in which people can operate, if there is to be any coherence of approach in dealing with the wide variety of social responsibility issues that already face companies – let alone those yet to emerge!

A viable, useful code provides a broad description of what is and is not acceptable, sets broad standards and, on occasion, challenging goals. Its value lies in providing a reference, against which conflicts of interest can be tested. In theory – and to a large extent in practice, in companies where the codes are widely disseminated and lived up to by senior management – employees at all levels will incorporate the values into the day-to-day decisions and actions they make.

The risk of a proliferation of codes and guidelines on different topics is real. However, companies can overcome this by distinguishing between an overreaching set of business values/ principles and the policies that emanate from them. Inevitably, there will be some overlap, but the greater the clarity, the easier the "right" thing to do.

In this appendix, we have brought together examples of some codes and policies at different levels as follows:

- codes of general business practice
- policy on equal opportunities
- policy on employee development
- policy on environment
- policy on educational development.

There are numerous other areas in which we could have selected policy statements. By and large, however, they will follow the same basic approaches.

"The process of drawing up codes and keeping them up to date can clarify issues, concentrate minds and build a common commitment. Their promulgation sets norms and standards against which lapses can be admitted and behaviour changed. Moreover, a corporate culture can then be more easily sustained by internal social pressures whereas, with nothing written, the informal cultures that develop are very difficult to deal with," writes Neville Cooper, chairman of the Top Management Partnership and chairman of the Institute of Business Ethics in an occasional paper "What's All This About Business Ethics?"

In another booklet "Company Philosophies and Codes of Business Ethics", also published by the institute, writer and researcher Simon Webley outlines a model code and gives advice on how to set about drawing it up.

He says that the statement and code should not be left to an enthusiast on the board or delegated to the personnel department. In practice, he maintains, companies which value their statements and make use of them in daily life involve the most senior officers in drawing up and publishing them.

Guidelines for a model code of business principles

Preface or introduction (signed by the chairman, chief executive officer or both)

Start with a sentence on the purpose of the statement. Mention the values which are important to the top management in the conduct of the business such as integrity, efficiency, professionalism and responsibility.

Set out the role of the company in the community and end with a personal endorsement of the statement and the expectation that the standards set in it will be maintained by all involved in the organisation.

Date the preface.

Include:

a. The object of the business
   The service which is being provided and the business's role in society as the company sees it.
b. Customer relations
   The importance of customer satisfaction and good faith in all agreements. The priority given to customer needs, fair pricing and after-sales service.

c. Shareholders or other providers of money
   The protection of investment made in the company and
   proper return on money lent. As commitment to effective
   communication with this group of people.
d. Suppliers
   Long-term co-operation. Prompt settling of bills. Joint actions
   to achieve quality and efficiency.
e. Employees
   How the business values employees. The company's policies
   towards recruitment, development and training, rewards,
   communication, work conditions, health and safety, industrial relations, equal employment opportunity, retirement,
   severance and redundancy.
f. The wider community
   Compliance with the spirit as well as the letter of the law. The
   company's obligation to conform to the environmental and
   safety standards. The involvement of the company and its
   staff in local affairs. The corporate policy on giving to
   education and charities. The leadership role of the business in
   maintaining high standards both within the organisation and
   in its dealings with others.
g. Other matters
   Relations with competitors, research and development policy
   and management responsibility. The ethical standards
   expected of employees.

The issue of ethical standards is often best expanded on in a
separate statement addressed primarily at staff, says Webley,
who suggests that a typical, effective version will be short and
written in simple language. It should be concerned with
problems experienced by employees and include something
about procedures to be followed when confronted with an ethical
dilemma. It should also make clear what will happen if the code is
breached.

1. Introduction
This should state the reason why the code has been produced. It
should state that it applies to everyone and that anyone found
breaching it will be subject to serious disciplinary action.

2. Conflicts of interest
A clause covering conflicts of interest – for example, in the
company's dealings with immediate members of the employee's
family. A directive that all potential conflicts should be reported

to their immediate superior and recorded. A ban on share dealing with information obtained while working.

3. *Giving and receiving gifts*
The code must contain guidance on giving and receiving cash, services, hospitality or bribes in any form. It should include a statement that all offers made as an inducement should be refused.

State company policy on giving gifts to others.

State that any gifts received must be reported to a superior and recorded. The fact that business entertainment should be on a reciprocal basis and on a scale consistent with the status of the employee within the organisation.

4. *Confidentiality*
A statement that all information obtained during work is the property of the company.

State that confidential information must not be disclosed to an unauthorised person and that this also applies when the employee has left the company.

Advise the steps to be taken to safeguard information that might be useful to competitors.

5. *Environment*
A standard for the working environment and the effect of business activity on local communities.

A statement that the health and safety of employees is paramount. State that staff are required to see that products and operations not only comply with legal requirements but take into account the well-being of the general public – especially those living in the general vicinity of manufacturing plants.

6. *Equal opportunity*
An undertaking that selections for posts shall be based only on suitability. State that there will be no discrimination on the grounds of race, religion, marital status, colour, nationality, disability or ethnic or national origin. Outline similar undertakings on promotion and security of employment.

7. *Other areas*
There are a number of other areas that might be covered in such a code.

These include:

- political activities
- obligations under competition or anti-trust laws
- moonlighting by employees
- sexual harassment.

Examples of codes of practice

The following examples have been chosen to illustrate some of the variety of statements which organisations have used to establish ethical values and principles within their organisations.

Case study: Forte plc

Forte plc has opted for a short written outline of company philosophy. It states:

The company philosophy

- To increase profitability and earnings per share each year in order to encourage investment and to improve and expand the business
- To give complete customer satisfaction by efficient and courteous service and value for money
- To support managers and their staff in using personal initiative to improve the profit and quality of their operations while observing company policies
- To provide good working conditions and to maintain effective communications at all levels to develop better understanding and assist decision-making
- To ensure no discrimination against sex, race, colour or creed and to train, develop and encourage promotion within the company based on merit and ability
- To act with integrity at all times and to maintain a proper sense of responsibility towards the public
- To recognise the importance of each and every employee who contributes towards these aims.

Case study: The Body Shop

The Body Shop Charter

We declare that:
1. The Body Shop's goals and values are as important as our products and our profits.
2. Our policies and our products are geared to meet the real people, both inside and outside the company.
3. Honesty, integrity and caring form the foundations of the company, and should flow through everything we do.
4. We care about each other as indiviudals: we will continue to endeavour to bring meaning and pleasure to the workplace.
5. We care about our customers, and will continue to bring humanity into the marketplace
6. We care about humanising the business community: we will continue to show that success and profits can go in hand with ideals and values.

In addition the Body Shop declares:

- We will demonstrate our care for the world in which we live, by respecting fellow human beings, by not harming animals, by working to conserve our planet
- We will continue to create products which show that we care: by not testing on animals, by using naturally-based ingredients that are close to source, by making products which work for our customers
- We will continue to search, to challenge, to question, to celebrate life and generate joy and excitement
- We embrace everyone who works for The Body Shop and with The Body Shop as part of our extended family. We are all the company: it is up to us to make it work.

Case study: Royal Dutch/Shell Group of Companies

The Royal Dutch/Shell Group of Companies has a general statement of business principles which was published in the Institute of Business Ethics booklet "Company Philosophies and Codes of Business Ethics". In the introduction to the detailed statement, the chairman of the Committee of Managing Directors of the Service Companies, Mr L.C. van Wachem, explains why such a document is important. He says: "The group is typified by decentralised, highly diversified and widespread operations, in which operating companies are given wide freedom of action. However, the upholding of the Shell reputation is a common bond which can be maintained only by honesty and integrity in all activities. A single failure, whether it be wilful or due to a misplaced zeal, or short-term expediency, can have very serious effects on the group as a whole."

Statement of general business principles

1. Objectives
The objectives of Shell companies are to engage efficiently, responsibly and profitably in the oil, gas, chemicals, coal, metals and selected other businesses, and to play an active role in the search for and development of other sources of energy. Shell companies seek high standards of performance and aim to maintain a long-term position in their respective competitive environments.

2. Responsibilities
Four areas of responsibility are recognised:

- a. To shareholders
  To protect shareholders' investment and provide an acceptable return.
- b. To employees
  To provide all employees with good and safe conditions of work, good and competitive conditions of service; to promote the development and best use of human talent and equal opportunity development; and to encourage the involvement of employees in the planning and direction of their work, recognising that success depends on the full contribution of all employees.
- c. To customers
  To develop and provide products and services which offer value in terms of price and quality, supported by the requisite technological, and

commercial expertise. There is no guaranteed future: Shell companies depend on winning and maintaining customers' support.

d. To society

To conduct business as responsible corporate members of society, observing applicable laws of countries in which they operate, giving due regard to safety and environmental standards and societal aspirations.

These four areas of responsibility can be seen as an inseparable whole.

3. Economic principles

Profitability is essential to discharging these responsibilities and staying in business. It is a measure both of efficiency and of the ultimate value that people place on Shell products and services.

It is essential to the proper allocation of corporate resources and necessary to support the continuing investment required to develop and produce future energy supplies to meet consumer needs. Without profits and a strong financial foundation it would not be possible to fulfil the responsibilities outlined above.

Shell companies work in a wide variety of social, political and economic environments over the nature of which they have little influence, but in general they believe that the interests of the community can be served most efficiently by a market economy.

Criteria for investment decisions are essentially economic but also take into account social and environmental considerations and an appraisal of the security of the investment.

4. Voluntary codes of conduct

Policies of Shell companies are consistent with the two internationally agreed voluntary codes of conduct for multinational enterprises, the OECD Declaration and Guidelines for International Investment and Multinational Enterprises and the ILO Tripartite Declaration of Principles.

5. Business integrity

Shell companies insist on honesty and integrity in all aspects of their business. All employees are required to avoid conflicts of interest between their private financial activities and their part in the conduct of company business. The offer, payment, soliciting and acceptance of bribes in any form are unacceptable practices. All transactions on behalf of a Shell company must be appropriately described in the accounts of the company in accordance with established procedures and subject to audit.

6. Political activities

a. Shell companies endeavour always to act commercially, operating within existing national laws in a socially responsible manner, abstaining from participation in party politics. It is, however, the legitimate right and responsibility to speak out on matters that affect the interests of employees, customers and shareholders, and on matters of general interest, where they have a contribution to make that is based on particular knowledge.

b. Political payments

As a policy, Shell companies do not make payments to political parties, organisations or their representatives.

c. Employees

Where employees, in their capacity as citizens, wish to engage in activities in the community, including standing for election to public office, favourable consideration is given to their being enabled to do so, where this is appropriate in the light of local circumstances.

7. Environment

It is the policy of Shell companies to conduct their activities in such a way as to take foremost account of the health and safety of their employees and of other persons, and to give proper regard to the conservation of the environment. In implementing this policy Shell companies not only comply with the requirements of the relevant legislation but promote in an appropriate manner measures for the protection of health, safety and the environment for all who may be affected directly or indirectly by their activities. Such measures pertain to safety of operations carried out by employees and contractors; product safety; prevention of air, water and soil pollution; and precautions to minimise damage from such accidents as may nevertheless occur.

8. Grants and general community projects

The most important contribution that companies can make to the social and material progress of the countries in which they operate is in performing their basic activities as efficiently as possible. In addition, the need is recognised to take a constructive interest in societal matters which may not be directly related to the business. Opportunities for involvement, for example, through community, educational or donations programmes, will vary depending upon the size of the company concerned, the nature of the local society and the scope for useful private initiatives.

9. Information

The importance of the activities in which Shell companies are engaged and their impact on national economies and individuals are well recognised. Full relevant information about these activities is therefore provided to legitimately interested parties, both national and international, subject to any overriding consideration of confidentiality proper to the protection of the business and the interests of third parties and the need to avoid wasteful information exercises.

Increasingly, the behaviour of large companies is subject to rigorous external scrutiny. The reputation of the Royal Dutch/Shell Group of Companies depends on the existence and acknowledgement of clearly understood principles and responsibilities and their observance in day-to-day practice in widely differing environments. Although individual operating companies may elaborate their own statements to meet their national situations, this statement of general business principles serves as a basis on which companies of the Royal Dutch/Shell Group, in their operations, pursue the highest standards of business behaviour. Shell companies also promote the application of these principles in joint ventures in which they participate.

Case study: British Gas

1. Financial or other interest

a. Conflict of interest

Anyone who has a personal interest in an organisation with which British Gas has or may have a business relationship is vulnerable to allegations of impropriety. If a personal interest or that of a member of one's immediate family might influence the company's business relationship, it should be formally declared in writing at the HQ to the company secretary or in a region to the regional secretary, who will record the declaration of interest in a register maintained for this purpose. Examples of personal interest that should be declared are a directorship, a large shareholding, promise of future employment or the employment of a close relative or friend in a position of influence in an organisation which may be given business or awarded contracts by the company.

b. Dealing in shares of British Gas plc
Some staff have access during their work to unpublished information about the company's activities or future prospects which, if published, might affect the share prices. If you are in this special position and you wish to buy or sell British Gas shares, you must first study the separate guidelines on share dealing which will be available from your head of department.

c. Dealing in shares of other companies
You should not deal in the securities of any company when, by virtue of your position as an employee of British Gas, you are in possession of information likely upon publication to affect the market price of those securities. This includes shares or debentures or options to subscribe for shares or debentures.

d. Purchasing and supplies department
In addition to the foregoing, if you are a senior officer or above within the purchasing department at headquarters or in a region, you will be required from time to time formally to declare in writing to your HQ or regional director or controller details of any shareholding, involvement or activity which could give rise to a conflict of interest. Everyone employed in the industry's purchasing function is expected to abide by the Institute of Purchasing and Supply's Code of Ethics.

e. Declaration of interest
In addition to the foregoing, if in any other department you are in a position to influence the choice of contractors or suppliers, you may be required to make a similar declaration at the discretion of your managing director, HQ director or regional chairman as appropriate.

2. Gifts, hospitality or benefits
It is a criminal offence to accept or solicit any gift or consideration from anyone as an inducement or reward for showing favour in connection with the company's business.

To avoid any possibility of misunderstanding, all such offers should be politely but firmly declined. Gifts delivered should be returned to the sender with an appropriately worded letter and the matter reported to your superior. The only exception is that gifts of a trifling nature such as calendars or diaries may be accepted.

Any approaches from contractors, suppliers or traders, seeking favoured treatment in consideration of any offers of benefits or hospitality must be firmly declined and the circumstances reported to your superior.

Business entertainment should be on a reciprocal basis and on a scale consistent with that which you, when host, would be authorised to arrange.

If you have the slightest doubt about accepting any offer of benefits or hospitality you have clearly recognised a potentially dangerous situation and should seek guidance from your superior.

3. Confidentiality of information
We all have a responsibility to safeguard the confidentiality of any information acquired during the course of our work, including information kept on computers and a duty never to use it for personal advantage. Such information should not be disclosed outside. Equally, we should all be on our guard and avoid careless and thoughtless talk which may damage the company's business or that of any of its customers.

4. Confidential disclosures
Any disclosure or similar communication made to management in accordance with this code will be treated as confidential although it may be discussed with your director or controller.

If in doubt
a. This code has been prepared to give guidance. If you are ever in any doubt about any matter concerning conduct, you should seek advice from your superior. You should also be aware that breaches of the code can result in disciplinary action.
b. Refer to examples of codes of practice in specific areas.

Policy on equal opportunities

Ford Motor Company's joint statement on equal opportunity

Ford Motor Company hands out the following statement, written in November 1988, to all employees. Signed by the company and its trade unions, entitled "Joint Statement on Equal Opportunity", it is one of the most comprehensive equal opportunities policy documents in the country:

1. Commitment to equal opportunity
1.1 The company and the trade unions are committed to the principle of equal opportunity in employment. The company and the trade unions declare their opposition to any form of less favourable treatment, whether through direct or indirect discrimination, accorded to employees and applicants for employment on the grounds of race, religious creed, colour, nationality, ethnic or national origins, marital status or sex.

1.2 The company and the trade unions similarly declare their opposition to any form of less favourable treatment accorded to employees and applicants for employment on the grounds of non-job related disabilities and unfair discrimination on the grounds of age.

1.3 The company and trade unions recognise their obligations under the Sex Discrimination Act 1975 and the Race Relations Act

1976 and support the spirit and intent of the related codes of practice:

- for the elimination of discrimination on the grounds of sex and marriage and the promotion of equality of opportunity in employment
- for the elimination of racial discrimination and the promotion of equality of opportunity in employment.

2. Employment practices
2.1 The company and the trade unions state their wholehearted support for the principle and practice of equal opportunity and agree that it is the duty of all employees to accept their personal responsibility for fostering a fully integrated community at work by adhering to the principles of equal opportunity and maintaining racial harmony. The company will, therefore, actively promote equal opportunity through the application of employment policies which will ensure that individuals receive treatment which is fair, equitable and consistent with their relevant aptitudes, potential, skills and abilities. The trade unions will seek to ensure that all members and representatives comply with these principles and practices.

2.2 The company will ensure that individuals are recruited and selected, promoted and treated on objective criteria having regard to relevant aptitudes, potential, skills and abilities. In particular, no applicant or employee will be placed at a disadvantage by the requirements or conditions which are not necessary to the performance of the job or which constitute indirect unfair discrimination.

2.3 The company and the trade unions recognise the problems that sexual harassment may cause in the workplace and are jointly committed to ensuring that such unacceptable behaviour does not take place. Sexual harassment includes unwanted physical contact; suggestive remarks or behaviour; compromis-ing invitations; demands for sexual favours and similar unwanted behaviour. Sexual harassment is regarded as unfair discriminatory conduct and will be dealt with in accordance with the procedures set out in 4.2 below.

3. Monitoring and review arrangements
3.1 The company and the trade unions recognise that regular monitoring of the ethnic origin and sex of employees is essential to the thorough review of the effectiveness of the joint statement and to this end the company will maintain and improve as

necessary the current equal opportunity monitoring arrangements. These may be extended where agreed by the company and trade unions for the purpose of completing jointly agreed special exercises at local or national level.

3.2 The successful implementation of this joint statement is dependent on the regular examination of progress towards equal opportunity and the development of local initiatives. To this end, local management and trade unions are expected to set up appropriate joint bodies at plant or equivalent level.

3.3 The company will send a copy of the company-wide annual review of equal opportunity statistics to the trade unions.

3.4 The practical application of this joint statement will be subject to regular review at national level to ensure that it continues to be fully effective.

4. *Grievance and disciplinary procedures*

4.1 The company and trade unions will ensure that individual employees or groups of employees who believe that they have experienced direct or indirect unfair discrimination are properly represented. Any employee who feels that he or she has been treated unfairly in connection with his or her employment should raise his or her grievance through the appropriate procedure when every effort will be made to secure a satisfactory resolution. In addition, both the company and the trade unions will ensure that any employees making a complaint of unfair discrimination will be protected from victimisation.

4.2 The company will continue to treat unfair discriminatory conduct by any employee as a disciplinary offence.

5. *Training and advertising*

5.1 The company will provide in agreement with the trade unions, suitable and relevant equal opportunity training, as necessary and on a jointly agreed syllabus, for employees and trade union representatives. The trade unions agree to support and participate in such training programmes and to encourage their representatives to attend where appropriate. These arrangements in no way preclude the separate provision of training by the company or the trade unions to meet particular needs.

5.2 When vacancies are advertised, the company will continue to ensure such advertising, both in placement and content, is compatible with the terms of this joint statement. To this end, opportunities will be taken through language, images or declarations, as appropriate, to show that the company is an equal opportunity employer.

6. Communications
6.1 The company and the trade unions undertake to bring the principles set out above to the attention of all employees and the trade union representatives.

Policy on employee development

Case study: PowerGen

Values for managing people in PowerGen

PowerGen's future depends on the efforts of all the people who work for the company, and our ability to work as a team.

The executive is committed to a management style which will establish a well-informed, well-trained and well-motivated team as the best basis for achieving our main goal of producing electricity at the lowest cost.

PowerGen's mission statement sets out our aims for three key interest groups:

- Customers – we intend to satisfy our customers by being innovative and responsive to their needs
- Shareholders – we aim to create value for our shareholders
- Staff – we intend to provide secure and rewarding jobs for our employees.

Only by meeting the needs of our customers and shareholders can PowerGen manage and develop the business so as to provide the means for meeting the needs of staff.

We operate in an environment of risk, as do all companies, including our competitors. If we do not succeed in our mission our competitors will take business away from us, and our plant will cease to make money. We plan to succeed, but success cannot be taken for granted. We must pursue our goal of lowest cost producer by a constant effort to improve our performance and a constant preparedness to manage change effectively.

In order to help deal with change and uncertainty, and as a foundation for our future success, PowerGen has chosen to adopt the following long-term values for managing our people. We believe these values will evolve and develop over time, but as basic principles for dealing with people they should not be affected by short-term fluctuations in the conduct of our affairs.

We will act with integrity and in a caring manner when dealing with employees when they join the company, while they are with us, and when they leave. We will seek to base our relationship with staff on mutual understanding and respect for the individual.

Managers and staff must be able to communicate with each other openly and freely. Everyone at PowerGen should understand what is needed of them and why.

We need people who understand the demands of a competitive market and who can take advantage of the opportunities it provides; people who can respond to new and complex technologies; people who realise the need to promote the highest safety standards and to care for the environment. We must encourage them to use their talent and initiative as well as their skills and experience.

We believe strongly in training and developing staff to improve the performance of the individual and the team. This makes us more adaptable and more able to succeed in meeting competitive challenge. Managers are responsible for planning the development of their staff and making provision for succession.

PowerGen provides equal opportunity in all aspects of employment. When we select staff for employment, promotion, training and development, our aim is to get the best match between the needs of the organisation and the ability of the individual.

We want to establish PowerGen's reputation as an excellent company to work for. We will seek to meet the aspirations of our employees for job satisfaction, opportunity to develop and realise their potential, to enjoy the quality of their working life, and to benefit from fair and competitive terms and conditions of employment.

High standards of safety are essential both to protect the interests of staff and to achieve business efficiency. PowerGen's safety standards and practices will rank with the best worldwide. PowerGen management recognises its accountability for achieving excellent standards of safety and fire prevention. Every PowerGen employee shares the responsibility for maintaining the highest standards of safety at work.

We recognise the benefit of good health to individuals and its benefits to the company as a whole, and will promote a positive programme of employee health care. Prevention of accidents and promotion of good health are recognised as positive contributions to ensuring that people are fit for work.

We respect employees' right to belong to trade unions. We will provide appropriate arrangements that enable recognised trade unions to represent the interest of their members.

Our employees can only give their best if the quality of their management is first class. PowerGen aims to develop mutual trust and common interest between all members of the team. This is achieved by creating a culture which motivates staff and helps them to perform well; and in which achievement is valued and rewarded.

All managers are accountable to the executive for their performance in managing people. Managers will be supported to provide leadership which develops the strength and commitment of their teams.

Policy on the environment

3M's official environment policy

Under its worldwide environmental policy 3M will continue to recognise and exercise responsibility to:

- solve its own environmental pollution and conservation problems
- prevent pollution at source wherever possible
- develop products that will have a minimum effect on the environment
- conserve natural resources through the use of reclamation and other appropriate methods
- ensure that its facilities and products meet and sustain the regulations of all federal, state and local environmental agencies
- assist wherever possible, governmental agencies and official organisations engaged in environmental activities.

Policy on educational involvement

The Wellcome Foundation Ltd's policy on links with education states:

Wellcome supports the view that a healthy business needs a healthy community. Education is critical to the vitality and prosperity of our society, especially its economic performance in increasingly international markets. The company knows that the long-term success of its business will require a more highly educated workforce capable of coping with rapid change and that, in order to respond to these needs, education will in turn need the company's support and involvement.

Wellcome's support has both local and national aspects, but the company believes that building links, that is establishing *partnerships* with local schools and colleges, must form the basis of work with education. This is the foundation for developing projects and material for national dissemination.

Partnership with education
The aims:

- better preparation of young people for the rapidly changing world of work
- better understanding between education and industry
- better knowledge of science and technology for all.

To help managers, employees and community partners to understand the relationship between company objectives and educational needs, it has published the tables on pages 314–317.

To assist the development of a strategy for the company at the local level, it is useful to relate company objectives to the educational motives. Tables 1 and 2 which follow suggest activities which are already taking place or which may be developed or expanded to satisfy these two parameters, in the short and medium term.

Educational motives:
- *Curriculum development*
- *Careers education*
- *Informed employers*

- *expert input on relevant subjects and themes in the curriculum*
- *a realistic input from industry*
- *major changes and new initiatives in education*
- *the role and value of the teacher*

- *Informed teachers*
- *Access to resources*

- *Advice and consultancy*

- *increased understanding of industry*
- *financial resources for prizes and sponsorship*
- *equipment*
- *on aspects of school management*
- *on business-related activity*

Table 1

SHORT-TERM COMPANY OBJECTIVES / EDUCATIONAL MOTIVES	UNDERSTANDING OF INDUSTRY AND PROMOTION OF PERSONAL CONTACTS	CONTRIBUTING TO LOCAL COMMUNITY RELATIONS	HELPING SCHOOL LEAVER/ GRADUATE RECRUITMENT	PROMOTING IMAGE OF PHARMACEUTICAL INDUSTRY
CURRICULUM DEVELOPMENT	• Work experience for students on employers' premises carrying out specific task for coursework. • Employees work with teachers to develop materials and strategies to meet national curriculum needs for economic and industrial understanding.	• Offer visits to sites and offices for students to see the application of what they are learning.	• Work with teachers to develop learning materials to encourage specific skills and knowledge needed.	• Wellcome pharmacists/ chemists/biologists work with science teachers to give relevance to course work. • Develop case studies on different facets of the industry.
CAREERS EDUCATION	• Support local careers conventions by staffing displays. • Work experience for 4th/5th/6th form students to enable them to see what industry is like.	• Make company site visits available for groups of students and careers teachers/officers to see the range of employment opportunities. • Hold an open day for parents, teachers and	• Employees carry out mock interviews for students on company sites. • Use work experience placements to identify potential recruits. • Provide case studies on	• Employees from different departments contribute to careers education courses. • Contribute to national promotions informing about opportunities and skills shortages.

EDUCATIONAL MOTIVES \ SHORT-TERM COMPANY OBJECTIVES	UNDERSTANDING OF INDUSTRY AND PROMOTION OF PERSONAL CONTACTS	CONTRIBUTING TO LOCAL COMMUNITY RELATIONS	HELPING SCHOOL LEAVER/ GRADUATE RECRUITMENT	PROMOTING IMAGE OF PHARMACEUTICAL INDUSTRY
MUTUAL UNDERSTANDING	• Employees spend time in educational institutions work-shadowing teachers/ lecturers. • Employee serves on governing body of school/ college. • Teacher work-shadows employee, has work placement on company site.	• Make Wellcome materials available to schools and colleges to display in their institutions. • Wellcome employee serves on local Business-Education Partnership forum or education industry liaison group.	• Work with local compact or partnership providing employment with training.	• Contribute to development of resource materials on the industry, for use in education – videos, simulations. • Work with ABPI, CIA and ASE.
ACCESS TO RESOURCES Financial and material	• Sponsor local training event for teachers on economic and industrial awareness. • Provide support to develop business simulation on industry's role in society.	• Provide redundant equipment and materials to school/college if appropriate. • Allow use of materials/ equipment on company site by students/teachers. • Sponsor local project on topical issue for different ages.	• Offer paid holiday employment. • Donate prizes for individual student achievements.	• Sponsor design project for corporate image of pharmaceutical industry. • Contribute to national programmes with ABPI, CIA, Royal Society of Chemistry, Royal Pharmaceutical Society, ASE.
ADVICE AND CONSULTANCY	• Wellcome provides support for local developments – financial management in schools, staff training, appraisal techniques. • Invite teachers onto company training courses.	• Institutions provide company sites with information and update on educational developments.	• Provide specific information on company needs, qualifications and progression routes.	

Table 2

EDUCATIONAL MOTIVES	HELPING TO PREPARE PUPILS FOR THE WORLD OF WORK	DEVELOPING YOUNGER EMPLOYEES THROUGH WORK WITH SCHOOLS	PUTTING INDUSTRY RELATED MATERIAL INTO THE CURRICULUM	ENCOURAGING INTEREST IN SCIENCE FROM AN EARLY AGE TO AVOID FUTURE SHORTAGES	ENABLING WELLCOME EMPLOYEES TO LEARN ABOUT EDUCATION SYSTEM AND SCHOOLS
CURRICULUM DEVELOPMENT	• Provide work experience, work-shadowing for students with identified aims. • Assist with preparation and de-briefing. Contribute to assessment. • Act as advisors for projects.	• Employees and teachers work together, in classroom and on company premises, using Wellcome as context for learning. e.g. Project work for: • humanities • health education • design and technology • problem-solving • prevocational and vocational training.	• Work with teachers/advisors to develop appropriate materials for all subjects including languages – problem-solving activities, role-play, simulations – printed matter, video, tape, computer program.	• Employees work with science teachers to develop exciting methods of delivering science and technology in National Curriculum. • Work with examination boards – on assessment targets.	• Information flow and absorption facilitated by employees' direct involvement in developments and support for and contact with education.
CAREERS EDUCATION	• Use employees from different departments and at a variety of levels in careers education courses as role-models.	• Involve employees from all parts of the company at careers conventions and displays. • Use case studies of employees' career progression to promote opportunities – in company/industry.	• Develop new or amend existing company material on self-awareness. • Invite teachers to assess existing company material for use in school. • Provide details of progression and career development.	• Provide exciting examples of the use of scientific knowledge and skills at all levels through people and materials.	• Support the local careers offficer/teacher/employers group. • Provide up-to-date information on company and industry to schools and careers service to reciprocate their contribution.

TABLE 2 *continued*

MEDIUM-TERM COMPANY OBJECTIVES / EDUCATIONAL MOTIVES	HELPING TO PREPARE PUPILS FOR THE WORLD OF WORK	DEVELOPING YOUNGER EMPLOYEES THROUGH WORK WITH SCHOOLS	PUTTING INDUSTRY RELATED MATERIAL INTO THE CURRICULUM	ENCOURAGING INTEREST IN SCIENCE FROM AN EARLY AGE TO AVOID FUTURE SHORTAGES	ENABLING WELLCOME EMPLOYEES TO LEARN ABOUT EDUCATION SYSTEM AND SCHOOLS
MUTUAL UNDERSTANDING	• Employees act as advisors for enterprise activities and business simulations.	• Identify skills and knowledge company is seeking and link with National Curriculum.	• Invite teachers to spend placement with company to identify possible areas for material development. • Employee spends time with teacher in school.	• Raise employees' awareness of content of science curriculum by working with teachers and using employees' experience to advise on approaches, applications etc.	• Link with a local school or set up a local partnership with a consortium of primary/ secondary schools and colleges. • Form a liaison group. • Hold an open day.
ACCESS TO RESOURCES Financial and material	• Make "relevant" employees available to contribute to school curriculum activities. • Fund work experience placement expenses, e.g. lunch and travel.	• Donate prizes/awards for skills achievements for students in different age groups. • Provide training courses for employees linked to school activities, e.g. interviewing skills.	• Provide financial and technical support for: • development • printing • dissemination and in-service teacher training.	• Sponsor young scientist competition. • Work with national projects – ABPI, CIA, ASE and other companies.	• Provide support for information sharing sessions. • Work with PTA. • Invite education input to company staff group meetings.
ADVICE AND CONSULTANCY	• Employees offer advice on professional career routes. • Invite teachers to join in-house training courses.	• Support local compact/ partnership.	• Work with ABPI, CIA, ASE.	• Use your local school-industry liaison officer to link into programme of activity, e.g. SATRO.	• Use a consultant/ advisor to develop training and awareness raising programme.

British Rail's education/industry liaison policy states five objectives:

- to increase the level of awareness among pupils and students of the industry's business needs and priorities
- to improve the calibre of potential recruits to the industry from school-leaver population
- to enhance the attractiveness of the industry as an employer against the background of greater competition for staff due to the declining labour force
- to secure for all young people the education, training, personal development and employment opportunities they need to become productive and responsible members of the community
- to have a greater understanding of the education system and to seek to influence the development of the curriculum.

BR's policy is to attain these objectives through a range of prescribed activities which form what it describes as a code of best practice. This includes:

- the establishment of effective local partnerships founded on a steering group of key leaders from education, employers and the community
- joint planning by education authorities and employers to achieve skill-matching
- curriculum and syllabus development to take account of economic and industrial awareness, enterprise and technology
- secondment of staff in both directions
- visits to schools by senior corporate managers and local managers
- the appointment of employers' representatives to school governing bodies
- the provision of work experience placements and work-shadowing opportunities for pupils
- visits by pupils and students to key BR sites and installations
- development programmes for teachers and local employees
- the establishment of local bargains known as "compacts", especially in areas of urban deprivation.

The policy statement goes on to state that "the mainstream of effort to be directed towards these activities should be at regional and/or area/depot level". It explicitly recognises that each region and function will need to develop its own approach within the policy framework and that local managers will need to take the initiative to make the policy stick. It further stresses that "these activities should be pursued in the context of positive encouragement from board headquarters".

To avoid duplication of effort each area should designate a manager – normally the area personnel manager – to be responsible for co-ordinating BR/education links.

Finally, and significantly, the BR policy document states: "It is recognised that this policy is designed to be illustrative of what can be achieved for the benefit of all parties – it is not prescriptive, but the board counsels the pursuit of it since the attachment of a better trained and motivated workforce from the ranks of school children and students is essential to the achievement of the industry's total business objectives."

Appendix 3: Useful addresses

For further information and help, contact:

Responsibilities towards customers

Committee of Advertising Practice (CAP)
Brook House
2-16 Torrington Place
London
WC1E 7HN
071-580 5555

The Advertising Standards Authority
Brook House
2 – 16 Torrington Place
London
WC1E 7HN

Responsibilities towards employees

Health Education Authority
Hamilton House
Mabledon Place
London
WC1H 9TX

Institute of Manpower Studies
Mantell Building
University of Sussex
Falmer
Brighton
BN1 9RF

Institute of Personnel Management
IPM House
Camp Road

Wimbledon
London
SW19 4UW
081-946 9100

New Ways to Work
309 Upper Street
London
N1 2TY
071-226 4026

Social Audit and Public Interest Research Centre
PO Box 111
London
NW1 8XG
071-586 7771

Department of Employment
Moorfoot
Sheffield
S1 4PQ

Women
The Equal Opportunities Commission
Overseas House
Quay Street
Manchester
M3 3HN
061-833 9244

Opportunity 2000
5 Cleveland Place
London
SW1Y 6JJ
071-321 6426

Training and enterprise
The Industrial Society
3 Carlton House Terrace

London
SW1Y 5DG
071-839 4300

National Training Task force
Room W719
Moorfoot
Sheffield
S1 4PQ
0742 593944

TEC Secretariat
0524 843566

Ethnic minorities
The Commission for Racial
Equality
Elliot House
10-12 Allington Street
London
SW1E 5EH
071-824 7022

Fullemploy
County House
Great Dover Street
London
SE1 5DG
071-378 1774

Disabled people
Susan Scott-Parker
Employers Forum on Disability
5 Cleveland Place
London
SW1Y 6JJ
071-321 6591

RADAR (Royal Association for
Disability and Rehabilitation)
25 Mortimer Street
London
W1N 8AB
071-637 5400

Ex-offenders
Apex Trust
12-18 Hoxton Street
London
N1 6NG
071-729 5979

NACRO
169 Clapham Road
London
SW9 0PU
071-582 5100

Young people
Prince's Trust
8 Bedford Row
London
WC1R 4BA
071-430 0524

Long-term unemployed
Community Industry
Head Office, Victoria House
Croft Street
Widnes
Cheshire
WA8 0NQ
051-495 2114

Purchasing

Better Made in Britain
39-40 St James Place
London
SW1A 1NS
071-491 0458

Business in the Community (BiC)
227a City Road
London
EC1V 1LX
071-253 3716

Furniture Industry Research
Association
Maxwell Road
Stevenage
Hertfordshire

Institute of Purchasing and
Supply
Easton House
Easton on the Hill
Stamford
Lincs
PE9 3NZ
0780 56777

Regain programme

Kirklees and Wakefield Chamber
of Commerce
0484 423455

Small Business Unit
Durham University
Durham
Co Durham
091-374 2000

Responsibilities towards shareholders

Proshare
Library Chambers
13-14 Basinghall Street
London EC2V 5BQ
071-600 0984

Responsibilities towards the broader community

Charity Commission
St Albans House
57-60 Haymarket
London
SW1Y 4QX

London Education Business
Partnership
c/o Whitbread & Co
The Brewery
Chiswell Street
London
EC1Y 4SD
071-606 4455

London Enterprise Agency
(LEntA)
4 Snow Hill
London
EC1A 2BS
071-236 3000

The Per Cent Club/BiC
227a City Road
London
EC1V 1LX
071-253 3716

Secondment
David Hemsworth
Action Resource Centre (ARC)
First Floor
102 Park Village East
London
NW1 3SP
071-383 2200

Charities
Charities Aid Foundation
8 Pembury Road
Tonbridge
Kent
TN9 2JD
0732 771333

Directory of Social Change
Radius Works
Back Lane
London
NW8 1HL
071-435 8171

Small business
Federation of Small Businesses
140 Lower Marsh
Westminster Bridge
London
SE1 7AE
071-928 9272

Prince's Youth Business Trust
5 Cleveland Place
London
SW1Y 6JJ
071-321 6501

Education
John Abbott
Education 2000
Garden City Corporation Offices
The Broadway
Letchworth Garden City
Hertfordshire
SG6 3AB
0462 482424

Peter Davies
Teacher Placement Service

Sun Alliance House
New Inn Hall Street
Oxford
OX1 2QE

Chris Lea or John Woolhouse
Centre for Education and
Industry
University of Warwick
0203 524330 or 524371

SCIP/MESP
Carol Kay
University of Warwick
0203 523950

Headteachers into Industry
David Coulson
University of Warwick
0203 524331

University of Warwick
Westwood Campus
Coventry
CV4 7AL

Peter Westgarth
Young Enterprise
Ewart Place
Summertown
Oxford
OX2 7B2
0865 311180

John Rennie
Community Education
Development Centre
Lyng Hall
Blackberry Lane
Coventry
CV2 3JS
0203 638660

Roger Opie
Industrial Society
Quadrant Court
49 Calthorpe Road
Birmingham
B15 1TH
021-454 6769

John Allum or David Merrel
Standing Conference on Schools'
Science and Technology (SCSST)
76 Portland Place
London
W1N 4AA
071-278 2468

John Williams
The Engineering Council
10 Maltravers Street
London
WC2R 3ER
071-240 7891

David Blandford
Careers Research and Advisory
Centre (CRAC)
Sheraton House
Castle Park
Cambridge
CB3 OAX
0223 460277

Keith Dexter
Trident Trust
91 Brick Lane
London
E1 6QN
071-375 0245

Alaine Low
Understanding British Industry
(UBI)
Sun Alliance House
New Inn Hall Street
Oxford
OX1 2QE
0865 722585

Antony Wood
Understanding Industry
Enterprise House
59 Upper Ground
London
SE1 9PQ
071-620 0735

Crime prevention
Nigel Whiskin MBE

Crime Concern
David Murray John Buildings
Brunel Centre
Swindon
SN1 1LY
0793 514596

Responsibilities towards the environment

Association of Environment
Conscious Builders
Windlake House
The Pump Field
Coaley
Gloucester
GL11 5DX

British Trust for Conservation
Volunteers
80 York Way
London
N1 9AG
071-833 8951

Business and the Environment
Unit
Ian Oakins DTI
Room 1016
Ashdown House
123 Victoria Street
London
SW1E 6RB
071-215 6082

The Civic Trust
17 Carlton House Terrace
London
SW1Y 6AW
071-930 0914

Community Service Volunteers
237 Pentonville Road
London
N1 9NG
071-278 6601

Friends of the Earth
26-28 Underwood Street
London
N1 7JQ
071-490 1555

Groundwork Foundation
Bennets Court
6 Bennets Hill
Birmingham
B2 5ST
021-236 8565

Institute of Waste Management
(IWM)
3 Albion Place
Northampton
NN1 1UD
0604 20426

International Institute for
Environment and Development
3 Endsleigh Street
London
WC1H 0DD

Network for Environmental
Technology Transfer
Square de Meeus 25
B-1040
Brussels
010 322 511 2462

The Tidy Britain Group
The Pier
Wigan
0942 824620

Warren Spring Laboratory, DTI
Gunnels Wood Road
Stevenage
Hertfordshire
SG1 2BX
Environmental enquiry point –
0800 585 794

Water Services Association of
England and Wales
(information on the water and
sewage businesses)
Queen Anne's Gate
London
SW1H 9BT
071-222 8111

Worldwide Fund for Nature – UK
Panda House
Weyside Park
Godalming
Surrey
048342 6444

Responsibilities towards suppliers

George Neil
Supply Chain Management Group
Glasgow University
59 South Park Avenue
Glasgow
G12 8LF
041-330 5696

How to organise social responsibility

Allied Dunbar
Allied Dunbar Centre
Swindon
SN1 1EL
0793 514514

Social responsibility auditing

The ITEM Group
Burnham House
High Street
Burnham
Bucks
SL1 7JZ

Confederation of British Industry
Centre Point
103 Oxford Street
London
WC1A 1DU

Urban renewal

Inner City Task Force Unit
Ashdown House
123 Victoria Street
London
SW1E 6RB
071-215 6734

Sports

The Sports Council
16 Upper Woburn Place
London
WC1H 0QH
071-388 1277

The arts

Association for Business
Sponsorship of the Arts (ABSA)
Nutmeg House
60 Gainsford Street
London
SE1 2NY
071-378 8143

Index of corporate case studies and examples